The Ecosystem Concept in Anthropology

AAAS Selected Symposia Series

Published by Westview Press, Inc.
5500 Central Avenue, Boulder, Colorado

for the

American Association for the Advancement of Science
1776 Massachusetts Ave., N.W., Washington, D.C.

The Ecosystem Concept in Anthropology

Edited by Emilio F. Moran

AAAS Selected Symposium **92**

TO THE MEMORY OF

PROFESSOR JULIAN STEWARD

AAAS Selected Symposia Series

This book is based on a symposium that was held at the 1982 AAAS National Annual Meeting in Washington, D.C., January 3-8. The symposium was sponsored by AAAS Section H (Anthropology).

Published in 1984 in the United States of America by
Westview Press, Inc.
5500 Central Avenue
Boulder, Colorado 80301
Frederick A. Praeger, President and Publisher

Library of Congress Catalog Card Number: 83-51458
ISBN: 0-86531-721-6

Printed and bound in the United States of America

5 4 3 2 1

About the Book

Critics of the ecosystem concept have noted the tendency of ecosystem-based studies to overemphasize energy flow, to rely on functionalist assumptions, to neglect historical and evolutionary factors, and to overlook the role of individuals as the locus of natural selection and decision making. In this volume, leading figures in the study of biological and human ecology evaluate these criticisms and propose ways to advance the state of knowledge in ecological research.

Most of the authors agree that the ecosystem concept has been a useful heuristic tool in conceptualizing the unity of physical abiotic and biotic systems, in promoting detailed quantitative data collection on a broad array of system components and relationships, and as a framework within which to test hypotheses on people/habitat relationships. Less valuable has been the use of the ecosystem as a spatial unit or as a unit whose behavior and evolution can be meaningfully analyzed in anthropology using shorthand methods such as energy-flow and nutrient cycling studies. Finally, the authors examine the loss of explanatory value when the ecosystem concept is applied to human systems, which are better dealt with by theoretical approaches in which microlevel phenomena can be more easily incorporated.

About the Series

The *AAAS Selected Symposia Series* was begun in 1977 to provide a means for more permanently recording and more widely disseminating some of the valuable material which is discussed at the AAAS Annual National Meetings. The volumes in this *Series* are based on symposia held at the Meetings which address topics of current and continuing significance, both within and among the sciences, and in the areas in which science and technology impact on public policy. The *Series* format is designed to provide for rapid dissemination of information, so the papers are not typeset but are reproduced directly from the camera-copy submitted by the authors. The papers are organized and edited by the symposium arrangers who then become the editors of the various volumes. Most papers published in this *Series* are original contributions which have not been previously published, although in some cases additional papers from other sources have been added by an editor to provide a more comprehensive view of a particular topic. Symposia may be reports of new research or reviews of established work, particularly work of an interdisciplinary nature, since the AAAS Annual Meetings typically embrace the full range of the sciences and their societal implications.

WILLIAM D. CAREY
Executive Officer
American Association for
the Advancement of Science

Contents

PART 2 NEW DIRECTIONS IN RESOLVING THE PROBLEM OF TIME AND OF BOUNDARY DEFINITION IN ECOSYSTEMS

PART 3 NEW DIRECTIONS IN RESOLVING THE PROBLEMS OF HIERARCHICAL LEVEL, SCALE, AND DATA COLLECTION

About the Editor and Authors

Emilio F. Moran *is associate professor and chairman of the Department of Anthropology and associate professor in the School for Public and Environmental Affairs at Indiana University at Bloomington. A specialist in ecological anthropology, resource management, and agricultural development, he has written on human adaptation and processes of change through time in the humid tropics. His books include* Human Adaptability *(Duxbury, 1979; reprinted by Westview, 1982),* Developing the Amazon *(Indiana University Press, 1981), and* The Dilemma of Amazonian Development *(Westview, 1982).*

John W. Adams *is associate professor of anthropology at the University of South Carolina, Columbia. A social anthropologist with a particular interest in the demographic factors of social organization, he has done research on the Northwest Coast Indians and on New England from 1620-1850. He is the author of* The Gitksan Potlatch *(Holt, Rinehart and Winston).*

Daniel G. Bates, *professor and chairman of the Department of Anthropology at Hunter College, City University of New York, has specialized in ecological and economic anthropology and has done field research in Africa and the Middle East. He is the author of* Nomads and Farmers: The Yoruk of Southeastern Turkey *(University of Michigan, 1971) and* Peoples and Cultures of the Middle East *(with A. Rassam; Prentice-Hall, 1982). He edited* Contemporary Anthropology: An Anthology *(with S. Lees; Knopf, 1979) and currently serves as coeditor, with Susan H. Lees, of the journal* Human Ecology.

John W. Bennett, *professor of anthropology at Washington University in St. Louis, Missouri, has specialized in economic and ecological anthropology. He has published on anthropological theory and methodology, agricultural decisionmaking and rural development, Third World development, cooperatives, Japanese society and modernization, and aspects of American culture. His books include* Northern Plainsmen *(Aldine, 1969),* The Ecological Transition *(Pergamon, 1976), and* Of Time and the Enterprise *(University of Minnesota Press, 1982).*

Francis Paine Conant *is professor of anthropology at Hunter College, City University of New York. His major fieldwork has been in West and East Africa where he studied the subsistence and settlement systems of farming and herding peoples. His specialization is ecological anthropology, including the application of remote sensing data (aerial photography as well as satellite digital data) to the study of resource utilization in the African sahel. He has published on anthropological method and theory as well as religion, kinship, community types, and the division of labor by gender in African societies.*

Neville Dyson-Hudson, *professor of anthropology at the State University of New York, Binghamton, has done research on food production systems and structure and infrastructure in primitive society in East Africa. Among his publications are* Karimojong Politics *(Clarendon, 1966) and* Perspectives on Nomadism *(edited with W. Irons; Leiden, 1972).*

Rada Dyson-Hudson *is associate professor of anthropology at Cornell University. A specialist in ecology, evolutionary biology, and human ecology, she has done research on East African pastoralism and social stratification, human territoriality, and land degradation. Recently she edited* Rethinking Adaptation *(with M. A. Little; Westview, 1983).*

Roy F. Ellen *is senior lecturer in social anthropology at the University of Kent at Canterbury, United Kingdom. He is currently interested in the application of ecological concepts to the study of small-scale populations and has studied the organization of indigenous knowledge and classifications; the social organization of trade; and the ethnography of Indonesia. His publications include* Social and Ecological Systems *(edited with P. Burnham) and* Classifications in Their Social Context *(edited with D. Reason; both published by Academic, 1979) and* Environment, Subsistence, and System *(Cambridge University Press, 1982).*

James E. Ellis, *a research associate at the National Resource Ecology Laboratory at Colorado State University, Fort Collins, is interested in systems ecology and social systems analysis. He has done studies of the structure and function of mammalian social systems, energy flow relationships in both man-managed and natural ecosystems, and the ecology of nomadic pastoralism.*

Frank B. Golley *is professor of zoology and environmental design and research professor of ecology at the Institute of Ecology, University of Georgia, Athens. A specialist in the structure and function of ecological systems, he is the author of numerous books and articles in his field and is ecology series editor for Dowden, Hutchinson & Ross and Springer-Verlag publishers. Currently he serves as president of the International Society of Tropical Ecology and secretary general of the International Association for Ecology, and he is a past president of the Ecological Society of America.*

Daniel R. Gross *is professor of anthropology at Hunter College, City University of New York. His major fields of interest include nutrition, adaptation, rural development, and energy policy. An ecological anthropologist with field experience mainly in Brazil and more recently in West Africa, he has published on the effects of technological change, method and theory in human ecology, and ecology and acculturation among peasants and native peoples of various regions in Brazil. He is the editor of* Peoples and Cultures of Native South America *(Doubleday/Natural History Press, 1969).*

Michael Jochim *is associate professor of anthropology at the University of California, Santa Barbara. His primary research interest is anthropological archeology, with emphasis on European prehistory and New World Paleoindian and Archaic tribal cultures. Among his publications are* Hunter-Gatherer Subsistence and Settlement: A Predictive Model *and* Strategies for Survival: Cultural Behavior in an Ecological Context *(Academic, 1976 and 1981, respectively).*

Alice Bee Kasakoff, *associate professor of anthropology at the University of South Carolina, Columbia, has done studies of kinship, marriage, and regional systems of social organization in Tikopia, China, and colonial New England. She has coauthored important articles in* Man *and the* Journal of Interdisciplinary History.

Susan H. Lees, *a specialist in human ecology, is professor of anthropology at Hunter College, City University of New York. She has written on various aspects of desertification, irrigation, environmental management, and rural development and change, particularly in Latin America. She shares the editorship of the journal* Human Ecology *with Daniel Bates.*

Michael A. Little, *professor of anthropology at the State University of New York, Binghamton, has specialized in biological anthropology, with emphasis on adaptations made to the environment. His publications include* Man in the Andes *(edited with P. T. Baker; Dowden, Hutchinson & Ross, 1976),* Ecology, Energetics, and Human Variability *(with G. E. B. Morren, Jr.; William C. Brown, 1976), and* Rethinking Human Adaptation *(edited with R. Dyson-Hudson; Westview, 1983).*

Robert McC. Netting *is professor of anthropology at the University of Arizona, Tucson, specializing in cultural ecology, social organization, and historical demography. He has published on household composition, intensive agriculture, warfare, and local politics, and his books include* Hill Farmers of Nigeria: Cultural Ecology of the Kofyar of the Jos Plateau *(University of Washington Press, 1968),* Cultural Ecology *(Benjamin/Cummings, 1977), and* Balancing on an Alp: Ecological Change and Continuity in a Swiss Mountain Community *(Cambridge University Press, 1981).*

Eric Alden Smith, *assistant professor of anthropology at the University of Washington, Seattle, is interested in ecological anthropology and evolutionary theory. He has written on foraging theory, energy flow and adaptation, human sociobiology and evolutionary ecology, hunter-gatherers, and subsistence and socioeconomics among the Inuit of Canada. He is coeditor of* Hunter-Gatherer Foraging Strategies *(with B. Winterhalder; University of Chicago Press, 1981).*

David M. Swift, *a specialist in grazing systems and the nutrition and ecology of ruminants, works as a simulation modeler at Colorado State University. He has done studies of grassland biomass trophic pyramids and comparisons of energy flow among grazing animals of different societies.*

Preface

In the past decade a growing number of anthropologists and biologists have questioned the value of the ecosystem concept in ecological explanation. The critiques have noted the tendency of ecosystem-based studies to over-emphasize energy flow; to rely on functionalist assumptions; to neglect historical and/or evolutionary factors; and to overlook the role of individuals as the locus of natural selection and decision-making. What all these criticisms suggest is that a reassessment of the ecosystem concept is necessary to determine when, and if, the concept is still relevant and productive for anthropology.

It was with such an assessment in mind that I organized an all-day symposium at the 1982 annual meeting of the American Association for the Advancement of Science. The eight papers presented at the meeting are included here in revised form (i.e., Golley, Jochim, Little et al., Lees and Bates, Moran, Ellen, Adams and Kasakoff, and Bennett). Additional contributions were invited from a number of colleagues whose expertise would make the published volume a more complete state-of-the-art assessment of the ecosystem concept in anthropology. Professor Roy Rappaport was originally included in the symposium but year-long fieldwork in New Guinea followed by pressing academic obligations did not permit him to share his thoughts with us. His absence is deeply felt given his crucial role in the debates that are at the heart of this assessment.

In the process of organizing the AAAS symposium, I encountered a response from a colleague that lends further credence to the timeliness of an assessment such as this. This colleague, a leading figure in the study of ecological anthropology, told me that he preferred not to participate because "ecosystem is not a terribly relevant concept for the analysis of human biobehavioral phenomena." This strongly negative view, coming from a scholar who had spent more than a decade executing some of the most sophisticated analyses ever produced in ecological anthropology, deserves to be systematically addressed and dealt with.

It has been twenty years since Clifford Geertz first proposed the ecosystem as a useful analytical concept for an ecological approach in anthropology. Geertz noted that the concept helped to specify the relations between selected human activities, biological transactions and physical processes (Geertz 1963:3). In the two decades since then, the paradigmatic gap between social and biological scientists has been increasingly bridged due to ecosystem research (cf. Little et al., this volume) but problems still remain in terms of the spatial dimensions studied (see Golley, this volume) and on the role of individuals in social systems (Orlove 1980). During this same period the ecological approach, and the concept of adaptation, have become fundamental to the field of anthropology--comparable in theoretical and methodological significance to the study of kinship and political systems. As a mode of analysis, the ecological approach has become the only paradigm capable of integrating social, cultural, biological and archeological anthropology. The reasons for the success of the ecological approach in anthropology are due in no small part to the appeal of the ecosystem concept to a discipline that adheres firmly to holism and which has always given an important place in its studies to the physical surroundings within which a population lives.

The volume that is before you begins with historical assessments of the ecosystem concept in biology and anthropology (Moran, Golley, and Smith) and with papers assessing the uses of the concept in archeology, physical anthropology, and social/cultural anthropology (Jochim, Little et al., and Lees and Bates). Each paper critically assesses past uses of the concept and proposes new directions being taken by researchers to deal with the problems identified.

Part two of the volume addresses one of the most persistent criticisms of the ecosystem concept: its neglect of historical factors and past vagueness in boundary definition. Adams and Kasakoff explore the evidence for "long waves" with characteristic fluctuations in Colonial New England and how a different view of ecosystem results from historically deep studies over large spatial units. Ellen explores the notion of "graded boundaries" through time as a way to cope with the problem of time-depth and system closure in human ecosystems. Finally, Netting discusses how a village that appears to be a relatively closed ecosystem through time is sustained by subtle flows of goods, money, and people in and out of the village that made the tight internal controls over access to land workable.

Part three of the volume explores additional issues in ecological theory and method. Conant presents us with the potential of remote sensing for boundary definition in ecosystems, Gross evaluates three research methods' potential for achieving valid generalizations about social and ecological process. Moran presents a model for nesting microecological studies within hierarchies to deal with the problem of level of analysis shifting. Bennett, in a final philosophical reflection, raises the troublesome question over the fundamental inconsistency between natural ecosystems and human ecosystems due to the latter's incorporation of human value systems that have become increasingly short-term in their goals.

The symposium at the AAAS was well attended and benefitted from a profitable dialogue between biologists and anthropologists out of which emerged a more sober perspective on ecosystems research. Most of those present spoke about the usefulness of the concept as a heuristic tool in conceptualizing the unity of physical and biological systems, in promoting detailed and quantitative data collection on a broad array of system components and relationships, and as a framework within which to test hypotheses on the relationship between people and the physical environment. Less useful, participants tended to agree, was the use of ecosystem as a spatial unit or as a unit whose behavior and evolution could be meaningfully analyzed in anthropology using shorthand methods such as energy flow or nutrient cycling studies. The ecosystem concept's use as the largest unit of aggregation in biological systems, while useful at the level of regional environmental resource management, lost explanatory power in dealing with evolutionary questions or when confronted with highly variable human factors better dealt with by theoretical approaches in which micro-level phenomena could be more easily incorporated.

I want to thank the contributors to the volume for the promptness with which they undertook the task of manuscript revisions and for the quality of the final papers. The Publications Office of AAAS, and especially Joellen Fritsche, were encouraging and helpful throughout the period of manuscript preparation. The anonymous reviewer of the volume for AAAS was detailed and thorough in providing useful suggestions for revision. I want to thank Dr. Priscilla

Reining for her helpful suggestions in the organization of the symposium. Funds for putting the manuscript on the word processor were provided by Dean John Lombardi and the President's Council on International Programs of Indiana University whose assistance is gratefully acknowledged. Rita Harper spent long hours setting up the camera-ready manuscript and deserves special recognition. This book is dedicated to the memory of Dr. Julian Steward, whose pioneer work in cultural ecology laid the foundations for the emergence of a distinct ecological approach in anthropology and for the ideas which form the subject of this volume.

Emilio F. Moran
Department of Anthropology
Indiana University
Bloomington, Indiana 47405

Part 1

Assessment of Past and Present Approaches

Emilio F. Moran

1. Limitations and Advances in Ecosystems Research

Twenty years have passed since the ecosystem concept was first applied to anthropological investigations. In that interim, both systems ecology and ecological anthropology have grown into substantial specialties within biology and anthropology respectively. Both disciplines, however, have come to recognize the limitations in the ecosystem concept for certain questions posed by biologists and anthropologists.

This introduction explores the biological and anthropological foundations of the ecosystem approach and the role that it came to play in each area. Some of the limitations of the concept are evaluated and suggestions offered to refine our use of the concept for more productive study of the patterns of mutual causality between people and their physical environment.

Foundations of the Ecosystem Approach

The historical foundations of the ecological approach in anthropology are dual: on the one hand, the rejection of environmental deterministic explanations led by anthropologists in the first decades of the twentieth century and, on the other, the adoption of biological concepts in the 1960's to avoid over dependence on the concept of culture. This polemic between culture and environment as the prime causes of observable social configurations and diversity forms the basis for the intellectual development of an ecological anthropology.

Ecosystems in Biology

The term ecosystem generally refers to the structural and functional interrelationships among living organisms and the physical environment within which they exist. Indeed, the ecosystem is the total context within which human adaptation and biological evolution take place (Moran 1982). Of all available ecological concepts, the ecosystem concept accords physical environmental factors the most attention. This attention to abiotic factors is, in itself, an important contribution to biology since evolutionary theory does not always recognize the importance of the physical environment in shaping species' behavior (Evans 1976). The physical environment tends to be viewed as a backdrop against which evolving species and adaptive responses are studied.

Authors agree that the ecosystem concept was formally defined by Sir Arthur Tansley in 1935 (see Golley, this volume). As a philosophical stance, however, the concept can be found in writings both past and present. Given the human capacity for language and culture--and the consequent need to categorize and simplify the infinite variety of the external world--all societies tend to develop systems of classification that represent associations of plants, animals, and landscapes (see review by Major 1969). Terms such as biocoenosis (Möbius 1877), ecotope (Troll 1950), biogeocoenosis (Sukkachev 1960) and many others such as _natürcomplex_, _holocoen_, and biosystem approximate the ecosystem concept but emphasize differing aspects of the physico-biological interaction of interest to each of its proponents.

The ecosystem concept took time to develop in Tansley's own writings and grew from his earlier notion of "circle of affinity"--defined as all those phenomena that are part of the total situation of an organism and that might influence it. The circle of affinity developed into the ecosystem concept--an elegant concept because of its comprehensiveness. The concept was most useful as a didactic device in arguing for the unity of Nature and the importance of conservation--rather than as a real research unit. It was conceived as applicable to the level of the plant community or biome, rather than lower levels of organization (Evans 1956).

Tansley's ecosystem concept was considerably ahead of the state of ecological theory when it was first formulated and thus was slow to be adopted. Two publications were particularly significant in influencing the adoption of the concept in biology: the first edition of Eugene Odum's _Fundamentals of Ecology_ (1953) and Evans' comment in _Science_ (1956) in which the ecosystem was proposed as the basic unit of ecology. Evans argued the ecosystem was a unit as important to ecology as species was to taxonomy and systematics. Odum's text offered the ecosystem as an organizing principle emphasizing interdependence, obligatory and causal relationships. It influenced a whole generation of ecologists despite the difficulties faced by those trying to implement the concept in actual research.

The time was ripe for the adoption of such a concept. It helped to bridge the then distinct fields of autecology and synecology.[1] Autecology, the study of the interrelations between individual organisms and two or three environmental variables, had been limited in the past by the difficulties of controlling experimental work due to the inconstancy of climate from one year to the next. Synecology, the study of groups of organisms, such as the community, had been characterized by two rather philosophical and deductive traditions: the American plant succession school led by F.E. Clements and the European plant sociology school of Braun-Blanquet, Cajander, and Sukkachev (Spurr 1969:5-7). Both of these traditions simplified the physical conditions of plant growth by postulating climatic stability and derived static taxonomies made up only of climax forms. Recognition of the role of climatic variation, of the in- and out-migration of organisms, and of ecological factors such as fire and animal browsing on biotic composition, however, led to abandonment of these approaches. Advances made since the 1940's, especially in cybernetics and engineering, for the first time allowed highly precise and controllable experimental research in growth chambers and the construction of large-scale deductive models through the use of computer simulations. The ecosystem concept provided an elegant basis for large-scale integrated modeling and a bridge between inductive and deductive modes of research in ecology.

Whereas the ecosystem concept, when defined by Tansley in 1935 and used by Odum in 1953, was presented mainly as a didactic device to emphasize the interaction between living and non-living components of a system, the introduction of systems engineering and cybernetics initiated conscious application of quantitative techniques to a purely theoretical statement of relationships, rather than a physical unit of study (Wiener 1948; Shinners 1967; Odum 1957). In the process, the concept became frequently equated with biome units (see Bennett, this volume).

The use of the ecosystem concept is rooted in the use of organic analogy (Spengler 1926; Odum 1971; Butzer 1980).

---

[1] Historically, autecology had been experimental and inductive in its approach, whereas synecology had been philosophical and deductive (Spurr 1969:5).

To study ecosystems as real units, it became necessary to study their internal metabolism since system metabolism is a measure of the collective processes which serve to maintain the integrity of the whole (Reichle and Auerbach 1979:91). Studies of trophic levels and energy flow, aided by the use of radioisotope techniques, were concerned with questions relevant to large scale ecosystems in units such as tundra, tropical forests and grasslands. This interest and orientation is reflected in the development during the 1960's of the International Biological Program (IBP) and the choice of biome-level units for systems ecology research. "The goal of ecosystem analysis is to develop quantitative ecosystem science which may provide new theoretical insights into the organization and function of natural systems <u>at their most complex level</u>" (Reichle and Auerbach 1979:92).

When reading the technical writings of systems ecologists such as Van Dyne (1969, 1979, orig. publ. in 1966), it becomes clear that the ecosystem was conceived as a complex level of organization above the levels of cell, tissue, organ, organism, population, and community (see Figure 2.1). The goal of ecosystem research was to overcome the microscopic approach then dominant in biology and enrich it with a macroscopic view of general principles applicable to higher levels of organization. Yet, even in its earliest usage systems ecologists had to grapple with the problem of boundary definition. Odum (1953) clearly noted that ecosystems were defined by the needs of the investigator, and could include anything from a pond to the biosphere. The only requirements to the application of the ecosystem concept would appear to be that at least several organisms were present and that the interaction of these organisms with the abiotic environment be taken into consideration.

Biologists developed clear criteria for defining an ecosystem: it must be a functional entity with internal homeostasis, have identifiable boundaries, and recognizable relationships between components (Reichle and Auerbach 1979:94-5). The goal was to focus on attributes of systems and to pose different questions than are normally undertaken by research on lower units or levels of analysis. Of concern are questions like: what homeostatic mechanisms ensure the self-perpetuation of ecosystems? What is the ecological significance of evergreenness? How does diversity relate to stability? One thing did emerge from the work of systems ecologists: the structural and functional characteristics of ecosystems may not be inferred from those of species, communities or populations.

Ecosystem analysis begins by organizing available knowledge into models of the system in question. This includes all important system components and interactions but focuses on the more important "driving" functions and aggregates the data so that it can be manipulated. Through modeling, systems ecologists seek to predict the behavior of a system from a basic understanding of its structural and functional relations. The problem is that modeling, particularly at the community and ecosystem levels, has the inherent weakness that afflicts all deductive modeling--it can only predict behavior under conditions for which the model was designed. Deductive models cannot predict the behavior of systems undergoing structural transformation, whether externally or internally generated. The tools of ecological modeling coming out of cybernetics and systems ecology proved excellent in describing an ecosystem under current and known conditions. However, difficulties arose in predicting future structural configurations and functional relationships.

Ecological Approaches in Anthropology

The ecosystem concept made its way into anthropology in the 1960's and seems to have been inspired by the writings of Eugene Odum (1953) and Marston Bates (1953). However, anthropological interest in ecology goes back to the very foundations of anthropology as a discipline. Actually, anthropology anticipated the now lively debates over causality in systems during the acrimonious debates over the relative impact of environment in bringing about particular social or political forms (Thomas 1925). Anthropology's origins are associated with an intellectual thrust to reject various forms of racial and environmental determinism and the over-generalizations of anthropogeography prevalent in the late nineteenth century (cf. review of this literature in Moran 1982; Ellen 1981; Glacken 1967; Thomas 1925). The early work of American anthropologists was characterized by an emphasis on historical and cultural descriptions which focused on the uniqueness of human groups (Goldenweisser 1937). According to this view, which has come to be known as "historical possibilism," environment was seen as a passive force that limited human options but which played no active role in the emergence of observable human traits or institutions. In *The Mind of Primitive Man* (1911) Boas noted that the environment furnished the materials out of which people shaped and developed the artifacts of daily life but it was historical forces and diffusion which predominantly explained the particular forms that given artifacts took.

The possibilist position was sympathetic to the "cultural area approach" (Wissler 1926). In this approach geographical regions were divided into culture "areas" based on shared cultural traits of residing cultures. This view was strongly espoused well into the 1930's. C.D. Forde (1934) and A. Kroeber (1939), for example, while acknowledging the need to collect ecological data because of its potential explanatory relevance, concluded that economic and social activities are products of the historical but largely unpredictable processes of cultural accumulation and integration.

Julian Steward was trained in this tradition in the 1930's but his views departed from that of his mentors. Whereas possibilism and cultural area approaches generated good descriptions of the historical past, they often failed in explaining the process that could be generalized beyond the particular case. Steward, on the other hand, was concerned with cross-cultural comparisons and with the causal connection between social structure and modes of subsistence. The crucial focus in Steward's approach was neither on environment nor culture. Rather, the process of resource utilization, in its fullest sense, was given research priority. The "cultural ecological" approach proposed by Steward involved both a problem and a method. The problem was to test whether the adjustment of human societies to their environments required specific types of behavior or whether there is considerable latitude in human responses (Steward 1955:36). The method involved three procedures: a) to analyze the relationship between subsistence system and environment; b) to analyze the behavior patterns associated with a given subsistence technology; and c) to ascertain the extent to which the behavior pattern entailed in a given subsistence system affected other aspects of culture (ibid. :40-1).

This research strategy is all the more impressive if one considers its historical backdrop. From the broad generalities of the environmental determinists and the detailed inductive findings of the possibilists, Steward proposed a research method that paid both careful attention to empirical details but that causally linked the cognized environment,[2] social organization, and the behavioral expressions of human resource use. Steward delimited, more

---

[2]Although the term "cognized environment" was introduced later, it is accurate in describing Steward's notion of "selected features of an environment of greatest relevance to a population's subsistence."

than anyone before him, the field of human/environment interactions. He viewed social institutions as having a functional unity that expressed solutions to recurrent subsistence problems. Steward's use of functionalism was concerned with the operation of a variable in relation to a limited set of variables, not in relation to the entire social system, and thus did not fall prey to the weaknesses of then current British functionalism. British functionalists emphasized the role of social institutions in the maintenance of structural equilibrium. Steward steered "cultural ecology" towards a concern with how single systems change through time and how the causal relationships within that system can actually lead to change.

Most attempts to operationalize the cultural ecological approach required modifications of the basic research strategy laid out by Steward (cf. Netting 1968; Sweet 1965; Sahlins 1961). His concept of the culture "core" proved to underestimate the scope, complexity, variability, and subtlety of environmental and social systems (Geertz 1963). The cultural ecological approach of comparing societies across time and space in search of causal explanations was judged to be flawed a decade later (Vayda and Rappaport 1968). Vayda and Rappaport, among others, found the concept of the culture core to give undue weight to culture as the primary unit of analysis, and found the presumption that organization for subsistence had causal priority to other aspects of human society and culture to be both untested and premature (cf. Geertz 1963).

Ecosystems in Anthropology

Critiques of Steward's cultural ecology paradigm led anthropologists towards a more explicitly biological paradigm. Geertz (1963) was the first to argue for the usefulness of the ecosystem as a unit of analysis. Its merits were eloquently stated: systems theory provided a broad framework, essentially qualitative and descriptive, that emphasized the internal dynamics of such systems and how they develop and change. The explicit adoption of biological concepts in anthropology led to provocative and sometimes productive results. As early as 1956 Barth applied the concept of the "niche" to explain the behavior of adjacent groups and the evolution of ethnic boundaries. Coe and Flannery (1964) noted the use of multiple ecological niches by prehistoric peoples of South Coastal Guatemala. Neither the niche nor other concepts from biology had as significant an impact on anthropological thinking, however, as did the ecosystem concept.

Each subfield of anthropology was differentially affected by the ecosystem concept. Archaeologists have always been conscious of the environmental context of society. However, in many cases the environment has been treated as a static background against which human dynamics occur (Butzer 1982:4). In part, the problem was the lack of "an adequate conceptual framework within which to analyze complex relationships among multivariate phenomena" (Ibid., p. 5). The seminal paper in archeology may have been Flannery's (1968) in which he postulated the useful applications of systems theory to archaeological investigations. According to systems'-oriented archeologists, "culture is defined not as aggregates of shared norms (and artifacts), but as interacting behavioral systems" (Plog 1975:208). Emphasis was given to variability, multivariate causality, and process (Clarke 1968).

In archeology, the concept has proved a useful heuristic device leading archaeologists to think in terms of systemic interrelationships but it was rarely used as a spatial unit of analysis. Thus, archaeology did not fall into the trap of making ecosystems coterminous with biogeographical units or sites. Rather, the ecosystem approach encouraged the study of the landscape at large, the use of catchment analysis and regional surveys (see Jochim, this volume). Ecological archaeology has benefitted from the breadth of the concept and appears not to have suffered from many of the problems that seem to have plagued ecosystem research in physical and social anthropology. Unlike energy flow studies (or decision-making studies) which emphasize present-time measurement, ecological archaeology deals with spatio-temporal variability. The long time frames of the archaeological record reflect aggregate changes in the physical environment and in the material manifestations of social and cultural change (Butzer 1982), thereby avoiding the pitfalls of synchronic equilibrium-oriented functionalism.

In another subdiscipline, physical anthropology, Little (1982) has noted that in the 1950's physical anthropologists began to take a special interest in the study of adaptation to environment. This "new physical anthropology" focused on studies of body morphology and composition, physiological response to environmental stress, demographic and health parameters of adaptation and genetic attributes of populations (Harrison et al. 1964).

The research of the new physical anthropologists found support in the International Biological Program (IBP) which began ca. 1964. A "human adaptability" section was included in the program, intended to cover "the ecology of mankind" from the perspectives of health, environmental physiology, population genetics, developmental biology and demography (Weiner 1965). Even though doubts were expressed at the 1964 symposium at Burg Wartenstein about the omission of social/cultural aspects of adaptability, the perceived gap between the methods of human biology and social science led to no solution to this problem (Weiner in Worthington 1975). Only a decade later did an IBP workshop begin to seek ways to bring together ecologists and social scientists so that humans could be incorporated into the IBP ecosystem approach (Little and Friedman 1973). This conference was followed by one on the application of energy flow to the study of human communities (Jamison and Friedman 1974).

Four important synthesis volumes have resulted from the human adaptability projects in the Arctic and high altitude ecosystems (Baker and Little 1976; Baker 1978; Jamison et al. 1978; Milan 1979). It is quite clear that the 1964-74 decade of research led to more sophisticated methods and greater awareness of the limitations of original formulations. Practitioners now go beyond evaluating systems in terms of a single flow and instead consider multiple flows and constraints. Indeed, energy flow analysis[3] is seen as a method quite distinct from an adaptive framework or any other theoretical stance (Thomas 1973). The flaws of human energy flow studies carried out in the 1960's and early 1970's (cf. critique in Burnham 1982) resulted from preliminary efforts to test the utility of the new methods for anthropology. Indeed, energy flow analysis is a convenient starting point in understanding the complexity of human systems--systems in which social relations and historical process play a primary role. To fully understand them, however, other methods are more appropriate to social and ideological analysis.

In social anthropology and human geography ecological studies became common in the 1970's, reflecting the influence of systems ecology and the ecological movement (see Bennett, this volume). The majority of studies focused on the flow of energy through small-scale societies (e.g., Rappaport 1967; Clarke 1971; Kemp 1971; Waddell 1972; Nietschmann 1973). For all intents and purposes, the use of "ecosystems," however defined by researchers, did not radically alter the units of analysis used: small non-urban communities continued to be

---

[3]Energy flow analysis refers to methods that attempt to measure the chemical transformation of solar energy into biomass and its gradual diffusion and loss through a food web (cf. Odum 1971; Moran 1982).

selected wherein the complexity of social and environmental interactions could be measured.

A generation of anthropologists, trained in ecology and systems theory, went to the field to measure the flow of energy through the trophic levels of the ecosystems of which humans were but a part (Rappaport 1967). The choice of research site was still a local community, and was often treated as a closed system for the purposes of analysis. Emphasis on micro-level study in ecology was well argued by Brookfield (1970) who pointed out that an adaptive system can best be studied at this level because such a system model "acquires the closest orthomorphism with empirical fact" (1970:20). Micro-level studies using the ecosystem as a "unit of analysis" have provided valuable insights into flow of energy, health and nutritional status of populations, relative efficiency rates of various forms of labor organization and cropping practices, and into social organizational aspects of subsistence strategies (cf. discussion in Netting 1977; Moran 1982; Ellen, Lees and Bates; and others, this volume).

The impact of the ecosystem approach in social and cultural anthropology may have been most strong in research methods and the degree of quantification thought desirable (see Gross, this volume). The earliest studies using the approach emphasized energy flow accounting, and more recent studies have emphasized the application of micro-economic approaches to adaptive strategies and choice-making by individuals and groups (see Orlove 1980; Lees and Bates, Gross, Bennett, and Smith, this volume).

Efforts to measure the flow of energy and the cycles of matter through human ecosystems served to detail more than before the environmental setting of specific populations. Energetics emphasizes the collection of data on a sample of components and flows so that the data may be aggregated and used in simulation models. The goal is to understand system dynamics by manipulating rates of flow given current conditions in the ecosystem. However, the value of these measures in studying small scale populations may have been overestimated in the 1960's. Flow of energy and cycles of matter are aggregate measures appropriate to macro-ecosystem description but provide little insight into human variation in resource use in given localities (see Moran, Chapter 12, this volume). These measures were never meant to address, or be relevant to, microecological explanation or to evolutionary questions as some critics of the ecosystem approach have suggested (see Smith, this volume).

Just as the ecosystem concept helped biology broaden its interests to include neglected physical environmental factors, so it affected anthropology. The ecosystem approach provided greater context and holism to the study of human society by its emphasis on the biological basis of productivity and served as a needed complement to the cultural ecology approach. By stressing complex links of mutual causality, the ecosystem concept contributed to the demise of environmental and cultural deterministic approaches in anthropology.

Limitations of the Ecosystem Concept

Perhaps no work has had a greater impact on the development of an ecosystem approach in anthropology than Rappaport's study of a New Guinea population (1967) nor has any other study attracted as many critics of an ecological approach. Originally many of the advocates of a more explicit ecological approach in anthropology were satisfied with this study. It argued that a human population was a species within the ecosystem; that the system operated according to laws of nature that could be understood in the light of systems theory. In this framework major cultural processes like ritual could be understood to play cybernetic functions.[4] The study was rich in ethnographic and quantitative data--despite the difficulties of collecting those data in the New Guinea Highlands of the early 1960's. Rappaport was able to relate the ritual cycle to the cycles of pig population growth, the fallow cycles of swidden fields, and cyclical warfare.

---

[4]Rappaport (1977) in a recent response to criticism of his Pigs for the Ancestors (1967) notes that it is not surprising that he, and others, found systems in relative homeostasis in preindustrial, small, self-sufficient populations. The imperative of individual existence tends to lead men into conflict with the social systems of which they are members. Those conflicts become more exaggerated with increasing size of the social system due to increased difficulties in social control--whereas cultural dimensions such as ritual can more effectively adjust small-scale populations to local perturbations. Contradictions between individual goals and social goals are inevitable and there is nothing in the ecosystem concept itself that suggests the presence or absence of such contradictions. It is simply not within the scope of the concept to deal with this important dimension of general systems. However, ecosystemic study of one level of aggregation allows one to discover contradictions between levels.

The merits of the ecosystem concept were evident in Rappaport's study: holism was stressed while, at the same time, specific relationships between human populations and the total environment served to give focus. The concept allowed Rappaport both to eliminate detail at the macro-level and to examine in detail components at the micro-level. Empirically, the ecosystem concept as employed by Rappaport contributed to the accumulation of data on subsistence systems, the appreciation of the impact of those same systems upon the environment and the social system, and led to the acquisition of more sophisticated techniques for data analysis such as modeling and computer simulation. It encouraged the move away from typologizing and correlation and towards integrative studies dealing with mutual causality (Ellen 1981).

A number of problems emerged in the process of applying the ecosystem concept to anthropology (see also the assessment by Vayda and McCay 1975): a) a tendency to reify the ecosystem and to give it the properties of a biological organism; b) an overemphasis on predetermined measures of adaptation such as energetic "efficiency"; c) a tendency for models to ignore time and structural change, thereby overemphasizing stability in ecosystems; d) lack of clear criteria for boundary definition, and e) level shifting between field study and analysis.

Reification of the Ecosystem

The tendency of some authors to reify the ecosystem and to transform the concept into an entity having organic characteristics appears to have been a product of the initial excitement generated by the concept. When the volume *The Ecosystem Concept in Natural Resource Management* (Van Dyne 1969) appeared, the editor and some of the contributors noted that they were at the threshold of a major development in the field of ecology. The concept was hailed as an answer to the divisions within bioecology and gained a large popular following during the "ecology movement" of the 1960's and early 1970's. It is evident that, for some, ecosystems have become a shorthand for the biome or community and that this heuristically useful physical/biological construct has been unwittingly endowed with purely biological attributes. As Golley has noted, it is generally understood that ecosystems are subject to the laws of biological evolution but they are also subject to laws not yet completely understood and that are not exclusively biological. The problem of reification persists to the present.

When an ecosystem is viewed as an organic entity it is assigned properties such as self-regulation, maximization of energy through-flow, and having strategies for survival. This view is similar to earlier "superorganic" approaches in anthropology (Durkheim 1915; Kroeber 1917; White 1949). Few ecological anthropologists today would accept the notion that ecosystems "have strategies" and even fewer would agree that energy maximization is always "adaptive" in human ecosystems. The notion of self-regulation is more problematic since it devolves around the question of whether ecosystems *per se* can by cybernetic, e.g., use information for self-regulation (Engelberg and Boyarsky 1979). Patten and Odum (1981) believe this to be a pseudoissue that distracts us from more fundamental concerns: e.g., how are we to think about ecosystems and how are we to place them within the scheme of known systems? Ecosystems do not seek to process energy and matter. Long-term selection favors as a matter of implicit design, structured relations or organization that creates order where there might be chaos. However, this does not reduce the potential for evolutionary change along orderly lines (Patten and Odum 1981:896). Anthropological ecosystem studies have tended to de-emphasize the capacity of *Homo sapiens* to transform the physical environment through organized social activity (Ellen 1981:91). Thus, studies have over-emphasized the self-regulatory features of ecosystems to the neglect of processes by which systems transform themselves in response to either external or internal dynamics. Inter-specific exchanges have been emphasized to the neglect of intra-specific exchanges and the role of labor exchange (Cook 1973:41-4). Cognitive dimensions of human behavior have been neglected despite the knowledge that cultural factors mediate such ecological dimensions as population size and resource use. Cognitive dimensions tended to be considered only under the aegis of "ethnoecology" and rarely incorporated into system analysis.

The Calorific Obsession

Perhaps no other problem has received more attention within anthropology in recent years than the charge that ecosystem studies were obsessed with calories. Many young scientists took great pains to measure energy flow through ecosystems under the assumption that energy was the only measurable common denominator that structured ecosystems and that could serve to define their function. Energy flow studies conducted in the 1960's and 1970's demonstrated the descriptive usefulness of energetics before, during, and after field investigations. What they also proved was that the forcing functions of ecosystems varied from site to site and that it was naive to postulate energy as the organizing basis for all extant ecosystems (e.g., Kemp 1971; Rappaport 1971; Thomas 1973; Moran 1973; Baker and Little 1976; Vayda and McCay 1975; Ellen 1978).

The seminal work on the energetic basis of society was that of Leslie White (1949) who proposed that cultural evolution is determined by the control of progressively greater amounts of energy. In his scheme, social systems are determined by the use of technology to control energy. While White's scheme was purely theoretical, his successors began to measure food production in an effort to specify the relationship between harnessing of energy and social evolution. For macro-modeling, there is little doubt that the energetic approach to social evolution has considerable merit (cf. Harris 1977). However, such an approach submerges the anthropologically important concerns with human variability in time and space, and issues of causality, evident by use of other kinds of analysis.

Today few would suggest that measurement of energy flow ought to be the central concern of ecosystem studies. Concern has shifted instead to nutrients and to the impact of external factors upon given ecosystems (Shugart and O'Neill 1979). Bioecologists are less concerned today with the calorific obsession than with the perception that there is overemphasis in training and research on systems engineering and a growing inadequacy in the biological training of systems ecologists (Innis 1977). Anthropologists use energy flow analysis as a preliminary research tool to organize data collection, model input-output relations, and to define hypotheses. Here energy flow analysis is not seen as a theoretical construct that explains human biobehavioral phenomena but rather as a convenient starting point that highlights the importance of environmental/human relations (see Little et al., this volume).

Ignoring Historical Factors

Next to the "calorific obsession," ecosystem research and modeling efforts have been limited by ignoring time and historical change. This emphasis on ahistorical models, in turn, led to an overemphasis on stability and homeostasis rather than on the cumulative change that occurs in social systems. The emphasis on the self-maintenance and self-regulating characteristics of ecosystems also contributed to a view that man's role was essentially disruptive of "natural processes." Ellen, Adams and Kasakoff, Bennett, Netting, Gross, Conant, Smith, and others in this volume discuss the consequences of overlooking transformations over time and in space. Recent inclusion of a historical dimension in ecosystem research provides for an appreciation of the processes of stability and change in human ecosystems. At any given period, systems appear to be seeking stability, whereas in the long run they suggest continuous and accumulating change leading away from stability under pressures from physical, demographic, and socio-economic variables that bring about a broad range of individual responses.

It is paradoxical that ecological anthropological studies have only rarely explored the changing population variable over time given the importance of demographics in population ecology. In part, the reason must be sought in the study of isolated small communities lacking historical records of births, deaths, and marriage. To see a human ecosystem in process, rather than as a synchronic snapshot, requires dependable, continuous, and relatively complete records of a population over a long period of time. Such ideal conditions are rarely found except in modern-period Western Europe and North America. Thus, it comes as no surprise that the few studies employing demographic data come from fieldwork in these areas, for example, Netting's (1981, 1979, 1976, 1974, this volume) site in the Swiss Alps and Adams and Kasakoff's (this volume) work in colonial New England.

Demographically-deep studies represent a relatively new direction in ecological anthropology (cf. N. Baker and Sanders 1971; Cook 1972; Polgar 1972; Zubrow 1976; Netting 1981). Demographic studies lead us away from models emphasizing closure, constraints to energy flow and negative feedback and toward questions emphasizing evolutionary change in systems (Zubrow 1976:21). Without such time depth, it is not possible to explain how systems come to be nor how they change. Additionally, population data have the advantage of being observable, replicable, quantifiable, and cross-culturally comparable (Zubrow 1976:4).

The change from a synchronic to a more diachronic ecological anthropology does not require an abandonment of the ecosystem concept (Diener et al., 1980). What it does imply is an extension of the tools of ecological study to include also the tools of historical demography. The seminal work on this topic is generally acknowledged to be Boserup's <u>The Conditions of Agricultural Growth</u> (e.g., Cohen 1977; Basehart 1973; Bayliss-Smith 1974; Berreman 1978; Harner 1970; Netting 1973, 1981; Vasey 1979; White 1973, to name but a few who sought to test the validity of Boserup's thesis). The tools of historical demography to date have required extensive records of property owned or controlled by households, records of household composition and labor supply, and both total production from agriculture and marketable production--found generally only in Western cultures. Whether what we learn about human population dynamics in these complex social settings can be applied to the human/habitat interactions of preindustrial foragers or isolated horticulturalists remains to be seen. It might be argued, however, that the worldwide incorporation of scattered socio-political units within larger economic and political systems makes it nearly impossible to treat local communities as closed systems for analytical purposes.

The change toward a demographic ecological anthropology is a natural extension of the more synchronic studies that characterized research in the 1960's and 1970's. Ecosystem analysis is more complete and more attuned to ecological theory when it moves beyond the detailed appraisal of how a population survives and how its members respond to various "perturbations" (Vayda and McCay 1975). Consideration of how they respond differently from one generation to the next, how they respond to novel and sometimes externally induced problems allows for explanations that are more consistent with our understanding of the adaptability of human populations. In fact, ecological analysis of this sort makes a distinct contribution to anthropology in that it can distinguish between real system change versus shifts in a group's mental categories, values or dominant symbols (Netting 1981). The change may be as subtle as a shift in statistically-observable fertility rates, outmigration or land tenure distribution. Yet, these shifts signal major structural transformations in human ecosystems which may or may not be accompanied by cultural change. An understanding of the lags between demographic and cultural change is a subject of considerable and continuing interest.

Vayda and McCay (1975) proposed that human ecology focus on life-threatening hazards such as drought, frost or disease as a way of dealing with real problems humans face and to understand adaptive strategies. Two problems result from this emphasis: how to predict the occurrence of a hazard with sufficient anticipation to carry out a baseline study and to study the hazard as it affects people, and how to evaluate the relative adequacy of coping strategies. Perhaps more realistic is the event-oriented approach proposed by Lees and Bates (this volume). The process of rural development, they would argue, and the interventions associated with it, provide an ideal context for testing hypotheses dealing with proximate causality. Such an approach does not free the investigator from the responsibility to seek, over time, additional evidence to gradually place the event-centered study within a historical matrix of physical, demographic, and social change.

Problems of Boundary Definition

Just as the time dimension was long overlooked, so was the problem of boundary definition. The common wisdom is that the ecosystem concept is flexible and that the boundaries are determined by the goals of the investigator. Clearly, any unit which provides the empirical conditions for defining a boundary may constitute an ecosystem for analytical purposes. However, most human ecosystems do not have the clear cut boundaries that a brook, a pond, or an islet offers (see Ellen, this volume).

Rappaport (1967) defined the boundaries of the ecosystem he studied by using the concept of "territoriality". The Tsembaga Maring of New Guinea, as horticulturalists and as the ecologically "dominant" species, attempted to construct anthropocentric ecosystems. Within their territories they played a dominant regulatory role. Thus, "the domain of the regulatory operations of a local group <u>defines</u> an ecosystem" (or territory) (Rappaport 1977:148). This is a basically satisfying solution to the question of boundary definition except for two implicit problems: how do ecosystem boundaries change through time and how do shifts in boundary definition relate to internal and external structural or functional relations?

The former problem can be addressed through the use of the notion of adaptation. All living systems seek to persist through time and their structures change in response to both external and internal change. How boundaries change through time is an empirical problem addressed by Netting, Ellen, and Adams and Kasakoff (this volume).

Bounding one's research area is an ever present challenge to be confronted by both biologists and anthropologists. By assuming that ecosystems are purely and subjectively definable yet also somehow coterminous with biomes or other biogeographical units, creates real problems in defining clear sampling criteria. Environmental "patchiness" and heterogeneity, animal mobility, and massive ecosystem change due to natural and man-made disasters has received little attention as they affect one's sample population, for example. There has been progress, however, and several papers deal with this problem in this volume. Ellen (1981) proposes "graded boundaries" that acknowledge temporal and spatial criteria for closure; Conant suggests the use of remote sensing over time to determine the boundaries of ecosystem components; Gross suggests the use of cross-sectional, comparative, and longitudinal analysis to deal with the processes of stability and change in human society. Clearly, time, space, and hierarchical level all need to be accounted for in ecosystem analysis.

Level Shifting

Whereas it is normal and quite common to understand one level of analysis in terms of the other, such a tack may not be appropriate. Indeed, this may be the most serious limitation of the ecosystem approach. All we have for most macro-ecosystems is data for a few sites, for a limited time period, and on only some aspects of the whole system of interactions. From an analytic perspective, one cannot confidently use site-specific studies as a basis for macro-ecosystem models. Geographers, of all scientists, have shown the most sensitivity to this constraint, particularly in reference to how one can understand a large region while only studying small areas within it (McCarthy et al. 1956; Dogan and Rokkam 1969).

Anthropology and ecology have shown less caution about the distinctness of each level. Odum (1971) and many others provide few cautions about the pitfalls of extrapolating evidence from single sites to macro-systems. Current trends in both ecology and anthropology suggest that the macro-ecosystem level may not be appropriate for dealing with questions of human impact and resource management except in a very broad and unspecific way. Resource management is a site-specific task in which social, political, legal, and historical dimensions are at least as important as environmental ones. A paper later in this volume provides an extended discussion of this basic problem that plagues all of science and which confuses debates over the causal process (see Moran, Chapter 12, this volume).

Advances in Ecosytem Studies

The above problems in past ecosystem studies do not justify that the ecological approach be discarded. There has been considerable progress in the sophisticated assessment of systems of production due in no small part to the research efforts of ecological anthropologists (cf. review in Ellen 1981). Research has shifted from an overemphasis on calories to a more multivariate approach to causality in human ecosystems (Lees and Bates, Netting, Moran, this volume). The static functionalism and "vulgar materialism" that have attracted so many critics is not evident in the papers found in this volume.

Golley's discussion of the historical origins of the concept in biology and of its contemporary understanding highlights the dynamic nature of ecosystems. For him, ecosystems provide a bridge between the principles of physics, chemistry, and biology and that relates these principles to actual processes. Ecosystems emphasize the dynamic rather than the static view of systems because of the role of feedback between components. His optimism about the utility of systems ecology for anthropology is not shared by Smith who proposes that evolutionary biology is a more powerful theoretical construct. This view reflects the ongoing debates in biology between system ecologists and evolutionary ecologists. For the latter, the theory of ecology is complete with the organism and its evolving population. The environment is there as a given that accommodates to changes in biotic populations. Smith's rejection of the ecosystem approach stems from his problems with the work of functionalist cybernetic ecological anthropologists. Most of the authors in this volume, while agreeing with much of Smith's critique, do not share his polemic view of the problem. Many ecological anthropologists make use of the ecosystem concept without attributing teleological qualities to it (e.g., Geertz 1963; Thomas 1973; Moran 1982; Jochim 1981; Ellen 1981; Netting 1981). The contributors to this volume highlight the conceptual usefulness of the concept while they reject its value as a physical unit for anthropological study.

This view is clearly stated by Jochim who sees in the concept a heuristic device that encourages systemic thinking and inclusiveness. Archaeology has not fallen prey to the error of making ecosystem a concrete unit of analysis due to the difficulty of reconstructing even small portions of past ecosystems. This limitation has proven to be a strength in that archaeologists are free to benefit from the concept without the unproductive debates over whether ecosystems "really exist." However, archaeological research has to deal with the problem posed by differences in scale of temporal resolution in archaeology and the modern studies used as analogies.

This archaeological attention to the problem of time in ecosystem research is also addressed in the work of social anthropologists. The paper by Netting subtly deals with the persistence of the Alpine community of Törbel as a relatively closed ecosystem due to the in and out flow of labor and capital side-by-side with legal principles of inheritance that prevented pressure on the land. What at first appeared a stable, even static, system was really a dynamic one. The value of historical demography for ecological anthropology is demonstrated by this elegant study executed over a ten-year period.

The demographic studies of Adams and Kasakoff in this volume further highlight the usefulness of incorporating temporal change in understanding ecological change. It is unlikely that ecological anthropologists can ever again carry out synchronic research in single communities. Rather, research is likely to be either diachronic or comparative or cross-sectional. The paper by Gross in this volume discusses the value and limitations that each of these three methods of ecological research offer. Conant's paper emphasizes the value of remote sensing for discovering interrelationships between habitat and humans, for defining boundaries, and for testing the extent to which local observations apply to a larger spatial unit.

The problem of temporal variability is compounded by that of spatial variability. The paper by Ellen quickly dissolves any naive notions about the "ease" of defining boundaries of ecosystems. His study of the Moluccas demonstrates that the spatial boundaries of ecosystems change over time and as a function of the parameters of interest to the researcher. Thus, he proposes the notion of "graded boundaries," with explicitly definable criteria used to establish the degree of reproductive autonomy of local populations.

Another and complementary proposal to how one might define and bound an ecosystem for study is presented by Lees and Bates. They suggest that focusing on events which pose particular problems to a human population is a useful way to study cumulative change and adaptation. The impact of modern economic development on ecological and social systems is of such magnitude that ecological research in both biology and anthropology have become increasingly oriented to assessing the environmental and social impact of development. There can be little doubt that the ecosystem concept is useful for holistic assessment of the impact of a project upon a habitat--whether humans are included or not. The event-oriented approach of Lees and Bates reflects the immediacy of these problems. The ecosystem approach is useful here although tools and theoretical stances from a broad array of disciplines may be called for, depending on the questions asked or the level of impact felt by the population.

In short, the ecological approach in anthropology has gone through various phases, each of which has seemed to overemphasize environment, culture, techno-environmental features, energy flow, or natural selection. Each generation of anthropologists has found considerable limits to the causal models proposed by those before them. The authors in this volume find reasons to reject the efforts to make ecosystems into superorganic systems, but affirm its conceptual usefulness as a device that helps us test hypotheses about cultural behavior in its environmental context.

The chief danger to practitioners of the ecosystem approach lies in allowing the concept to harden into fixed biotic boundaries, or to rely on any single index of adaptability. Science must maintain flexibility in its theoretical and methodological concepts, while at the same time providing the detailed context of an investigation. Just as Tansley in the 1930's proposed that the entire context of vegetational studies be investigated as a means of evaluating the adequacy of any analysis (i.e., his circles of affinity), so too must practitioners of the ecosystem approach consider the entire context of human society--before drawing the boundaries for their study using appropriate methods for the given study and level of analysis. The consideration of that context, however, is an important contribution to the ecological approach in biology and anthropology. Although it is no panacea for the difficulties of integrating the complex linkages between biotic and abiotic components of Nature, it is a helpful concept that reminds us that all systems are far more complex than our deductive or inductive models can ever conceive.

References Cited

Baker, P. and M. Little (eds.)
1976 Man in the Andes. Stroudsburg, PA: Dowden, Hutchinson and Ross.

Baker, P. and W. Sanders
1971 Demographic Studies in Anthropology. Annual Review of Anthropology 1:151-78.

Barth, F.
1956 Ecologic Relationships of Ethnic Groups in Swat, N. Pakistan. American Anthropologist 58:1079-89.

Basehart, H.W.
1973 Cultivation Intensity, Settlement Patterns, and Homestead Forms among the Matengo of Tanzania. Ethnology 12:57-73.

Bates, M.
1953 Human Ecology. In Anthropology Today. A. Kroeber, ed. Chicago: Univ. of Chicago Press.

Bayliss-Smith, T.
1974 Constraints on Population Growth: The Case of the Polynesian Outer Atolls in the Pre-contact Period. Human Ecology 2:259-95.

Bennett, J.
1967 Microcosm-Macrocosm Relationships in North American Agrarian Society. American Anthropologist 69:441-54.
1969 Northern Plainsmen. Chicago: Aldine.
1976 The Ecological Transition. London: Pergamon.

Berreman, G.D.
1978 Ecology, Demography and Domestic Strategies in the Western Himalayas. Journal of Anthropological Research 34:326-68.

Boas, F.
1888 The Central Eskimo. Washington, DC: Smithsonian.
1911 The Mind of Primitive Man. New York: Macmillan.

Boserup, E.
The Conditions of Agricultural Growth. Chicago: Aldine.

Brookfield, H.C.
1970 Dualism and the Geography of Developing Countries. Presidential Address at the Australian and New Zealand Assoc. for the Advanc. of Sci.

Burnham, P.
1982 Energetics and Ecological Anthropology: Some Issues. Energy and Effort. G. Harrison, ed. New York: International Publication Service.

Butzer, K.W.
1980 Civilizations: Organisms or Systems? American Scientist 68:517-23.
1982 Archeology as Human Ecology. New York: Cambridge University Press.

Clarke, D.
1968 Analytical Archeology. London: Methuen.

Clarke, J.
1976 Population and Scale: Some General Considerations. In Population at Microscale. L. Kosinski and J. Webb, eds. New Zealand: Commission on Populat. Geog.

Clarke, W.
1971 Place and People. Berkeley: Univ. of California Press.

Coe, M. and K. Flannery
1964 Microenvironments and Mesoamerican Prehistory. Science 143:650-54.

Cohen, Mark
1977 The Food Crisis in Prehistory: Overpopulation and the Origins of Agriculture. New Haven: Yale University Press.

Cook, S.
1973 Production, Ecology and Economic Anthropology: Notes Toward an Integrated Frame of Reference. Social Science Information 12(1):25-52.

Cook, S.F.
1972 Prehistoric Demography. Reading, Mass.: Addison-Wesley Publishing Co.

Diener, P., et al.
1980 Ecology and Evolution in Cultural Anthropology. Man 15(4):1-32.

Dogan, M. and S. Rokkam (eds.)
1969 Social Ecology. Cambridge, MA: MIT Press.

Durkheim, E.
1915 The Elementary Forms of the Religious Life. London: Allen and Unwin.

Ellen, R.
1978 Problems and Progress in the Ethnographic Analysis of Small Scale Human Ecosystems. Man 13:290-303.
1981 Environment, Subsistence, and System. Cambridge: Cambridge Univ. Press.

Engelberg, J. and L. Boyarski
1979 The Noncybernetic Nature of Ecosystems. American Naturalist 114:317-24.

Evans, F.C.
1956 Ecosystems as the Basic Unit in Ecology. Science 123:1127-8.

Evans, G.
1976 A Sack of Uncut Diamonds: The Study of Ecosystems and the Future Resources of Mankind. Journal of Ecology 64:1-39.

Flannery, K.
1968 Archaeological Systems Theory and Early Mesoamerica. In Anthropological Archaeology in the Americas. B. Meggers, ed. Washington, D.C.: Anthropological Society of Washington.

Forde, C.D.
1934 Habitat, Economy and Society. New York: Dutton.

Friedman, J.
1974 Marxism, Structuralism, and Vulgar Materialism. Man 9:444-69.

Geertz, C.
1963 Agricultural Involution. Berkeley: Univ. of California Press.

Glacken, C.
1967 Traces on a Rhodian Shore. Berkeley: University of California Press.

Goldscheider, C.
1971 Population, Modernization, and Social Structure. Boston: Little, Brown.

Goldenweisser, A.
1937 Anthropology. New York: F.S. Crofts.

Harner, M.
1970 Population Pressure and the Social Evolution of Agriculturalists. Southwest Journal of Anthropology 26:67-86.

Harris, M.
1977 Cannibals and Kings. New York: Vintage Books, Random House.

Harrison, G. et al.
1964 Human Biology. London: Oxford.

Innis, G.S. (ed.)
1977 New Directions in the Analysis of Ecological Systems. La Jolla, CA: Society for Computer Simulation, Proceedings Series. Vol. 5.

Jamison, P. and S. Friedman
1974 Energy Flow in Human Communities. University Park, PA: US-IBP Human Adaptability Coordinating Office.

Jochim, M.
1981 Strategies for Survival. New York: Wiley.

Jordan, C.F.
1981 Do Ecosystems Exist? American Naturalist. 118:284-87.

Kemp, W.
1971 The Flow of Energy in a Hunting Society. Scientific American 224:104-15.

Kroeber, Alfred
1939 Cultural and Natural Areas of Native North America. Berkeley: University of California Press.
1917 The Superorganic. American Anthropologist 19:163-213.

Lee, R.B.
1979 The !Kung San. New York: Cambridge Univ. Press.

Little, M. and S. Friedman
1973 Man in the Ecosystem. University Park, PA: US-IBP Human Adaptability Coordinating Office.

Little, M. and G. Morren
1976 Ecology, Energetics and Human Variability. Dubuque, Iowa: W.C. Brown.

Little, M.
1982 The Development of Ideas on Human Ecology and Adaptation. In A History of American Physical Anthropology, 1930-80. F. Spencer, ed. New York: Academic Press.

Major, J.
1969 Historical Development of the Ecosystem Concept. In The Ecosystem Concept in Natural Resource

Management. G.M. Van Dyne, ed. New York: Academic Press.

McCarthy, H.H., J.C. Hook and D.S. Knos
1956 The Measurement of Association in Industrial Geography. Dept. of Geography. Univ. of Iowa.

Milan, F.
1979 Human Biology of Circumpolar Populations. Oxford: Cambridge University Press. Vol. 21. IBP Synthesis volume.

Möbius, K.
1877 Die Auster und die Austernwirtschaft. Berlin: Wiegundt, Hempel and Payey.

Moran, E.F.
1973 Energy Flow Analysis and Manihot esculenta Crantz. Acta Amazonica 3(3):28-39.
1981 Developing the Amazon. Bloomington: Indiana Univ. Press.
1982 Human Adaptability: An Introduction to Ecological Anthropology. Boulder: Westview Press. Originally published in 1979 by Duxbury Press.

Netting, R.
1968 Hill Farmers of Nigeria. Seattle: University of Washington Press.
1973 Fighting, Forest and the Fly: Some Demographic Regulators among the Kofyar. Journal of Anthropological Research 29:164-79.
1974 The System Nobody Knows: Village Irrigation in the Swiss Alps. In Irrigation's Impact on Society. T. Downing and M. Gibson, eds. Tucson: University of Arizona Press.
1976 What Alpine Peasants Have in Common: Observations on Communal Tenure in a Swiss Village. Human Ecology 4:135-46.
1977 Cultural Ecology. Menlo Park, Ca: Cummings.
1979 Household Dynamics in a 19th Century Swiss Village. Journal of Family History 4:39-58.
1981 Balancing on an Alp. New York: Cambridge Univ. Press.

Nietschman, B.
1973 Between Land and Water. New York: Seminar Press.

Odum, E.
1953 Fundamentals of Ecology. Philadelphia: Saunders.
1977 The Emergence of Ecology as a New Integrative Discipline. Science 195:1289-93.

Odum, H.T.
1957 Trophic Structure and Productivity of Silver Springs, Florida. Ecol. Monogr. 27:55-112.
1971 Environment, Power and Society. New York: Wiley.

Odum, H.T. and E.C. Odum
1976 Energy Basis for Man and Nature. New York: McGraw-Hill.

Orlove, B.
1980 Ecological Anthropology. Annual Review of Anthropology 9:235-73.

Patten, B. and E. Odum
1981 The Cybernetic Nature of Ecosystems. American Naturalist 118:886-95.

Plog, F.
1975 Systems Theory in Archaeological Research. Annual Review of Anthropology 4:207-224.

Polgar, Steven
1972 Population History and Population Policies from an Anthropological Perspective. Current Anthropology 13:203-11.

Rappaport, R.
1967 Pigs for the Ancestors. New Haven: Yale Univ. Press.
1971 The Flow of Energy in an Agricultural Society. Scientific American 224:116-32.
1977 Ecology, Adaptation and the Ills of Functionalism. Michigan Discussions in Anthropology 2:138-90.

Reichle, David and S. Auerbach
1979 Analysis of Ecosystems. In Systems Ecology. Shugart, H.H. and R.V. O'Neill, eds. Stroudsburg, PA: Dowden, Hutchinson and Ross. Orig. Publ. in 1972 by the Amer. Inst. of Biol. Sciences.

Ricklefs, R.
1973 Ecology. Portland, OR: Chiron Press.

Sahlins, Marshall
1961 The Segmentary Lineage: An Organization for Predatory Expansion. American Anthropologist 63:322-345.

Schneider, J. and R. Schneider
1976 Culture and Political Economy in Western Sicily. New York: Academic Press.

Shinners, S.M.
1967 Techniques of Systems Engineering. New York: McGraw-Hill.

Shugart, H.H. and R.V. O'Neill, eds.
1979 Systems Ecology. Stroudsburg, PA: Dowden, Hutchinson and Ross. Benchmark Papers in Ecology, Vol. 9.

Spengler, O.
1926 Decline of the West. New York: Knopf.

Spurr, S.H.
1969 The Natural Resource System. In The Ecosystem Concept in Natural Resource Management. G. Van Dyne, ed. New York: Academic Press.

Steward, J.
1955 The Concept and Method of Cultural Ecology. In Theory of Culture Change. Urbana: Univ. of Illinois Press.

Sukkachev, V.N.
1960 Relationship of biogeocoenosis, ecosystem and facies. Soviet Soil Science 6:579-584.

Sweet, Louise
1965 Camel Pastoralism in North Arabia and the Minimal Camping Unit. In Man, Culture and Animals. A. Leeds and A.P. Vayda, eds. Washington, D.C.: AAAS.

Thomas, F.
1925 The Environmental Basis of Society. New York: Century Press.

Thomas, R.B.
1973 Human Adaptation to a High Andean Energy Flow

System. Univ. Park, PA: Penn. State Univ., Dept. of Anthropology, Occasional Papers.

Troll, C.
1950 Die Geographische Landschaft und ihre Erforschung. Studium Gen. 3:163-181.

Van Dyne, G.M.
1979 Ecosystems, Systems Ecology and System Ecologists. In Systems Ecology. H.H. Shugart and R.V. O'Neill, eds. Stroudsburg, PA: Dowden, Hutchinson and Ross. Reprinted from the orig. publ. in 1966 by Oak Ridge Nat. Lab.

Van Dyne, G.M. (ed.)
1969 The Ecosystem Concept in Natural Resource Management. New York: Academic Press.

Vasey, D.E.
1979 Population and Agricultural Intensity in the Humid Tropics. Human Ecology 7:269-83.

Vayda, A.P. and R. Rappaport
1968 Ecology, Cultural and Non-cultural. In Introduction to Cultural Anthropology. J. Clifton, ed. Boston: Houghton and Miffling.

Vayda, A.P. and B. McCay
1975 New Directions in Ecology and Ecological Anthropology. Annual Review of Anthropology 4:293-306.

Waddell, E.
1972 The Mound-Builders. Seattle: Univ. of Washington Press.

Watson, W.
1964 Social Mobility and Social Class in Industrial Communities. In M. Gluckman, ed. Closed Systems and Open Minds. Chicago: Aldine.

Weiner, J.S.
1965 IBP Guide to the Human Adaptability Proposals. London: ICSU, Special Committee for the IBP.

White, B.
1973 Demand for Labor and Population Growth in Colonial Java. Human Ecology 7:217-36.

White, L.
1949 The Science of Culture. New York: Farrar, Straus and Giroux.

Wiener, N.
1948 Cybernetics. New York: Wiley.

Wissler, Clark
1926 The Relation of Nature to Man in Aboriginal America. New York: Oxford.

Worthington, E.
1975 The Evolution of the IBP. Cambridge: Cambridge University Press.

Zubrow, Ezra (ed.)
1976 Demographic Anthropology. Albuquerque: University of New Mexico Press.

Frank B. Golley

2. Historical Origins of the Ecosystem Concept in Biology

Tansley and the Ecosystem

Sir Arthur Tansley (1871-1955), an English botanist, coined the term ecosystem in 1935. In order to appreciate the concept denominated by the word, it is useful to know a little about Tansley as a person and the context in which he worked. I think it is fair to say that Tansley was the father of modern British plant ecology. He was one of the founders of the British Ecological Society, the world's first ecological society, the founder of the journal The New Phytologist, an editor of The Journal of Ecology from 1916 to 1936, the author of several authoritative books on British vegetation, a gifted teacher with several textbooks on plant ecology, a student of Sigmund Freud and author of a successful interpretive work titled The New Psychology, and a conservation advocate who helped establish the Nature Conservancy of the United Kingdom. These few remarks, based on long accounts of Tansley by Godwin (1977) and Evans (1976), suggest something of his character. Tansley was a scientist with broad interests, with a deep understanding and appreciation of field botany, and a special concern about philosophy and the processes of thought and research methodology. In addition to botany, he had a background in geology.

One focus of Tansley's research was the plant community, which he defined as the collection of plant species in a particular place and time that live together and interact through a complex of competitive and cooperative interactions. He recognized that soils, climate, and animals have an effect upon the distribution and abundance of these plants.

The plants and animals together with the physical features of the environment (i.e., the soils and climate), then, comprise an ecological system or ecosystem. In Tansley's own words (Tansley 1939):

> Since animals depend upon plants, directly or indirectly, for their food and often for indispensable shelter and since vegetation is affected by animals in varied and far-reaching ways and some species of plants depend upon animals for their maintenance, it is clear that animal and plant populations inhabiting the same unit of space are very closely knit together. For this reason a wider concept has been formulated, the biome or biocenosis (which some have called the "biotic community"), applying to animals and plants taken together. I myself have preferred a wider concept still, the ecosystem, which includes the inorganic as well as the living components in the whole to be considered.

Evans (1976), reviewing Tansley's contributions to ecology comments:

> The elegance of the idea of the ecosystem is that it is comprehensive, including within itself all those elements, physical, chemical and biological, which could conceivably affect the organisms being studied.

It is important to note that Tansley did not develop the ecosystem concept entirely or even mainly as a classification device. Rather, the concept was introduced as an analog to a physical system. This allowed Tansley to focus on a major concept--that of equilibrium. He stated in 1949:

> . . . the key concept which must govern all our efforts to formulate the phenomena of vegetation in a rational system is the idea of progress toward equilibrium, which is never, perhaps, completely attained, but to which approximation is made whenever the factors at work are constant and stable for a long enough period of time. This leads us to include the units of vegetation in a general conception of physical systems of which the universe is composed.

Tansley (1935) said:

> Such a system may be called an ecosystem, because it is determined by the particular portion, which we may call an ecotope (Greek topos, a place), of the physical world

> that forms a home (oikos) for the organisms which inhabit it.

Clearly, we see here a juxtaposition of Tansley with his broad interests, his focus on plants growing in natural habitats, his rigorous habits of thought and method within a social-cultural-scientific environment where physics had made great advances in understanding the dynamic nature of physical systems and where progress and equilibrium were not only of scientific interest but were important cultural ideas. The intersection of man and environment produced the concept we are considering here.

Of course, Tansley did not operate in an ecological vacuum, nor was he the first to deal with biological-environment systems. There were similar men thinking in similar patterns elsewhere both before and after Tansley. Major's (1969) review provides us with some of their names.

Alternative Concepts

Probably the most important and widely used alternative to ecosystem is the word biogeocoenosis. This term arose in the USSR and is derived from the Greek word koinos, meaning common, and the prefixes bio or life and geo or earth (Sukachev 1960). The term biocoenosis was employed by Mobius (1877) in his study of oyster beds and associated organisms in the north sea. It is widely used as a synonym of community in continental Europe. The Russian insertion of the prefix geo into biocoenosis served to emphasize the Russian longstanding interest in dynamic soil processes and their understanding of the interactive roles of plants, animals, geology and climate in creating a specific soil.

Excerpts from Sukachev's (1960) analysis of terminology illustrate this pattern of thought.

> In addition, biogeocoenosis has quite concrete content. Just as a phytocoenosis . . . is not a general expression for all categories of plant taxons, so too a biogeocoenosis is not a general expression for all the taxonomic subdivisions of a biotic community. . . . a biogeocoenosis is an area characterized throughout by a well defined, even more complex system of interactions between its living and dead natural components that remains uniform, i.e., a uniform system of obtaining and transforming matter and energy and exchanging them with neighboring biogeocoenoses and other natural bodies.

These processes

> depend on 1) the properties of their primary constituents and their distribution within the biogeocoeonosis; 2) the conditions under which these constituents become active, e.g., the relief and time of their existence; 3) the nature of the environment of the biogeocoenosis; and 4) the soil, a secondary constituent of bioinert character, which is the sum total of all the interactions.
>
> This idea was well expressed 35 years ago by the leading Soviet soil scientist B.B. Polynov. Using the phrase "elementary landscape" in a sense close to that of "biogeocoenosis," Polynov wrote "The soil is a total reflection of the landscape; it differs significantly from animals, plants, and rocks in not having, strictly speaking, its own original material. It does not come from without to adapt itself in one way or another to the landscape. From the very beginning of its formation it is a product of the landscape and therefore reflects the properties of the landscape to a greater extent than any other element." In a sense soil is the resultant of the processes taking place in the biogeocoenosis.
>
> Therefore a biogeocoenosis may be defined as any portion of the earth's surface containing a well defined system of interacting living (vegetation, animals, microorganisms) and dead (lithosphere, atmosphere, hydrosphere) natural components, i.e., a system of obtaining and transforming matter and energy and exchanging them with neighboring biogeocoenoses and other natural bodies that remain uniform.

Finally, Sukachev (1960) emphasizes the evolutionary character of the biogeocoenosis.

> The biogeocoenosis as a whole develops through the interaction of all its variable components and in accordance with special laws. The very process of interaction among the components constantly disrupts the established relationships, thereby affecting the evolution of the biogeocoenosis as a whole. Therefore, investigation of the specific laws governing the evolution of each component does not preclude the need of studying the laws of evolution of the biogeocoenosis as a whole. The latter is more than the single sum of its components and laws of development. The biogeocoenosis as a whole has its own distinctive qualities.

The comparison of ecosystem and biogeocoenosis makes a point familiar to anthropologists. Each discipline recognizes the several fundamental ideas inherent in these terms, but each also adds to the concept some special features of its own discipline and culture. Ecosystem and biogeocoenosis are not exact synonyms. Ecosystem emphasizes the mechanical view of nature characteristic of English-speaking cultures, especially that of the USA. It also emphasizes a connection with physics and chemistry--sciences with high status in these cultures. In contrast, biogeocoenosis emphasizes soil and the interaction of living and nonliving components to produce a soil. It also focuses on evolutionary processes and fits dialectical materialism. The basic stress on interaction and a wholistic entity are the same, but the terms are cast in quite different environments and cultures and therefore mean something different to the reader and user.

We could trace similar developments in the study of lakes or limnology [for example, Forbes (1887) wrote of the lake as a microcosm], geography or human ecology but the point is clear. The terminology of science is relative to specific scientific disciplines and to the cultures in which that science is practiced.

This account brings the ecosystem concept to the post-World War II period. By that time the concept was well founded: it expressed the integration of plants, animals, and environment, and it formed a link between biology and the physical sciences. It was not, however, especially well known or used in research.

Odum and Post-World War II Usage

It remained for Eugene Odum to bring the concept to the attention of the ecological community and to make it a fundamental idea in society. Odum in 1953 published the first edition of his text, Fundamentals of Ecology. This text was not only one of the first modern ecology textbooks but was also extremely well organized and innovative. Odum divided the book into sections concerned with ecosystems, and with communities and populations. He presented key concepts under the three sections in a standard format, with a description of the concept, a discussion of its meaning and significance and then gave several examples of the concept, often with field data. It is characteristic of Odum's thought that the ecosystem came first in his text as an organizing principle and not last as a synthetic concept. Odum (1953, p. 10) stated:

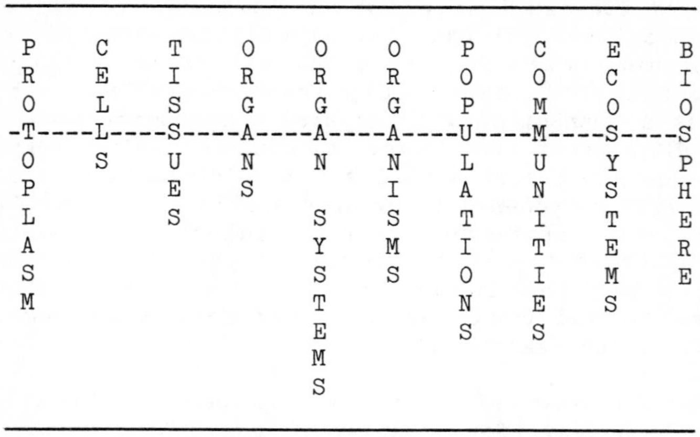

```
 P    C    T    O    O    O    P    C    E    B
 R    E    I    R    R    R    O    O    C    I
 O    L    S    G    G    G    P    M    O    O
-T----L----S----A----A----A----U----M----S----S
 O    S    U    N    N    N    L    U    Y    P
 P         E    S         I    A    N    S    H
 L         S         S    S    T    I    T    E
 A                   Y    M    I    T    E    R
 S                   S    S    O    I    M    E
 M                   T         N    E    S
                     E         S    S
                     M
                     S
```

Figure 2.1. Diagram showing ecological organization from Odum (1959)

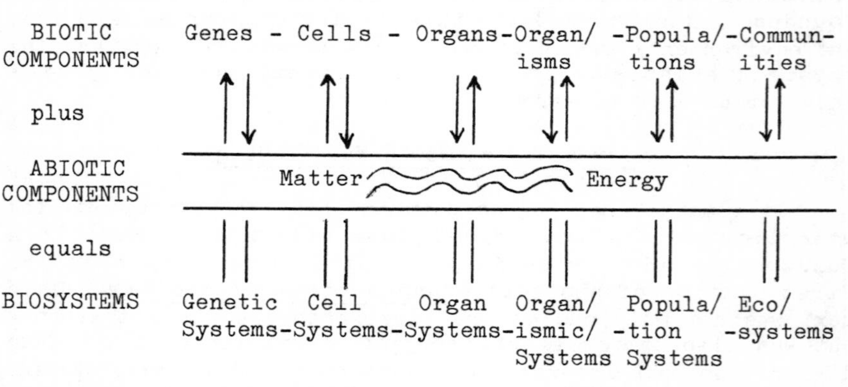

Figure 2.2. Diagram showing ecological organization from Odum (1971)

> The concept of the ecosystem is and should be a broad one, its main function in ecological thought being to emphasize obligatory relationships, interdependence, and causal relationships. Ecosystems may be conceived and studied in various sizes. Thus, the entire biosphere may be one vast ecosystem with numerous more or less circular systems within it. Obviously, smaller systems must be studied before the entire biosphere can be understood. A pond, a lake, a tract of forest, or a chemical cycle is a convenient unit of study.

Odum's text has been enlarged and rewritten in two additional editions.

In the second edition of his text (1959) Odum introduced the ecosystem in a diagram showing the relation of individuals, populations, communities and then in the same linear sequence, the ecosystem and biosphere (Fig. 2.1). This sequence mixed biological systems (individuals and populations) with systems containing biological and physical components (ecosystems). Evans (1956) and others had pointed out earlier that individuals, populations and communities and other biological units, with their physical environment form individual ecosystems, population ecosystems, community ecosystems, and so on. Odum adapted this format in the third edition of his text (Fig. 2.2). However, Odum's mixture of biological and ecological systems has been widely copied, especially in popular presentations. Most ecologists when they use the term ecosystem without a qualifier mean the biocoenosis or biotic community and its environment.

Odum is a biologist, with a strong zoological bias, but his experience with the ecosystem concept has led him to promote the ecosystem as the center point around which holistic sciences, as contrasted with reductionistic sciences, should concentrate (Odum 1977). What Odum calls the "new ecology" becomes linked with the social sciences, economics, and political science to directly address human problems.

After Eugene Odum it is impossible to identify single contributors to the ecosystem concept. Most ecologists educated in universities after 1950 were taught from Odum's or similar texts which featured the ecosystem concept. The concept passed into the mainstream of ecological thought and became operative in both the pedagogic and research spheres. Even so, it was difficult to implement the concept in actual research. Ecosystem studies required teams of scientists focused on a particular habitat or biotope. This type of research was not only contrary to the conventional pattern of biology, where a single individual with graduate students was the norm, but it was also very expensive. It thus came as a surprise to many that the major source of support for the implementation of this new concept turned out to be the U.S. Atomic Energy Commission (AEC). The AEC was faced with a series of problems that required a systems perspective. First, radioactive fallout injected into the atmosphere fell in unexpected places and concentrated in unexpected organisms and habitats. The AEC needed to be able to predict where and how much radioactivity would be accumulated from nuclear explosions and accidents. Second, the AEC operated several large industrial and test complexes. Initially, they required ecological surveys of the sites and then systems of monitoring the site to determine potential buildup of radioactivity. The ecosystem concept was essential here too.

The late John Wolf of the AEC put together teams of research workers which included groups working in major facilities such as the Savannah River Plant, Oak Ridge, Brookhaven, Hanford and Los Alamos. Studies were also started in Puerto Rico and Argonne National Laboratory, as well as in numerous universities. A large proportion of the active ecosystem ecologists in the U.S. came through these AEC programs sometime in their careers.

Another element in the development of the ecosystem concept at this time was the application of systems analysis and cybernetics to ecology. This development was significant because it gave ecologists a mathematical language which was common to other sciences and a conceptual framework within which to think about systems in general. This led quickly to the development of ecological modelling. Systems ecology developed at Oak Ridge where Bernard Patten, George Van Dyne and Jerry Olson formed a formidable group; at Florida and North Carolina under H.T. Odum; in California with Kenneth Watt; and in Canada under C.S. Holling.

The next step was the development of the International Biological Program (IBP). This was an international, nongovernmental program developed by biologists and modeled on the successful International Geophysical Year. It was formally presented at the General Assembly of the International Union of Biological Sciences (IUBS) in 1964, after a five-year preparatory period, and then continued as an active scientific program for about ten years. According to Worthington (1975), IBP held about 200 international scientific meetings, published 24 handbooks mainly on research methodology, published 25 issues of IBP News, had nation-based programs operating in 44 countries, with additional participation from 53 countries, with more than

2000 scientific research projects and thousands of technical papers and books published as a result of research. An international effort to synthesize results across national programs has resulted already in about 25 books published by Cambridge University Press. In addition, many national programs published their own synthesis volumes. This huge effort is still not finished, ten years after the program ended, as further evaluation of data continue to be published under the IBP imprint.

This international program was defined as studying "the biological basis of productivity and human welfare" and its object was to ensure world-wide study of organic production of the land, freshwaters and seas, the potentialities and uses of new, as well as existing, resources and human adaptability to changing conditions. It was organized into seven sections: productivity terrestrial, production processes, conservation terrestrial, productivity freshwater, productivity marine, human adaptability, and use and management of resources.

Worthington (1975) described the uniqueness of the program in these words:

> It is the ecosystem approach which distinguishes much of IBP research from what had dominated ecology before. Essentially it consists of the careful selection of a number of variables--biological, chemical and physical--about which data are collected quantitatively as well as qualitatively. Thereby the ecosystem can be analyzed in order to ascertain which factors and processes are important in causing the dynamics of the whole. In this, the application of systems analysis to biological systems has been one of the major innovations developing during IBP. Some would go further and say that it has been one of IBP's major achievements.

The ecosystem approach was especially used in the biome program of the terrestrial productivity section in its comparison of patterns of productivity across broad geographic regions. Of course, the ecosystem approach was not developed specially for IBP; rather, there was a convergence in the application of systems analysis to ecological problems and the development of the international program to focus on ecological processes underlying environmental problems. Since ecologists were approaching natural systems from a dynamic, in contrast to a static, viewpoint, systems analysis was the appropriate tool to use. In turn, the experience of IBP with large, complex ecosystems made it possible to test a variety of modeling approaches, to try different methods of management of teams of scientists, and to attempt to organize very large sets of data on biological, chemical and physical phenomena.

The contributions of the terrestrial productivity research activities were many, including accumulation of a greatly expanded data base on the structure and function of the world's terrestrial ecosystems, gradual evolution of techniques and methods including development of standard units and symbols, emergence of a group of scientists familiar with team research, and the development of the foundations of what some in the post-IBP era would call ecosystem engineering.

Of course, IBP was also criticized by biologists. These critics frequently belonged to subdisciplines which had relatively little interest in the problems of organic production and human adaptability. Others were philosophically opposed to team research or systems science. And a few others feared that IBP would reduce the flow of funds to their particular topic of interest. Unfortunately, in the United States of America there was a misguided effort to evaluate three biome programs of IBP by the National Science Foundation immediately as the program ended and before the full spate of synthesis volumes had appeared (Mitchell et al. 1976). This analysis had many conclusions, but what was significant to the critics of the IBP was that it found that systems analysis and modeling had not been able to reach the goals set for it and that the papers produced by these biome programs (up to 1974 about 500 papers had been published from the three biome programs) were "only slightly different with respect to breadth of coverage and attention to dynamic relations than the average paper published in *Ecology*" (Mitchell et al. 1976). While NSF had its reasons for examining the program when it did, an appraisal of the IBP is justified only after the synthesis volumes have all appeared and sufficient time has elapsed so that the connections between advances in science and their sources can be traced. I suspect that IBP will emerge as one of the major scientific events in biology in the century--at least for the ecological sciences, if not for other parts of science as well.

As one example, the IBP was managed in the U.S. by a committee of the U.S. National Academy of Sciences. It was designed to be a program of interest to many governmental agencies but ultimately its funding and direction were housed in the National Science Foundation. As the research matured, management of the proposals became more complicated and a new program in NSF was created. This program is called The

Ecosystem Studies Program in the Division of Environmental Biology and is responsible for support of ecosystem studies in the U.S. with an annual budget of around $11 million.

The most recent event in this program was the initiation of the Long-Term Studies in Ecological Research (LTER) project in 1980. This project received proposals from the community and then selected 10 to 12 sites where long-term ecosystem studies will be carried out. These sites represent a reasonable cross section of the nation's ecosystems (defined broadly) and are expected to provide new opportunities to trace the biological response to environmental and ecological parameters with long-term time dynamics, as well as to compare structure and function across a wide range of systems.

Contemporary Understandings

It is useful, at this point, to summarize the historical development of the concept and then to attempt a modern operational definition. The term ecosystem has become widely used in English-speaking countries. It expresses technically the common sense idea that everything is related to everything else. It is culturally useful since it expresses nature in physical mechanical terms, deemphasizing the biological-evolutionary aspect, and links directly to computer science and information theory. It is therefore a manipulative, in contrast to a relational, term. I suspect that these systems-relative features of the term have been influential in making it so widely acceptable.

In this context, the ecosystem may be defined operationally as follows. First, the ecosystem is conceived as a black box, containing both biological and nonbiological elements. These are the elements found together in a biotope. The boundaries of this box are difficult to define because the biological and nonbiological elements are usually distributed over space in continuous rather than discrete patterns, but the boundaries must be stated nevertheless. In most studies boundary problems are solved arbitrarily, being defined to fit the objectives of the study.

Second, the behavior of the ecosystem is defined as the ratio of inputs to and outputs from the blackbox. This process of conversion of a set of inputs into a set of outputs is an expression of the system's behavior. Inputs and outputs are in terms of energy or materials. This set of behaviors of an ecosystem is influenced by external factors--the environment of the system--and by internal factors--the interactions between the biota and between the biotic and abiotic elements of the system. Observation of the behavior of a series of ecosystems leads to identification of consistent and inconsistent patterns, which in turn lead to formulation of hypotheses which state the relationship between internal and external factors and the input-output ratios. Hypotheses may be tested experimentally.

Third, the patterns of ecosystem behavior, then, are interpreted in the context of a larger ecosystem of which the ecosystem of interest is an element and through the behaviors of subsystems of components within the black box. Thus, one can arrange ecosystems in a hierarchy of systems, as Tansley (1939) pointed out. The problems of ecosystem boundaries, significance and application are all solved when one considers the ecosystem of interest as one of a set of systems which collectively make up a system at the next higher level in the hierarchy of organization.

In point number two above, the interactions between the biological and physical components of ecosystems involve feedback and complex networks across which material, energy, and information flow. However, recently ecosystems have been described as noncybernetic systems by Engelberg and Boyarsky (1979). These authors argue that ecosystems do not contain information networks that connect all parts of the system and forge the parts of the system into an integrated whole. Further, the dominant interactions in ecosystems, they assert, involve high energy phenomena giving rise to other high energy phenomena, rather than low energy (informational) phenomena giving rise to high energy phenomena as in cybernetic systems. And finally, cycles in ecosystems, they state, merely trace movement of material or energy from one compartment to another. They conclude that ecosystems are not cybernetic systems.

This analysis raises questions about how we are to think about ecosystems and, as Patten and Odum (1981) commented in their rebuttal to Engelberg and Boyarsky, how we are to place ecosystems within the scheme of known systems. Both Patten and Odum (1981) and Jordan (1981) provide examples to refute the criticisms of Engelberg and Boyarsky. Jordan reasons from coevolutionary examples that it is inconceivable that such complex networks described by ecologists could have arisen by accident, while Patten and Odum present an elegant systematic analysis of the issue with ecological examples. They conclude:

> We believe that to understand the organism in nature, its other half, environment, will have to be

> understood as well. To us, "environment" means environment unspecified, but "ecosystem" is environment specified. The ecosystem is the level of organization concerned with orderly, not chaotic, processing of energy-matter in the biosphere. We do not believe that it is the goal of ecosystems to do this. They are not superorganisms. Rather, it is a constraint of existence that if living processes are not orderly, antientrophic, then they will not persist. The balance of nature calls for a conjugate action-reaction kind of organization that creates order where there could be chaos as a matter of implicit design that simply evolved over geological time.

This leaves us the final topic to consider; the key questions that deserve attention by students of ecosystems. I feel that there is a large set of such questions. They include the following:

1. Tansley (1939) introduced the ecosystem concept in the context of <u>system equilibrium</u>.

> What I have called an ecosystem is far less integrated than an individual animal or plant, but it shows itself capable, nevertheless, of a certain degree of integration of a certain resistance to disintegrating forces, and thus in maintaining; in certain cases, a <u>relative</u> dynamic equilibrium for centuries or even for millenia.

Tansley appears to have been influenced in part by Clements' concepts of succession toward an equilibrium or climax state and by physicists' concepts of equilibrium. In operational terms as described above, we would define an equilibrium as a state where the inputs and outputs balance and the storage within the system remains constant. Does an equilibrium occur?

Technically this is a difficult question because the response of an ecosystem to the environment may require hundreds of years before a semblance of balance is achieved. But further, is it more realistic to conceive of a directional process which has a built-in linear force toward an equilibrium state or is it more reasonable to consider an ecosystem as an adaptive system responding to the external environment and changing its behavior as the environment shifts and as biological evolution occurs within it? (See Smith in this volume.) The adaptive model appeals to me, but the question is open.

2. Do ecosystems undergo senescence and death? Clearly, ecosystems go extinct. Those of past geological epochs can only be recreated in an abstract sense with great difficulty from fossil and pollen records. Equally clearly, some ecosystems become senile. For example, organic matter builds at a rate faster than the rate of decomposition and system behavior becomes slower and slower. Ultimately the system changes. Is this analogous to senility and death?

3. Ecologists generally neglect the question of the boundaries of ecosystems, establishing them for convenience where an apparent discontinuity occurs. However, the location of a system boundary is not a trivial problem (see Netting, Adams and Kasakoff, Ellen, and Moran in this volume). A boundary implies a discontinuity in either the nature of the system structure or in the rate processes, or both. Watershed studies have been especially effective because the watershed, by definition, is limited by the flow of water into and out of the system. Lakes are also easily bounded systems; but this is not true of other common systems. How does adoption of arbitrary boundaries in a continuous universe bias the study of system behavior?

4. We understand that both physical and biological processes are operative within the ecosystem. We do not understand the balance between these different forces as the environment and habitat changes. In systems which are strongly regulated by physical process--the open ocean, for example--are the behaviors of ecosystems and their components more predictable than in a tropical rain forest where biological processes are dominant? Patten (1982) has recently argued that direct cause and effect is not very significant in explaining ecosystem behavior. Rather, he finds that indirect causality stemming from the interactions and feedback in the networks explains a larger, actually much larger, proportion of the behavior. If so, does this effect vary in systems under physical versus biological control (see Bates and Lees in this volume)?

5. Finally, I will ask, what are the hierarchies of subsystems between what the ecologist would call the community ecosystem and the population? The subdivision used in IBP was the trophic level (that is, the primary producers, the consumers and decomposers). The supralevel used by the population ecologist is the food chain, in which three or more populations are coupled together through the exchange of food and being eaten. There is a gap between trophic levels and food chains so that the ecosystem scientist and the population ecologist/biologist find less in common than they should. What are the hierarchical levels between ecosystems

and populations? This is an area where substantial advance might be possible once we have adequate data on the entire food web of a community. But to describe an entire food web is a very difficult task and has not been completely carried out anywhere as far as I know.

Man in the Ecosystem

Let me finish by making a few comments about anthropology. I have consciously avoided saying anything about man because I have emphasized the biological ecologists', rather than the human ecologists', perspectives. Frankly, I find no problem in including man in the ecosystem concept. However, for most biological ecologists, the systems of interest are spatially so small that man can only be an external factor--part of the system's environment.

When the ecologist moves to larger systems--regional systems or landscapes--man becomes an actor within the system and can be treated as such. However, man is unique in creating culture. This unique ability of man requires the ecosystem analyst to include history within the study and that makes it more difficult (see Netting, Ellen, and Adams and Kasakoff in this volume).

The word "ecosystem" now can be found in legislation, in regulations and in the popular press. In these usages it frequently conveys a concept of interaction or of integration of units into an interacting system. As such, it is a code word to express the common sense idea that everything is interacting with everything else. While this element is in the ecologist's concept of ecosystem, the technical concept is actually much richer in association and meaning. It reflects the hierarchy of organization from the universe to the atom; it emphasizes the dynamic, as contrasted to the static, element of systems; and it provides a bridge where principles of physics, chemistry and biology can all be brought together and related to actual processes. I conclude by observing that ecologists have never been especially interested in creating a taxonomy of ecosystems (as they did for plant communities and geographical regions). The fact that the concept is used in a variety of ways may be a sign of immaturity. It may also be a sign of its dynamic utility.

References Cited

Engelberg, J. and L.L. Boyarsky
1979 The Noncybernetic Nature of Ecosystems. Amer. Nat. 114:317-324.

Evans, F.C.
1956 Ecosystem as the Basic Unit in Ecology. Science 123:1127-8.
1976 A Sack of Uncut Diamonds: The Study of Ecosystems and the Future Resources of Mankind. J. Ecol. 64:1-39.

Forbes, S.A.
1887 The Lake as a Microcosm. Bull. Peoria Sci. Assoc., Illinois Nat. Hist. Surv. Bull. 15:537-550.

Godwin, A.
1977 Sir Arthur Tansley: The Man and the Subject. J. Ecol. 65:1-26.

Jordan, C.
1981 Do Ecosystems Exist? Amer. Nat. 118:284-287.

Major, J.
1969 Historical Development of the Ecosystem Concept. In G.M. Van Dyne, ed. The Ecosystem Concept in Natural Resource Management. New York: Academic Press. pp. 9-22.

Mitchell, R., R. Mayer and J. Downhower
1976 An Evaluation of Three Biome Programs. Science 192: 859-865.

Mobius, K.
1877 Die Auster und die Austernwirtschaft. Berlin: Wiegundt., Hempel and Parey.

Odum, E.P.
1953 Fundamentals of Ecology. First edition. Philadelphia: W.B. Saunders Co.
1959 Fundamentals of Ecology. Second edition. Philadelphia: W.B. Saunders Co.
1971 Fundamentals of Ecology. Third edition. Philadelphia: W.B. Saunders Co.
1977 The Emergence of Ecology as a New Integrative Discipline. Science 195 (4284):1289-1293.

Patten, B.C.
1982 Environs: Relativistic Elementary Particles for Ecology. Amer. Nat. 119(2):179-219.

Patten, B.C. and E.P. Odum
1981 The Cybernetic Nature of Ecosystems. Amer. Nat. 118:886-895.

Sukachev, V.N.
1960 Relationship of biogeocoenosis, ecosystem, and facies. Soviet Soil Science, No. 6. pp. 579-584. (English translation)

Tansley, A.G.
1935 Introduction to Plant Ecology. London: George Allen and Unwin, Ltd.
1939 British Ecology During the Past Quarter Century: The Plant Community and the Ecosystem. J. Ecol. 27:513-530.
1949 The British Islands and Their Vegetation. Volume 1. Cambridge: University Press.

Worthington, E.B.
1975 The Evolution of the IBP. Cambridge: Cambridge University Press.

Eric Alden Smith

3. Anthropology, Evolutionary Ecology, and the Explanatory Limitations of the Ecosystem Concept

Introduction

The ecosystem concept has had a substantial impact on research and theory in anthropology and other social sciences. The central thesis of this paper is that this concept, and the theoretical and methodological framework of systems ecology that nurtured it, have made and can only make a very limited contribution to anthropology.

In support of this thesis, the first section of the paper discusses the fundamental differences in scope and logic between systems ecology and anthropology as well as serious deficiencies in certain explanatory arguments advanced by many systems ecologists and their anthropological colleagues. Briefly, I argue that whereas anthropology seeks to elucidate the causes of variation in human society and culture, systems ecology is primarily concerned with describing the structure and function of much larger systems (i.e., ecosystems; see Moran and Golley in this volume). When systems ecology does venture into causal explanations, these are either at a level inappropriate for explaining the strategies of particular ecosystem components (e.g., a human population), of a teleological nature, or both. Hence, at best, the ecosystem concept offers a macro-scale descriptive framework for human ecology with little explanatory utility

[1] I thank the following colleagues for useful comments--not always heeded--on the first draft of this paper: Eric Fischer, Frank Golley, Raymond Hames, Donald Hardesty, Emilio Moran, Gordon Orians, Peter Richerson, Stephen Stearns, and Bruce Winterhalder. Support from a National Science Foundation postdoctoral fellowship is gratefully acknowledged.

for anthropology. Essentially, I conclude that whenever we are concerned with explaining social/cultural or behavioral diversity within and between human societies--which I take to be the fundamental goal of anthropological analysis--ecosystem approaches are of limited use.

The second section of this paper summarizes an alternative body of ecological theory--evolutionary ecology--that does not suffer from the particular defects of the ecosystem approach. There I briefly discuss the logic and method of evolutionary ecology as well as recent applications of this approach to anthropological problems. A third section summarizes the outstanding differences between systems ecology and evolutionary ecology--differences in theoretical principles, analytical methods, and research objectives. In conclusion, I argue that an awareness of the explanatory goals of anthropology, plus a fuller appreciation of the structure of current ecological theory, suggests anthropologists should reorient their attempts to derive explanatory insights from ecology.

Systems Ecology and its Role in Anthropology

The thesis that systems ecology has inherently little explanatory value to offer anthropology is one that must be defended in analytical terms. It will be helpful, however, to briefly review the historical development of the ecosystem concept and the process by which it was incorporated into the independently-developed tradition of ecological anthropology.

Until mid-century, ecology consisted of two loosely-related approaches to organism-environment interactions: natural history studies of ecological communities and the more theoretically-oriented tradition of population ecology which emphasized mathematical models and laboratory experiments. In the 1950's, the discipline underwent a major transformation, resulting in the gradual decline of the atheoretical "natural history" approach and the development of two highly divergent theoretical schools--systems ecology and evolutionary ecology. The contrasting sources and analytical methods of the "two ecologies" (summarized in a later section of this paper) are not generally recognized by ecological anthropologists, but they present very different frameworks for analyzing human ecology. (Additional foci of ecological research--such as physiological ecology and some areas of population ecology--persist outside the orbit of these two dominant theoretical schools of ecology, but because they have had little influence on anthropology, they can be ignored here.)

Major Features of Ecosystems Ecology

The substantive principles and methods of systems ecology are discussed elsewhere in this volume as well as in a series of articles, textbooks, and collections (Halfon 1979; Major 1969; E.P. Odum 1962, 1969, 1971; H.T. Odum 1971; Patten 1971-76; Shugart and O'Neill 1979). Certain basic assumptions and orientations of the approach need to be emphasized here, however. The primary assumption is that ecosystems are cybernetic entities--that is, that they are self-regulating and self-organizing systems controlled by information-carrying feedback loops (Margalef 1968; Patten and Odum 1981). This view holds that ecosystems are entities with internal coherence, expressed in terms of patterns of energy flow, nutrient cycling, and species composition. It furthermore argues that these coherent patterns are integrated and controlled by an information network--the "invisible wires of nature" vaguely delimited as "all the factors, processes and interactions that we collectively know as natural history which serve to mediate the movement or transformation of energy-matter" (Patten and Odum 1981:890).

In keeping with the cybernetic view, ecosystems are portrayed as orderly, stable, homeostatic, functional, and antientropic. In most versions, the primary "function" of ecosystems is held to be their survival or self-perpetuation; some versions, however, argue that ecosystems exhibit more definite purposes than that, as we shall see in a moment. The cybernetic view of ecosystems and related issues of ecosystem design and stability remain quite controversial (Colinvaux 1973:549ff; Whittaker 1975:261ff; Engelberg and Boyarsky 1979). Ecologists committed to the systems approach continue to affirm it, however, though disagreeing with their critics over the degree of systemic organization and teleological behavior necessary to qualify a system as cybernetic (Patten and Odum 1981).

The major methodological strategy in systems ecology involves descriptive modeling and detailed simulation. The classical approach--which continues to dominate many research projects on ecosystems analysis, such as the International Biological Program (IBP) projects (see Little et al., in this volume)--is to construct elaborate "compartmental models" of energy flow and nutrient cycling. These descriptive models may be represented graphically via hydrological (E.P. Odum 1971:64) or electrical (H.T. Odum 1972) symbols, or they may be expressed in the form of a system of differential equations. The models may be almost purely inductive efforts, based on detailed empirical observations of an ecosystem (e.g., Bliss 1977). Alternatively, especially in the case of highly complex ecosystems, abstract models of ecosystem structure and function may provide the basis for simulations that are simplified versions of reality (Paulik 1972).

Regardless of the particular form of modeling employed, systems ecology analyses are primarily aimed at constructing detailed descriptive generalizations about particular ecosystems. This research strategy has two major implications for ecological anthropology.

First, there is very little attempt to develop explanatory theory--general principles that account for why systems take the form they do. This results in part from the problems of assembling and analyzing the massive quantities of data needed to represent the workings of complex natural ecosystems and partly from a philosophical or pragmatic bias towards quantitative prediction of ecosystem behavior, regardless of the elusive causal mechanisms responsible for such behavior. In the words of one systems ecologist, the approach represents

> a move away from the explanatory or cognitive criterion of truth, a soft criterion which heuristically lends intellectual points of leverage for seeking understanding, and toward the predictive criterion, a hard one with the potential of leading ultimately to optimal design and control of ecosystems (Patten 1971:xiii).

Furthermore, predictions generated by the systems approach are generally short-term, system-specific, and inductive (that is, dependent on a unique simulation model and large inputs of empirical data drawn from the system being studied). As a result, anthropologists seeking to understand why different human populations vary in their ecological and social characteristics will find little explanatory guidance in systems ecology per se. At best, principles of thermodynamics and nutrient cycling may provide insights into some of the constraints within which sociocultural patterns must vary. (I am indebted to Peter Richerson for suggesting this last point).

Second, systems ecology focuses on a higher or more inclusive level of organization than that of a component population (such as a human population). Indeed, in most models species do not even appear as such but are lumped with other species at a particular trophic level or as a reservoir in the carbon cycle. This is an approach unlikely to yield understanding into the causes of cultural or biobehavioral variation in human populations.

While most systems ecologists have stuck to the descriptive, inductive approach just noted, a few prominent theoreticians have boldly looked beyond the cybernetic network of functioning ecosystems in search of theories or generalizations that explain why ecosystems exhibit the patterns they have uncovered. The resultant accounts have a highly functionalist flavor and, in some cases, go further and ascribe purposive as well as cybernetic qualities to ecosystems.

Presumably because of the cybernetic orientation and macrosystem focus of systems ecology, the explanatory arguments that have emerged emphasize a "top-down" view of causality. In other words, the focus in such explanations has been on how an ecosystem's component parts maintain the "self-organizing" system, rather than on how the parts evolve to form the whole. In its most extreme form, this "top-down" view holds that the populations comprising the ecosystem each play a definite role, subordinate to the smooth functioning of the whole system (Margalef 1968:81ff; H.T. Odum 1971:95ff). In less thoroughgoing varieties of ecosystem functionalism, the evolutionary strategies of each component species are simply taken as "givens," evolving within the constraints of ecosystemic perpetuation.

It is but a short step from a functionalist view of ecosystems to a teleological one. In the 1960's, systems ecologists developed a fairly elaborate set of generalizations about the evolutionary dynamics of ecosystems, thus venturing beyond the purely functionalist view. As exemplified in the synthesizing statements of E.P. Odum (1962, 1969) and Ramon Margalef (1968), ecosystems were portrayed as carrying out definite strategies. Building on earlier work on succession by natural-history era ecologists like Clements (1932), empirical generalizations about the direction of succession in many ecological communities were transmuted into conclusions that ecosystems were selected to maximize efficiency of energy flow and nutrient cycling, diversity, stability, and "information content." It was proposed that "succession in any self-organizing system involves the substitution of some piece of the system by some other piece that allows the preservation of the same amount of information at some lower cost, or the preservation of more information at the same cost" (Margalef 1968:81). That the goal is system improvement and that the "pieces" that are replaced in such improvement are component species is made clear when Margalef (1968:93) speaks of "the whole system of which the evolving population is an expendable part. In other words, selection is controlled by the cybernetic mechanism at the level of the ecosystem."

The idea that ecosystems exhibit functional design and goal-directed behavior is, of course, a highly controversial one (Williams 1966:248ff; Richerson 1977:9-11; Engelberg and Boyarsky 1979). As long as the features of ecosystem succession are proposed as empirical generalizations only, the controversy remains fairly muted; but when these trends are said to be explained by cybernetic principles, serious questions arise. The primary question is how such features of ecosystems could have evolved, especially if and when they conflict with the predicted outcomes of evolution by natural selection acting on the component populations of the ecosystem. There have been few attempts to establish the mechanisms by which ecosystem design of the sort postulated by Margalef _et al_. could arise (Dunbar 1960, 1972; Wynne-Edwards 1962; Wilson 1980; Patten 1981), and these are not widely accepted by evolutionary biologists at this time. Recently, some prominent systems ecologists have significantly qualified the assertion that ecosystems have strategies of development (e.g., Patten and Odum 1981:889; Margalef 1975). As a rule, however, most systems ecologists remain unconvinced that "reductionist" views of ecological communities as the product of competing individuals and species are sufficient to explain what they observe (Patten and Odum 1981:891, 894).

One of the most influential attempts to generate explanatory propositions from ecosystems ecology has been the thermodynamic scheme proposed by H.T. Odum (1971). The primary causal principle advocated in this case was stated as follows:

> In the last century, Darwin popularized the concept of _natural selection_, and early in this century Lotka (1922) indicated that the maximization of power for useful purposes was the criterion for natural selection. Darwin's evolutionary law thus developed into a general energy law (H.T. Odum 1971:31-32).

But whereas Darwin (and Lotka, for that matter) conceived of "useful purposes" primarily in terms of the reproductive interests of individuals or species, Odum followed the top-down bent of ecosystems ecology and argued that selection favored thermodynamic maximization for the ecosystem as a whole, even at the expense of the component species (e.g., H.T. Odum 1971:95, 150). The logical and empirical criticisms that can be raised against this scheme have been discussed at length by Slobodkin (1972) and myself (Smith 1979), among others. Suffice it to say that there is no currently accepted basis in evolutionary theory for viewing ecosystems as selected to maximize useful power, or any other global measure, and good reason to doubt the possibility.

The Incorporation of Ecosystems Ecology into Anthropology

Ecological anthropology originated independently of, and prior to, the development of the ecosystem concept in general ecology. The roots of the approach can be traced back to the nineteenth century (Anderson 1973; Vayda and Rappaport 1968), but it was Julian Steward's work in the 1930's (Steward 1936, 1937, 1938) that marked the development of a coherent system of ecological explanation in anthropology.

Steward developed the approach he termed "cultural ecology" as a framework for causal explanation of cultural differences and similarities. He seized on ecological considerations and environmental influences as an antidote to the sterile cultural relativism and "the fruitless assumption that culture comes from culture" that pervaded anthropology in the first half of this century (Steward 1955:36). Steward was generally familiar with the ecological and biological principles of his time and felt that "the principal meaning of ecology is 'adaptation to environment'" (ibid., p. 34). Indeed, his whole approach is framed in terms of adaptation and "the adaptive processes through which a historically derived culture is modified in a particular environment," arguing on analytical and empirical grounds that "over the millenia, cultures in different environments have changed tremendously, and these changes are basically traceable to new adaptations required by changing technology and productive arrangements" (p. 37). In this light, Steward's approach anticipates in many ways the current views of evolutionary ecology (Dyson-Hudson and Smith 1978:22; and below).

Many studies in ecological anthropology continue in the Stewardian tradition of cultural ecology without making any use of the ecosystem concept--or of any formal ecological theory, for that matter (reviews in Anderson 1973; Netting 1977; and Heider 1972). By the late 1960's, however, many ecological anthropologists (and human ecologists in other disciplines, such as geography) began emphasizing the ecosystem concept (see Moran, this volume). Such analyses vary in their uses of the concept. Many ecological anthropologists make use of the concept without attributing explanatory power or teleological qualities to the ecosystem itself (e.g., Geertz 1963; Thomas 1973; Moran 1982), simply viewing the ecosystem as the broad context within which human populations adapt. Compartmental models of energy flow have been quite influential in research on human ecology, and most studies have employed the energy-flow framework in an essentially descriptive manner (e.g., Kemp 1971; Nietschmann 1973) or to organize analyses of the subsistence adaptations of various human populations (e.g., Little and Morren 1976; Thomas 1973, 1976; Moran 1982).

None of the studies cited above attempt to employ the ecosystem concept as an explanatory device. Some anthropologists, however, have been influenced by the notion that ecosystems exhibit strategies and cybernetic design and even by the view that sociocultural variation is part of a grander scheme of nature, with human societies serving the interests of the ecosystems that they form a part of. Vayda and Rappaport (1968) were perhaps the first anthropologists to argue that the cybernetic approach to ecosystems ecology should be adopted in analyzing the "regulating or *homeostatic* functions of cultural practices" (p. 495; italics in original). Through the work of Rappaport (1967, 1968, 1971, 1977; see also Flannery 1972) in particular, the cybernetic/ecosystemic view became a dominant trend in ecological anthropology, though this view has recently suffered sustained criticism and defection (Jorgensen 1972; Friedman 1974, 1979; Vayda and McCay 1975; Brush 1975; Salisbury 1975; Bates and Lees 1979; Orans 1975; Orlove 1980).

To cybernetic ecological anthropologists, adaptation of ecological units does not refer to Darwinian struggle for reproductive success or efficient resource utilization, but rather to maintenance of equilibrium, homeostasis, and above all an undegraded ecosystem. Rappaport, for example, defines adaptation as "the process through which living systems maintain homeostasis" (1977:168), and he explicitly includes ecosystems within this class of adaptive systems, arguing that "the proper goal of adaptive systems is merely to persist" (ibid., p. 178). No sustained attempt to defend the validity of this view in the face of the logic of natural selection has been proposed, but at times reference is made to the group-selection argument of Wynne-Edwards (1962) (also a favorite with systems ecologists) or the philosophical views of Bateson (1972) and Slobodkin (1968; Slobodkin and Rappaport 1974).

The emphasis on homeostatic regulation derives in part from a concern with the dangers to population persistence if the environmental carrying capacity is exceeded, but it also seems to derive inspiration from the teleological view of ecosystem self-regulation propounded by many systems ecologists (see above). It can also be argued that ideas of systemic purpose and group-selection have been very attractive to anthropologists because of their heritage of similar views concerning culture developed by Durkheim, Radcliffe-Brown, Leslie White, and others (Raymond Hames, personal communication). Durkheim's (1915, 1933) concepts of "social solidarity" and "collective consciousness," Radcliffe-Brown's (1952) emphasis on the function social institutions play in maintaining the social "superorganism," and White's (1949, 1959) energy-based scheme of the evolution of culture, all no doubt served to pre-adapt anthropologists to the viewpoint of systems ecology. The cybernetic view of ecosystems is actually quite consistent with the functionalist, superorganic tradition in anthropology; all that is necessary to bring the two approaches into conformity is to postulate that social systems are functional components of much larger systems--ecosystems (viz. Rappaport 1968:224-33).

The primary problem that arises with ecological functionalism is the lack of a coherent theory that can predict the outcome of any conflict between "ecosystem imperatives" (Rappaport 1977:141) and the short-term adaptive interests of component individuals and populations, including human ones. While both systems ecologists and anthropologists generally recognize that such conflicts can occur--and indeed, may be inevitable--they too often _assume on principle_ that the resolution will favor the interests of the most inclusive level (the ecosystem). Since theoretical consensus on the outcome of conflicting selection pressures at different levels of organization has not yet been achieved (cf. Williams 1966; Lewontin 1970; Maynard Smith 1976; Wade 1978; Alexander and Borgia 1980; Uyenoyama and Feldman 1980; Wilson 1980), there is no clear basis in evolutionary theory for assuming that evolutionary processes will favor subordination of the adaptive interests of component individuals or populations to maintenance of ecosystem homeostasis or efficiency. In summary, assumptions of ecosystemic adaptation are premature at best and at worst quite misleading. Furthermore, such assumptions are not a necessary attribute of ecological theories of adaptation, a fact that is exemplified by the alternative body of ecological theory known as evolutionary ecology.

Evolutionary Ecology and Its Anthropological Uses

Evolutionary ecology offers a body of theory based on neo-Darwinian premises that clearly contrast with the assumptions of ecosystems ecology, and it appears to have considerable anthropological promise. What follows is a brief review of the basic logic of evolutionary ecology and a summary of potential and extant applications to anthropological problems.

The Logic and Structure of Evolutionary Ecology

Evolutionary ecology approaches topics by building mathematical models derived from the basic postulates of natural selection theory (and the analytical methods of microeconomics), deducing from these models testable hypotheses concerning behavioral and ecological processes. While empirical research has lagged somewhat behind theory formulation, a great deal of empirical research on animal and plant populations has been guided by theories and models developed in evolutionary ecology. Excellent overviews of this rapidly expanding discipline are now available (Cody and Diamond 1975; Emlen 1973; Krebs and Davies 1978; May 1981; Pianka 1983; Roughgarden 1979; Stearns 1982).

Currently at least four main areas of research in evolutionary ecology with clear anthropological implications can be discerned: 1) the study of foraging strategies; 2) research on mating systems and life-history strategies; 3) the study of spatial organization and group formation; and 4) the interrelated topics of niche theory, population dynamics, and community structure. I will discuss each area very briefly, referring the interested reader to the basic theoretical literature and to published anthropological applications (see also Smith and Winterhalder 1981; Smith 1982).

Foraging Theory. In evolutionary ecology, the study of subsistence strategies has led to the development of a group of models labelled "optimal foraging theory" (reviews in Krebs 1978; Pyke et al. 1977; Schoener 1971). This body of theory is concerned with several topics, including prey choice and diet breadth, foraging group size, habitat utilization, and optimal patterns of movement and time allocation during foraging. Given the strong anthropological interest in subsistence strategies, any systematic body of theory dealing with food procurement has obvious relevance. Hence, it is not surprising that the bulk of anthropological applications of evolutionary ecological theory have been concerned with foraging strategies--particularly those of hunter-gatherers, where the connection with extant ecological models is the most direct (Winterhalder 1981a).

The optimal diet model of MacArthur and Pianka (1966) can be used to illustrate the manner in which foraging theorists (and evolutionary ecologists in general) employ models to generate explanatory hypotheses. This particular model, illustrated graphically in Figure 3.1, assumes what is termed a fine-grained relationship between forager and prey, such that foragers search for all prey types simultaneously and encounter the different types "randomly"--in direct proportion to their environmental abundance. Since in this model search is not charged to particular prey types, the available types can be rank-ordered by a ratio of average value (e.g., in calories) per unit of handling time, where "handling" includes pursuit, capture, processing, and consumption. The forager's goal is to choose the array of prey types that will maximize the total expected benefit per unit of foraging time, including both pursuit times (for all prey types chosen) and search time. As illustrated in the graph, the division into search time and pursuit time generates two opposing cost curves. As a forager widens its diet by adding prey types of lower and lower rank, pursuit costs averaged over the entire array of types taken increases; with a widened diet breadth, however, less time is "wasted" in search because a smaller proportion of all types encountered are rejected. How generalized or specialized should one be? The solution generated by the model is that prey types should be "added" (in descending rank order) until the sum of the decreasing search costs and the increasing pursuit costs are minimized (see arrow, Fig. 3.1). This maximizes the total returns per unit foraging time.

This model yields many predictions, only two of which will be noted here (see Pyke et al. 1977 and Winterhalder 1981a for further discussion). First, since changes in abundance affect only the search curve, the decision to add or drop an item from the diet should be based only on the abundance of higher-ranked prey types already included in the optimal diet and <u>not</u> on the abundance of that prey type itself: in other words, inefficiently-pursued prey types should not be taken if they lie to the right of the intersection of the two curves (i.e., if adding this type will depress the overall rate of return from foraging) no matter how common they become. Second, when high-ranked resources are abundant, diets should become highly specialized, while scarcity of such resources selects for generalized diets--irrespective of the overall number of prey types available. These and other predictions have obvious implications for research on hunter-gatherer subsistence (Winterhalder and Smith 1981).

There are a substantial number of anthropological applications of optimal foraging models. These range from qualitative and heuristic applications of "optimal foraging

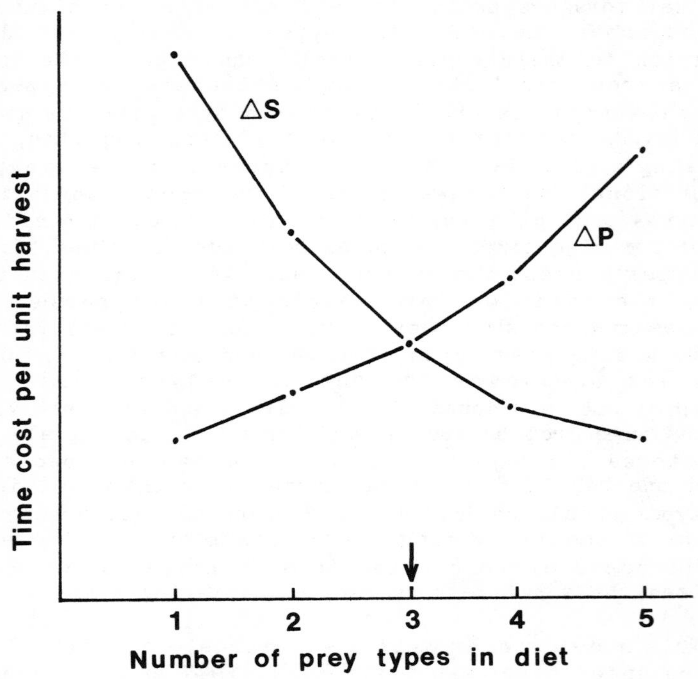

Figure 3.1 The MacArthur-Pianka optimal diet breadth model. The ΔS curve plots the change in search costs, and the ΔP curve the change in pursuit and processing costs, per unit of harvest, as prey types are added to the diet in descending rank order of net return (e.g., in calories) per unit of pursuit and processing time. Since expanding the diet breadth increases per unit pursuit costs but decreases per unit search costs, the optimal diet occurs at the intersection of the two curves, where total foraging time per unit harvest is minimized (MacArthur and Pianka 1966).

logic" to detailed, quantitative empirical tests and include both ethnographic and archaeological applications. The major studies are those by Winterhalder (1977, 1980a, 1981b) on contemporary Boreal Forest Cree Indians, Hawkes et al. (1982; Hill and Hawkes 1983) on the Ache (a semi-nomadic South American Indian group), Hames and Vickers (1982; Hames 1979, 1980) on several Amazonian forager/horticultural peoples, Perlman (1976, 1980) on prehistoric Indians of the Atlantic Coast, and Smith (1980, 1981) on contemporary Inuit (Canadian Eskimo) hunters.

These studies, and others not cited here for lack of space, indicate that much of the variation in human foraging behavior--dietary specialization or diversity, solitary vs. co-operative foraging, changing technology and production methods, patterns of habitat choice and time allocation--can be predicted in detail by foraging strategy models and hence understood as attempts to forage efficiently within a variety of environmental and cultural constraints. Equally important, an awareness of this relatively sophisticated set of models has prompted a growing number of anthropologists to re-examine some currently popular but rather unproductive approaches to human subsistence behavior. For hunter-gatherer studies in particular, optimal foraging theory offers a partial resolution to the dilemma of how to account for the diversity of human foraging adaptations without abandoning the search for general theory (a point developed in detail in Smith and Winterhalder 1981).

Spatial Organization. Ecological study of spatial organization is concerned with such topics as territoriality, resource competition, and predator defense as these relate to group formation or dispersion (reviews in Brown and Orians 1970; Bertram 1978; Davies 1978). As in optimal foraging theory, the evolutionary ecological approach to explaining diversity in spatial organization is to construct models and hypotheses that predict the strategic "choices" individuals should make, given information on their capabilities and key features of their environment--in this case, spatio-temporal resource distributions and the problems and opportunities presented by predators, competitors, and potential mates and co-operators.

Wilmsen (1973) was perhaps the first anthropologist to apply an evolutionary ecological model to human spatial organization; he argued that Horn's (1968) model of group formation in relation to resource dispersion and predictability helped account for the range of sizes observed in hunter-gatherer bands. Hypotheses derived from Horn's model have been tested with ethnographic data from several

Subarctic Amerindian societies (Winterhalder 1977, 1981b; Heffley 1981). A different but related approach was developed by Harpending and Davis (1977), though they did not test their model. Moore (1981), combining concepts from evolutionary ecology and locational theory in geography, presented a framework for analyzing regional settlement patterns and employed it to simulate a variety of possible patterns.

Dyson-Hudson and Smith (1978) adapted evolutionary ecological theory, especially the "economic defendability" model of territoriality (Brown 1964), to analyze cross-cultural variation in spatial organization. We argued that territoriality should be expected to develop only when the benefits of exclusive use outweigh the costs of territory defense and that this is only likely to occur when key resources are relatively predictable in space and time and of moderate density. Unpredictable and/or scarce resources do not repay a territorial strategy, while superabundant resources can be shared at no cost. Preliminary applications of this model to a number of human societies indicated that it could account for the presence or absence of territorial behavior given data on the spatio-temporal resource distribution. In light of the long history of anthropological debates concerning the origins of territoriality, further research is needed to assess whether ecological models of spatial organization can provide general explanations for the diversity of human settlement patterns (cf. Richardson 1982; Cashdan 1983).

Life History Strategies and Mating Systems. The general theory of life history strategies has developed rapidly through the hybridization of population ecology and natural selection theory. The impetus for developing this theory comes from the insight that "in the game of life, an animal stakes its offspring against a more or less capricious environment" (Horn 1978:411). Since both environments and reproductive/life history tactics vary tremendously in nature, the goal of this theory is to account for such variation in ecological terms.

The basic questions considered by life history theory proper include: 1) At what age(s) should reproduction occur? 2) How many offspring should be produced, and in what temporal distributions? 3) How much parental care should be given, and what is the optimal ratio of quantity to quality in offspring? 4) What is the optimal dispersal pattern for the young? and 5) What patterns of senescence and mortality are selected for in different environments? These core issues in life history theory are analyzed with a series of models derived from population ecology, especially the Euler-Lotka (life table) equation, the venerable logistic growth equation and its derivative concepts of "r- and K-selection" (MacArthur and Wilson 1967; Pianka 1970), and Fisher's (1930) concept of "reproductive value." Reviews of various aspects of the theory are provided by Giesel (1976), Horn (1978), Southwood (1981), and Stearns (1976, 1977, 1982). The topically-related area concerning the evolutionary ecology of mating systems differs from life-history theory in a greater concern with social behavior and a lesser emphasis on demographic processes (reviews in Clutton-Brock and Harvey 1977; Emlen and Oring 1977; Halliday 1978; Orians 1969; Wittenberger 1979).

Although attempts to apply life history theory to humans in a rigorous manner have scarcely begun, these models should offer new explanatory insights into certain problems in demographic and ecological anthropology (Kellum 1982). Furthermore, since explanation of variation in mating systems addresses matters of longstanding interest to sociocultural anthropologists, the ecological models are deserving of wider examination. For example, the wide birth-spacing of certain contemporary hunter-gatherer groups such as the !Kung San has drawn a great deal of anthropological attention (Lee 1972, 1979; Howell 1979). Utilizing data on !Kung birth-spacing and mobility costs collected by Lee and Howell, Blurton Jones and Sibly (1978) have demonstrated that !Kung reproductive rates approach optimality (where optimal is defined as the rate that maximizes offspring raised to maturity, in congruence with theory from evolutionary ecology) and have identified such factors as child weight, back strain, heat stress, and foraging requirements as the environmental factors selecting for wide birth-spacing. Further research on human life history tactics is both possible and desirable.

Theory of the Niche and Community Structure. The most dynamic and complex area of inquiry in evolutionary ecology is the study of niche evolution, competition, and community structure (reviews in Cody and Diamond 1975; Diamond 1978; May 1981; Schoener 1974; Stearns 1982; and Wiens 1977). This literature is far too extensive and complex to survey here. However, it seems likely that this branch of evolutionary ecology has great potential for anthropological applications, especially with regard to the evolution of complex social systems, for unlike the three areas of evolutionary ecology surveyed above, niche and community theory is concerned not with individual strategies per se but rather with tracing the consequences of individual and populational trends for larger systems. This "bottom up" orientation contrasts markedly with that taken by systems ecology and leads to very different approaches to understanding ecological communities--and hence to very different implications for those of us concerned particularly with human ecology.

The predictions and insights generated by niche and community theory have been employed in the analysis of modes of production and cultural diversity among both archaeological and ethnographic populations (e.g., Chasko and Cashdan 1978; Gage 1979; Hardesty 1980; Terrell 1977; Yellen 1977). Application to problems of human evolution also shows great promise, as well as illustrating some potential pitfalls. Paleoanthropologists have long drawn on concepts from evolutionary ecology, such as the competitive exclusion principle (e.g., Wolpoff 1971). All too often, however, the theory has been poorly understood and misused. Recently, attempts have been made to employ the theory in a more appropriate fashion (Shaklee and Shaklee 1975; Winterhalder 1980b, 1981c). As demonstrated by Winterhalder in particular, theory from evolutionary ecology is a rich source for developing testable hypotheses for explaining the human evolutionary record.

In summary, evolutionary ecology has developed theory in several areas that appears to have much relevance for analyses of human behavior and ecology. In this approach, abstract deductive models are constructed in order to represent variability in a set of environmental and behavioral parameters. The models are used to generate hypothetically optimal solutions to adaptive problems, such as resource acquisition, competitive interactions, reproduction, and spatial organization. The underlying physiology (and technology) of the study species and any unmodifiable environmental characteristics are taken as "givens"--that is, as constraints on the optimal solution. Cost-benefit currencies are generally operationally-defined correlates of fitness, such as net rate of energy capture or reproductive output. Hence the approach allows one to predict variation in behavioral strategies on the basis of particular environmental features and then to test these predictions with empirical data.

Conclusions

Contrasting Systems and Evolutionary Ecology

Having sketched out the basic assumptions and analytical methods of systems ecology on the one hand and evolutionary ecology on the other, it is now possible to summarize the fundamental contrasts between the "two ecologies"--contrasts that have major implications for the uses of ecological theory in anthropological research. Although what follows may exaggerate these contrasts somewhat, this might well have some heuristic value in light of the frequent tendency of anthropologists to perceive ecological theory as if it were a monolithic entity unified by the ecosystem concept.

Theoretical sources. The most fundamental contrast between systems and evolutionary approaches is found in the primary theoretical principles they each draw on. For systems ecology, the principles of cybernetics and general systems theory, in conjunction with certain physical laws (thermodynamics, geochemistry) and concepts from engineering and computer science, are of paramount importance. For evolutionary ecology, neo-Darwinian theory is primary, of course, but models and concepts from microeconomics and decision theory are increasingly employed. These contrasts in theoretical foundations are no doubt the outcome of complex influences, including historical factors, differences in empirical scope, and certain philosophical predilections of key researchers. As J.M. Emlen (1973:vii) has suggested, insofar as ecology, like any science, builds theory by deduction from basic axioms it must rely on the fundamental laws of physical science on the one hand and evolutionary change on the other. Perhaps the division into "two ecologies" reflects above all these disparate sources for theory-building. It may be that a synthesis of these two approaches into a truly general ecological theory will be attained in the near future (cf. Brown 1981).

Primary causal processes. In accordance with its theoretical foundations, in systems ecology causality is attributed primarily to thermodynamic and chemical processes and to cybernetic processes of feedback and homeostatic or dynamic "self-organization." In evolutionary ecology adaptation via natural selection in a finite environment is the primary causal force as expressed in various types of interactions (e.g., foraging, resource partitioning, predator-prey cycles); certain demographic and statistical (nonadaptive) forces affecting population dynamics and species composition in heterogeneous environments are also emphasized, however.

Theory development at different levels of organization. The "two ecologies" differ in the relative development of theory concerning individual strategies--what we might call "microecology" (Pulliam 1976)--and that concerning population- and community-level (multi-species) interactions or "macroecology." As might be expected, microecological theory is poorly developed in systems ecology, reflecting the "top-down" bias and concern with large-scale ecological processes of the systems approach. The emphasis of systems ecologists on macroecology centers around trophic structure, energy flow, nutrient cycling, and succession, with all but the last of these viewed as essentially physical processes.

Theory development in evolutionary ecology exhibits a contrasting pattern. Microecological theory is well developed in the form of optimal foraging theory, life history theory, and the like; and as a result, evolutionary ecology is becoming increasingly integrated with behavioral biology and general evolutionary theory. Theory concerning pairwise (two-species) interactions such as interspecific competition, predator-prey interactions, and co-evolution is also well developed, but theory concerning multi-species interactions is in a more formative stage (the areas of most active research being resource partitioning, species diversity and abundance, and the rules governing assembly of communities and "species packing"). Again, this differential development of theory by level of organization reflects the "bottom-up" orientation of evolutionary ecology and the inherent difficulties of explaining community-level processes by rigorous argument from lower levels (Brown 1981:880). Nevertheless, a basic goal of evolutionary ecology remains "the development of theories about the properties of communities on the basis of selection for the attributes of their component individuals" (Orians 1973:1239). At this point, it appears to be an open question whether existing theories in either evolutionary or systems ecology will be capable of explaining the way in which ecological communities are constructed.

Typical analytical methods and research objectives. The "two ecologies" differ in analytical methods and research objectives as well as in theoretical orientation. Compartmental models, computer simulations, and complex (multi-equation) mathematical models are typical of systems ecology. Evolutionary ecologists favor simpler analytical models (graphical or mathematical) and rely on hypothesis testing as the primary way of applying the models, rather than on simulation studies or large-scale data processing. The key difference here is not in the importance or sophistication of mathematical analysis per se--a paper in evolutionary ecology may contain a large number of equations, but typically these are mathematical proofs or derivations of the model being presented, not components of the model itself. Rather, what we see here is a contrast in basic research strategy (Levins 1977).

The primary research objective in systems ecology is precise, numerical prediction of the structure and function of particular types of ecosystems--hence, the emphasis on intensive data collection and on detailed, realistic models. Research projects in evolutionary ecology generally aim at testing rather general theoretical explanations for specific ecological processes; the class of data collected is generally much narrower in focus. In summary, where ecosystems research is data-intensive and concerned with prediction as an end in itself, research in evolutionary ecology is problem-oriented and concerned with prediction only insofar as it is useful in testing general theoretical explanations (Levins 1977).

The Implications for Anthropology

The points reviewed above suggest that ecological theory is complex and that certain types of ecological explanation are more appropriate for the usual range of anthropological problems than those that have often been emphasized. The ecosystems concept, and systems ecology in general, does not seem to be an adequate vehicle for explaining sociocultural differences and similarities, the patterns of human adaptation and evolution, or the reasons why humans (or any other particular species) pursue specific strategies of subsistence and reproduction in specific ecological contexts. Nevertheless, the findings of systems ecology (concerning thermodynamics, nutrient flow, productivity, and the like) are likely to be a useful complement to the explanatory models of evolutionary ecology, in that the variables studied by systems ecology must act as important constraints on the adaptation of particular populations to particular environments. And if one's interest in human ecology lies in policy formulation and evaluation rather than in general explanation and theory building per se, then the predictive tools of systems ecology may be highly relevant and useful (cf. Little et al., this volume).

My criticisms of the extension of systems ecology into anthropology are focused on inappropriate uses of this approach in attempting to explain cultural variation by adding dubious elements to the ecosystems framework (such as group selection, the Odum-Lotka energy theory, homeostatic functionalism, and cybernetic teleology). These efforts greatly overextend the valid role of systems ecology in anthropology and confuse the appropriate levels for macro- and micro-explanation (cf. Moran in this volume), much as if one were to apply predator-prey models in an attempt to explain class struggle or international relations. A colleague reading this paper has suggested that evolutionary and systems ecology might be complementary in that the former is best suited for studies of foraging populations and the latter for agricultural and industrial societies. I do not find this argument convincing. While evolutionary ecology certainly lacks models designed to analyze agricultural subsistence strategies (for obvious reasons of academic resource partitioning!), I do not see that there are any models or theories in systems ecology that offer explanatory insights into agricultural economies comparable in scope or power to what optimal foraging theory offers the student of hunter-gatherer societies. I suspect that anthropologists wishing to explain variation in agricultural subsistence strategies will do best either by utilizing models developed in microeconomics (e.g., Clark and Haswell 1967; Green 1980)--a discipline that shares the "bottom-up" orientation of evolutionary ecology--or by adapting theories from evolutionary ecology to fit the agricultural context (e.g., Gage 1980; Hardesty 1980).

Both evolutionary and systems ecology can be abused and misapplied, but I have tried to show that the former has much greater potential for generating interesting, general, and perhaps reliable explanations of sociocultural and behavioral diversity. It seems likely that because the unique properties of cultural transmission make human adaptation quite different than that of noncultural species (Richerson and Boyd 1978, n.d.; Durham 1979, 1982; Pulliam and Dunford 1980) evolutionary ecology by itself will not be sufficient to understand why cultures vary. Nevertheless, evolutionary ecology suffers considerably less explanatory poverty in an anthropological context than does systems ecology.

It is ironic that Vayda and Rappaport (1968) ushered in the cybernetic era in ecological anthropology with the admonition that the subdiscipline had too long suffered "from its isolation from developments in the field of general ecology." From the start, the cybernetic approach to human ecology suffered from a misunderstanding of the structure of evolutionary and ecological theory and overlooked the potential contribution of evolutionary ecology. As Rappaport (1971:242) has argued:

> If we wish to understand how the automobile works, we go to physics. If, on the other hand, we wish to understand its uses and functions, we go to economics, sociology, anthropology, and political science.

To bring the analogy home, I suggest that if we wish to do more than describe the position humans occupy in any ecosystem--if we wish to actually explain variation in the processes and adaptations we observe--we will find much more that is of use in theory from evolutionary ecology than we have been able to derive from systems ecology and the ecosystem concept.

References Cited

Alexander, Richard D. and Gerald Borgia
1978 Group Selection, Altruism, and the Levels of Organization of Life. Annual Review of Ecology and Systematics 9:449-474.

Anderson, James N.
1973 Ecological Anthropology and Anthropological Ecology. In Handbook of Social and Cultural Anthropology. J. Honigmann, ed. Chicago: Rand McNally. Pp. 179-239.

Bates, Daniel and Susan Lees
1979 The Myth of Population Regulation. In Evolutionary Biology and Human Social Organization. N. Chagnon and W. Irons, eds. North Scituate, Mass.: Duxbury Press. Pp. 273-289.

Bateson, Gregory
1972 Steps to an Ecology of Mind. New York: Ballantine.

Bertram, Brian C.R.
1978 Living in Groups: Predators and Prey. In Behavioral Ecology: An Evolutionary Approach. J.R. Krebs and N.B. Davies, eds. Oxford: Blackwell. Pp. 64-96.

Bliss, L.C. (ed.)
1977 Truelove Lowland, Devon Island, Canada: A High Arctic Ecosystem. Calgary: Univ. of Alberta Press.

Blurton Jones, Nicholas G. and R.M. Sibly
1978 Test Adaptiveness of Culturally Determined Behaviour: Do Bushmen Women Maximize Their Reproductive Success By Spacing Births Widely and Foraging Seldom? In Human Behavious and Adaptations. N.B. Blurton Jones and V. Reynolds, eds. Symposium No. 18, Society for the Study of Human Biology. London: Taylor & Francis. Pp. 135-157.

Brown, James H.
1981 Two Decades of Homage to Santa Rosalia: Toward a General Theory of Diversity. American Zoologist 21:877-888.

Brown, Jerram L.
1964 The Evolution of Diversity in Avian Territorial Systems. Wilson Bulletin 76:160-169.

Brown, Jerram L. and Gordon H. Orians
1970 Spacing Patterns in Mobile Animals. Annual Review of Ecology and Systematics 1:239-262.

Brush, Stephen B.
1975 The Concept of Carrying Capacity for Systems of Shifting Cultivation. American Anthropologist 77:799-811.

Cashdan, Elizabeth
1983 Territoriality Among Human Foragers: Ecological Models and an Application to Four Bushman Groups. Current Anthropology 24:47-66.

Chasko, William J., Jr., and Elizabeth Cashdan
1978 Competitive Interactions Between Human Populations. Paper presented at the annual meeting of the American Anthropological Association, Los Angeles, November 1978.

Clark, C. and M. Haswell
1967 The Economics of Subsistence Agriculture. NY: St. Martin's Press.

Clements, Frederick K.
1932 Nature and Structure of the Climax. Journal of Ecology 24:252-284.

Clutton-Brock, T.H. and Paul Harvey
1977 Mammals, Resources, and Reproductive Strategies. Nature 273:191-195.

Cody, Martin L. and Jared M. Diamond (eds.)
1975 Ecology and Evolution of Communities. Cambridge, Mass.: Harvard University Press.

Colinvaux, P.A.
1973 Introduction to Ecology. New York: Wiley.

Davies, Nicholas B.
1978 Ecological Questions About Territorial Behavior.

In Behavioural Ecology: An Evolutionary Approach. J.R. Krebs and N.B. Davies, eds. Oxford: Blackwell. Pp. 317-350.

Diamond, Jared M.
1978 Niche Shifts and the Rediscovery of Interspecific Competition. American Scientist 66:322-331.

Dunbar, M.J.
1960 The Evolution of Stability in Marine Environments: Natural Selection at the Level of the Ecosystem. American Naturalist 94:129-136.
1972 The Ecosystem as a Unit of Natural Selection. In Growth by Intussusception: Ecological Essays in Honor of G. Evelyn Hutchinson. E.S. Deevey, ed. Transactions of the Connecticut Academy of Arts and Sciences, Vol. 44. Pp. 111-130.

Durham, William H.
1979 Toward a Coevolutionary Theory of Human Biology and Culture. In Evolutionary Biology and Human Social Behavior. N. Chagnon and W. Irons, eds. North Scituate, Mass.: Duxbury Press. Pp. 39-59.
1982 The Relationships of Genetic and Cultural Evolution: Models and Examples. Human Ecology 10:289-323.

Durkheim, Emile
1915 The Elementary Forms of the Religious Life. J.W. Swain, translator (original French edition, 1912). London: Allen and Unwin.
1933 Division of Labor in Society. G. Simpson, translator (original French edition, 1893). New York: Macmillan.

Dyson-Hudson, Rada and Eric Alden Smith
1978 Human Territoriality: An Ecological Reassessment. American Anthropologist 80:21-41.

Emlen, J. Merritt
1973 Ecology: An Evolutionary Approach. Reading, Mass.: Addison-Wesley.

Emlen, Stephen T. and Lew Oring
1977 Ecology, Sexual Selection, and the Evolution of Mating Systems. Science 197:215-223.

Engelberg, J. and L.L. Boyarsky
1979 The Noncybernetic Nature of Ecosystems. American Naturalist 114:317-324.

Fisher, Ronald A.
1930 The Genetical Theory of Natural Selection. Oxford: Oxford University Press.

Flannery, Kent
1972 The Cultural Evolution of Civilizations. Annual Review of Ecology and Systematics 3:399-426.

Friedman, Jonathan
1974 Marxism, Structuralism, and Vulgar Materialism. Man 9:444-469.
1979 Hegelian Ecology: Between Rousseau and the World Spirit. In Social and Ecological Systems. P.C. Burnham and R.F. Ellen, eds. London: Academic Press. Pp. 253-270.

Gage, Timothy B.
1979 The Competitive Interactions of Man and Deer in Prehistoric California. Human Ecology 7:253-268.
1980 Optimal Diet Choice in Samoa. Paper presented at the 49th annual meeting of the American Association of Physical Anthropologists, Niagra Falls, April 1980.

Geertz, Clifford
1963 Agricultural Involution. Berkeley: University of California Press.

Giesel, J.T.
1976 Reproductive Strategies as Adaptations to Life in Temporally Heterogeneous Environments. Annual Review of Ecology and Systematics 7:57-79.

Green, Stanton W.
1980 Broadening Least-Cost Models for Expanding Agricultural Systems. In Modeling Subsistence Change in Prehistoric Economies. T.K. Earle and A.L. Christenson, eds. New York: Academic Press. Pp. 209-241.

Halfon, Efraim (ed.)
1979 Theoretical Systems Ecology: Advances and Case Studies. New York: Academic Press.

Halliday, Timothy R.
1978 Sexual Selection and Mate Choice. In Behavioural Ecology: An Evolutionary Approach. J.R. Krebs and N.B. Davies, eds. Oxford: Blackwell. Pp. 180-213.

Hames, Raymond B.
1979 A Comparison of the Efficiencies of the Shotgun and the Bow in Neotropical Forest Hunting. Human Ecology 7:219-252.
1980 Game Depletion and Hunting Zone Rotation Among the Ye'kwana and Yanomamö of Amazonas, Venezuela. Working Papers on South American Indians 2:31-66.

Hames, Raymond B. and William T. Vickers
1982 Optimal Diet Breadth Theory as a Model to Explain Variability in Amazonian Hunting. American Ethnologist 9:357-78.

Hardesty, Donald L.
1980 Ecological Explanation in Archaeology. In Advances in Archaeological Method and Theory, Vol. 3. M.B. Schiffer, ed. New York: Academic Press.

Harpending, Henry and Herbert Davis
1977 Some Implications for Hunter-Gatherer Ecology Derived from the Spatial Structure of Resources. World Archaeology 8:275-283.

Hawkes, Kristen, Kim Hill, and James O'Connell
1982 Why Hunters Gather: Optimal Foraging and the Ache of Eastern Paraguay. American Ethnologist 9:379-398.

Heffley, Sheri
1981 Northern Athapaskan Settlement Patterns and Resource Distributions: An Application of Horn's Model. In Hunter-Gatherer Foraging Strategies. B. Winterhalder and E.A. Smith, eds. Chicago: University of Chicago Press. Pp. 126-147.

Heider, Karl B.
1972 Environment, Subsistence, and Society. Annual Review of Anthropology 1:207-226.

Hill, Kim and Kristen Hawkes
1983 Neotropical Hunting Among the Aché of Eastern

Paraguay. In Adaptive Responses of Native Amazonians. R. Hames and W. Vickers, eds. New York: Academic Press.

Horn, Henry S.
1968 The Adaptive Significance of Colonial Nesting in the Brewer's Blackbird (Euphagus cyanocephalus). Ecology 49:682-694.
1978 Optimal Tactics of Reproduction and Life-History. In Behavioural Ecology: An Evolutionary Approach. J.R. Krebs and N.B. Davies, eds. Oxford: Blackwell. Pp. 411-430.

Howell, Nancy
1979 Demography of the Dobe !Kung. New York: Academic Press.

Jorgensen, Joseph G.
1972 A Variation on Traditional Concerns: The Neofunctional Ecology of Hunters, Farmers, and Pastoralists. In Biology and Culture in Modern Perspective. J.G. Jorgensen, ed. San Francisco: W.H. Freeman. Pp. 328-331.

Kellum, Mary Jane
1982 Life History Tactics: Environmental Uncertainty and Human Reproductive Tactics. M.A. Thesis in Anthropology, University of North Carolina, Chapel Hill.

Kemp, William B.
1971 The Flow of Energy in a Hunting Society. Scientific American 224(3):104-115.

Krebs, John R.
1978 Optimal Foraging: Decision Rules for Predators. In Behavioural Ecology: An Evolutionary Approach. J.R. Krebs and N.B. Davies, eds. Oxford: Blackwell. Pp. 23-63.

Krebs, John R. and Nicholas B. Davies (eds.)
1978 Behavioural Ecology: An Evolutionary Approach. Oxford: Blackwell.

Lee, Richard B.
1972 Population Growth and the Beginnings of Sedentary Life Among the !Kung Bushmen. In Population Growth: Anthropological Implications. Brian Spooner, ed. Cambridge, Mass.: MIT Press. Pp. 329-342.

1979 The !Kung San. Cambridge: Cambridge University Press.

Levins, Richard
1977 The Search for the Macroscopic in Ecosystems. In New Directions in the Analysis of Ecological Systems. Part 2. G.S. Innis, ed. LaJolla, CA: Soc. for Computer Simulation. Pp. 213-221.

Lewontin, Richard C.
1970 The Units of Selection. Annual Review of Ecology and Systematics 1:1-18.

Little, Michael A. and George E.B. Morren, Jr.
1976 Ecology, Energetics, and Human Variability. Dubuque, Iowa: W.C. Brown.

Lotka, A.J.
1922 Contributions to the Energetic of Evolution. Proceedings of the National Academy of Sciences 8:147-188.

MacArthur, Robert H.
1960 On the Relation Between Reproductive Value and Optimal Predation. Proceedings of the National Academy of Sciences 46:143-145.
1961 Population Effects of Natural Selection. American Naturalist 95:195-199.

MacArthur, Robert H. and Eric R. Pianka
1966 On Optimal Use of a Patchy Environment. American Naturalist 100:603-609.

MacArthur, Robert and E.O. Wilson
1967 The Theory of Island Biogeography. Princeton: Princeton University Press.

Margalef, Ramon
1968 Perspectives in Ecological Theory. University of Chicago Press.
1975 Diversity, Stability and Maturity in Natural Ecosystems. In Unifying Concepts in Ecology. W.H. van Dobben and R.H. Lowe-McConnell, eds. The Hague: Junk. Pp. 151-160.

Major, Jack
1969 Historical Development of the Ecosystem Concept. In The Ecosystem Concept in Natural Resource Management. G.M. Van Dyne, ed. New York:

May, Robert M. (ed.)
1981 Theoretical Ecology: Principles and Applications. Oxford: Blackwell.

Maynard Smith, John
1976 Group Selection. Quarterly Review of Biology 51:277-283.

Moore, James A.
1981 The Effect of Information Networks in Hunter-Gatherer Society. In Hunter-Gatherer Foraging Strategies. B. Winterhalder and E.A. Smith, eds. Chicago: University of Chicago Press.

Moran, Emilio F.
1982 Human Adaptability: An Introduction to Ecological Anthropology. Boulder, Co.: Westview Press. Originally published in 1979 by Duxbury Press.

Netting, Robert McC.
1977 Cultural Ecology. Menlo Park: Benjamin Cummings.

Nietschmann, Bernard
1973 Between Land and Water. The Subsistence Ecology of the Misquito Indians, Eastern Nicaragua. New York: Seminar Press.

Odum, Eugene P.
1962 Relationships Between Structure and Function in the Ecosystem. Japanese Journal of Ecology 12:108-118.
1969 The Strategy of Ecosystem Development. Science 164:262-270.
1971 Fundamentals of Ecology. 3rd Edition. Philadelphia: Saunders.

Odum, Howard T.
1971 Environment, Power, and Society. New York: Wiley-Interscience.
1972 An Energy Circuit Language for Ecological and Social Systems: Its Physical Basis. In Systems Analysis and Simulation in Ecology, vol. 2. B.C. Patten, ed. New York: Academic Press. Pp. 140-212.

Orans, Martin
1975 Domesticating the Functional Dragon: An

Analysis of Piddocke's Potlatch. American Anthropologist 77:312-328.

Orians, Gordon H.
1969 On the Evolution of Mating Systems in Birds and Mammals. American Naturalist 103:589-603.
1973 A Diversity of Textbooks: Ecology Comes of Age. Science 181:1238-1239.

Orlove, Benjamin S.
1980 Ecological Anthropology. Annual Review of Anthropology 9:235-273.

Patten, Bernard C.
1981 Environs: The Superniches of Ecosystems. American Zoologist 21:845-852.

Patten, Bernard C. (ed.)
1971-1976 Systems Analysis and Simulation in Ecology. Vols. 1-4. New York: Academic Press.

Patten, Bernard C. and Eugene P. Odum
1981 The Cybernetic Nature of Ecosystems. American Naturalist 118:886-895.

Paulik, G.J.
1972 Digital Simulation Modeling in Resource Management and the Training of Applied Ecologists. In Systems Analysis and Simulation in Ecology. B.C. Patten, ed. New York: Academic Press. Pp. 373-418.

Perlman, Stephen M.
1976 Optimum Diet Models and Prehistoric Hunter-Gatherers: A Test on Martha's Vineyard. Ph.D. dissertation, University of Massachusetts at Amherst.
1980 An Optimum Diet Model, Coastal Variability, and Hunter-Gatherer Behavior. In Advances in Archaeological Method and Theory. Vol. 3. M.B. Schiffer, ed. New York: Academic Press. Pp. 257-310.

Pianka, Eric R.
1970 On r- and K- Selection. American Naturalist 104:592-597.
1983 Evolutionary Ecology. 3rd Edition. New York: Harper and Row.

Pulliam, H. Ronald
1976 The Principle of Optimal Behavior and the Theory of Communities. In Perspectives in Ethology. Vol. 2. P.P.G. Bateson and P.H. Klopfer, eds. New York: Plenum Press.

Pulliam, H. Ronald and Christopher Dunford
1980 Programmed to Learn. An Essay on the Evolution of Culture. New York: Columbia University Press.

Pyke, G.H., H.R. Pulliam, and E.L. Charnov
1977 Optimal Foraging: A Selective Review of Theory and Tests. Quarterly Review of Biology 52:137-154.

Radcliffe-Brown, A.R.
1952 Structure and Function in Primitive Society. Oxford: Oxford University Press.

Rappaport, Roy A.
1967 Ritual Regulation of Environmental Relations Among a New Guinea People. Ethnology 6:17-30.
1968 Pigs for the Ancestors. New Haven: Yale University Press.
1971 Nature, Culture, and Ecological Anthropology. In Man, Culture, and Society. L. Shapiro, ed. 2nd Edition. Oxford: Oxford University Press. Pp. 237-267.
1977 Ecology, Adaptation, and the Ills of Functionalism. Michigan Discussions in Anthropology 2:138-190.

Richardson, Allan
1982 The Control of Productive Resources on the Northwest Coast of North America. In Resource Managers: North American and Australian Hunter-Gatherers. N.M. Williams and E.S. Hunn, eds. Boulder, Colo.: Westview Press. Pp. 93-112.

Richerson, Peter J.
1977 Ecology and Human Ecology: A Comparison of Theories in the Biological and Social Sciences. American Ethnologist 4:1-26.

Richerson, Peter J. and Robert Boyd
1978 A Dual Inheritance Model of the Human Evolutionary Process. I. Basic Postulates and a Simple Model. Journal of Social and Biological Structures 1:127-54.

n.d. Cultural Inheritance and the Evolution of Human Behavior. Chicago: University of Chicago Press (forthcoming).

Roughgarden, Jonathan
1979 Theory of Population Genetics and Evolutionary Ecology: An Introduction. New York: Macmillan.

Salisbury, Richard
1975 Non-equilibrium Models in New Guinea Ecology. Anthropologica 17:127-147.

Schoener, Thomas W.
1971 Theory of Feeding Strategies. Annual Review of Ecology and Systematics 2:369-404.
1974 Resource Partitioning in Ecological Communities. Science 185:27-39.

Shaklee, Alfred B. and Robert B. Shaklee
1975 Ecological Models in Relation to Early Hominid Adaptations. American Anthropologist 77:611-615.

Shugart, H.H. and R.V. O'Neill (eds.)
1979 Systems Ecology. Benchmark Papers in Ecology, Vol. 9. Stroudsburg, PA: Dowden, Hutchinson and Ross.

Slobodkin, Lawrence B.
1968 Toward a Predictive Theory of Evolution. In Population Biology and Evolution. Richard Lewontin, ed. Syracuse: Syracuse University Press. Pp. 187-205.
1972 On the Inconstancy of Ecological Efficiency and the Form of Ecological Theories. In Growth By Intussusception: Ecological Essays in Honor of G. Evelyn Hutchinson. E.S. Deevey, ed. Transactions of the Connecticut Academy of Arts and Sciences, Vol. 44. Pp. 291-305.

Slobodkin, Lawrence B. and Anatol Rapoport
1974 An Optimal Strategy of Evolution. Quarterly Review of Biology 49:181-200.

Smith, Eric Alden
1979 Human Adaptation and Energetic Efficiency. Human Ecology 7:53-74.
1980 Evolutionary Ecology and the Analysis of Human Foraging Behavior: An Inuit Example from the

East Coast of Hudson Bay. Ph.D. dissertation, Cornell University.

1981 The Application of Optimal Foraging Theory to the Analysis of Hunter-Gatherer Group Size. In Hunter-Gatherer Foraging Strategies. B. Winterhalder and E.A. Smith, eds. Chicago: University of Chicago Press. Pp. 35-65.

1983 Evolutionary Ecology and the Analysis of Human Social Behavior. In Rethinking Human Adaptation. R. Dyson-Hudson and M.o. Little, eds. Boulder, Colo.: Westview Press. Pp. 23-40.

Smith, Eric A. and Bruce Winterhalder

1981 New Perspectives on Hunter-Gatherer Socioecology. In Hunter-Gatherer Foraging Strategies. B. Winterhalder and E.A. Smith, eds. Chicago: University of Chicago Press. Pp. 1-12.

Southwood, T.R.E.

1981 Bionomic Strategies and Population Parameters. In Theoretical Ecology. R.M. May, ed. Oxford: Blackwell. Pp. 30-52.

Stearns, Stephen C.

1976 Life-History Tactics: A Review of the Ideas. Quarterly Review of Biology 51:3-47.

1977 The Evolution of Life History Traits: A Critique of the Theory and a Review of the Data. Annual Review of Ecology and Systematics 8:145-171.

1982 The Emergence of Evolutionary and Community Ecology as Experimental Sciences. Perspectives in Biology and Medicine 25:621-48.

Steward, Julian H.

1936 The Economic and Social Basis of Primitive Bands. In Essays in Honor of A.L. Kroeber. R.H. Lowie, ed. Berkeley: University of California Press. Pp. 331-350.

1937 Ecological Aspects of Southwestern Society. Anthropos 33:87-104.

1938 Basin-Plateau Aboriginal Sociopolitical Groups. Bureau of American Ethnology, Bulletin 120.

1955 Theory of Culture Change. Urbana: University of Illinois Press.

Terrell, John
1977 Geographic Systems and Human Diversity in the North Solomons. World Archaeology 9:62-81.

Thomas, R. Brooke
1973 Human Adaptation to a High Andean Energy Flow System. Occasional Papers in Anthropology (No. 7), Department of Anthropology, Pennsylvania State University, University Park, PA.
1976 Energy Flow at High Altitude. In Man in the Andes. P.T. Baker and M.A. Little, eds. Stroudsburg, PA: Dowden, Hutchinson and Ross. Pp. 379-404.

Uyenoyama, M. and M.W. Feldman
1980 Theories of Kin and Group Selection: A Population Genetics Perspective. Theoretical Population Biology 17:380-414.

Vayda, Andrew P. and Bonnie J. McCay
1975 New Directions in Ecology and Ecological Anthropology. Annual Review of Anthropology 4:293-306.

Vayda, Andrew P. and Roy A. Rappaport
1968 Ecology, Cultural and Non-Cultural. In Introduction to Cultural Anthropology. James Clifton, ed. Boston: Houghton-Mifflin. Pp. 477-497.

Wade, Michael J.
1978 A Critical Review of the Models of Group Selection. Quarterly Review of Biology 53:101-114.

White, Leslie
1949 The Science of Culture. New York: Farrar, Straus, and Giroux.
1959 The Evolution of Culture. New York: McGraw-Hill.

Whittaker, Robert H.
1975 Communities and Ecosystems. 2nd Edition. New York: Macmillan.

Wiens, John A.
1977 On Competition and Variable Environments. American Scientist 65:590-597.

Williams, George C.
1966 Adaptation and Natural Selection. Princeton: Princeton University Press.

Wilmsen, Edwin N.
1973 Interaction, Spacing Behavior, and the Organization of Hunting Bands. Journal of Anthropological Research 29:1-31.

Wilson, David Sloan
1980 The Natural Selection of Populations and Communities. Series in Evolutionary Biology, Institute of Ecology, University of California at Davis. Menlo Park: Benjamin/Cummings.

Winterhalder, Bruce
1977 Foraging Strategy Adaptations of the Boreal Forest Cree: An Evaluation of Theory and Models from Evolutionary Ecology. Ph.D. dissertation, Cornell University.
1980a Canadian Fur Bearer Cycles and Cree-Ojibwa Hunting and Trapping Practices. American Naturalist 115:870-879.
1980b Hominid Paleoecology: The Competitive Exclusion Principle and Determinants of Niche Relationships. Yearbook of Physical Anthropology 23:43-63.
1981a Optimal Foraging Strategies and Hunter-Gatherer Research in Anthropology Theory and Models. In Hunter-Gatherer Foraging Strategies. B. Winterhalder and E.A. Smith, eds. Chicago: University of Chicago Press. Pp. 13-35.
1981b Foraging Strategies in the Boreal Environment: An Analysis of Cree Hunting and Gathering. In Hunter-Gatherer Foraging Strategies. B. Winterhalder and E.A. Smith, eds. Chicago: University of Chicago Press. Pp. 66-98.
1981c Hominid Paleoecology: Limiting Similarity, Foraging and Niche Differentiation, and the Effects of Cultural Behavior. Yearbook of Physical Anthropology 24:101-121.

Winterhalder, Bruce and Eric A. Smith (eds.)
1981 Hunter-Gatherer Foraging Strategies: Ethnographic and Archaeological Analyses. Chicago: University of Chicago Press.

Wittenberger, James F.
1979 The Evolution of Mating Systems in Birds and Mammals. In Handbook of Behavioral Biology. P.

Marler and J. Vandenbergh, eds. Vol. 3. New York: Plenum Press. Pp. 271-349.

Wolpoff, M.H.
1971 Competitive Exclusion Among Lower Pleistocene Hominids. Man 6:601-614.

Wynne-Edwards, V.C.
1962 Animal Dispersion in Relation to Social Behavior. Edinburgh: Oliver and Boyd.

Yellen, John E.
1977 Long-Term Hunter-Gatherer Adaptation to Desert Environments: A Biogeographical Perspective. World Archaeology 8:262-274.

Michael Jochim

4. The Ecosystem Concept in Archaeology

Current Ecological Research in Archaeology

Although archaeology has a long history of interest in environmental and cultural relationships, only the most recent project designs and field techniques have begun to allow for the complexity involved in an ecological approach to past behavior. Ecology is the study of dynamic relationships between organisms and their total environments. An ecological approach to cultural behavior requires, consequently, that any particular aspect of behavior be examined within its cultural and natural context, keeping in mind that this context may be varying in space and time. With the realization that past behavior must be explained, in part, in relation to its context, the concept of the ecosystem, as the structure of dynamic interrelationships of population behavior and its context, has emerged as important in archaeological method and theory.

The ecosystem concept has been useful to archaeologists primarily as an heuristic device, encouraging us to think in terms of the systemic interrelationships among cultural and natural factors. A knowledge of the characteristic structural elements and processes of natural ecosystems has directed our attention to such features as the flow of energy and the diversity of interacting species in prehistoric human ecosystems. As a concrete unit of analysis, however, the ecosystem has had little role in archaeological research. In dealing with the past we must recognize that we can hope to reconstruct only small portions of past ecosystems. We are limited by differential preservation and by our present inability to resolve fine-scale environmental variability in time and space.

Nevertheless, the use of the ecosystem concept has had many positive implications for archaeology. First of all, new data have become relevant to prehistoric behavior. Archaeological research designs now often seek to include the gathering of information pertinent to the study of ecosystem traits and processes, such as the spatial distribution of environmental characteristics and the stability of their distribution through time. From this standpoint, new interactions among variables emerge and new determinants of behavioral variation may be examined.

Secondly, archaeology has moved away from the emphasis on prime movers to a systems orientation in explaining prehistoric behavior. For a greater understanding of a variety of features of prehistoric societies, archaeologists are now examining certain aspects of behavior which directly entail interaction with the environment. Monumental construction projects, for example, require the procurement of building materials and the organization of labor. The former, in turn, depends on the structure of raw material distributions and trade routes and networks, while the latter is affected by population distribution and the seasonal scheduling of subsistence activities. Neither the Pyramids of Egypt nor Stonehenge are comprehensible without consideration of such factors. Similarly, the development of complex political bureaucracies is increasingly being examined in light of governmental roles in coordinating the distribution of materials and personnel and in monitoring and buffering environmental fluctuations (Isbell 1978; Jorde 1977). Increasingly, the spatial and temporal structure of the environment has become an important set of factors in explaining cultural behavior.

A third implication of the use of the ecosystem concept in archaeological research is that many projects now regularly include such procedures as regional surveys and the analysis of site surroundings (or "catchments") in order to investigate more fully the nature of human interaction with the environment. These approaches represent an improvement over the use of simple site locations as the object of study since they attempt to deal with the distribution of activities throughout the environment, rather than at a few points in space. Furthermore, a host of physical techniques have been developed to help determine more precise chronological and seasonal relationships among sites. Archaeological methods are increasingly attempting to gather information about spatial and temporal variation in prehistoric human behavior.

Examples

A commitment to ecological archaeology, therefore, with its unifying concept of the ecosystem, introduces spatio-temporal variability and complex interrelationships as important elements of the problems investigated. These requirements of an ecological approach have significant implications for both techniques of archaeological research and the types of explanation acceptable. In order to illustrate the research demands and the potential of such an approach, three problems of European prehistory will be discussed. In each case, conflicting interpretations will be presented along with their support in the current data and their implications for future research.

Development of Microlithic Technology. The first problem represents a change in lithic technology. Beginning in the late Pleistocene and accompanying a general miniaturization of stone implements, there begin to appear small microblades and microliths throughout much of Europe. These implements were probably inserted into shafts to form composite tools, and they increase in frequency until they form the dominant characteristic of the early postglacial Mesolithic industries. A variety of hypotheses have been advanced to explain this change in technology, but these may be combined into two general views according to emphasis.

The first view sees this change as related to a modification of traditionally important activity--hunting. That is, microliths are interpreted largely as points, barbs, and cutting edges forming part of the hunting and butchering equipment and thus represent functional replacements for earlier points and knives (Chard 1969:173; Clark 1967:104). Suggestions about the reasons for this replacement have been varied. Most emphasize the development of the bow and arrow and its requirements for projectiles of lighter weight. Additional factors of possible importance may include a need for new and more complex projectile shapes made possible by composite tools, a need for more efficient use of smaller sources of stone raw material, and a need for the more efficient repair and replacement costs of composite tools.

A second, more recent, view is that this technological change represents not a modification of an existing activity but the development of an essentially new activity altogether--the collection and processing of plant foods (Clarke 1976). In this view, the development of microliths met the need for longer and more complex cutting edges required for harvesting and shredding activities. Of course, these two views are not mutually exclusive: microliths may represent multipurpose inserts. For simplicity, however, the two extreme views will be considered.

In both views, the technological change can be related to changes in the natural environmental context. With the late and postglacial warming and reforestation of central and northern Europe, mobile and gregarious animals of open country became rarer and were gradually replaced by more sedentary and solitary species of closed forests. Hunting methods and equipment may have changed accordingly, such that stalking became more efficient than driving or ambushing. If so, an advantage would have been presented by the bow and arrow with its longer striking distance and by projectiles with more complex barbs to hold fast despite snagging in the denser vegetation. Moreover, the use of arrows in forests would probably have resulted in more frequent breakage of points as they hit the trees, so that the ease of replacing only a portion of a composite tool may have been an additionally significant factor. Simultaneously, the economic adjustments of this period, including the shift to less mobile game and a broadening of the resource base, may have led to a smaller effective range of the local groups, perhaps causing a shift to local but smaller and less abundant sources of stone.

It is undeniable, on the other hand, that the postglacial warming led to an increase in the variety and abundance of plants and thus to an increase in the potential plant foods available. If this potential was utilized, then some technological accommodations may have been necessary. Since game was becoming both less productive and riskier, a shift to the more secure plant foods may have occurred.

Both views have some *a priori* probability, therefore, and the existing archaeological evidence offers meager support to both. Scattered finds show microliths clearly mounted as points and barbs of arrows or embedded in the bones of animals but also hafted to form knives of unknown function. The two hypotheses, however, should have some contrasting implications that should be considered in further research. The overall role of plant foods in the diet could be approached through the techniques of bone strontium analysis applied to Mesolithic skeletal material (Brown 1973). Techniques developed in Germany promise to allow the identification of concentrations of animal and plant fats in site sediments and could be used where possible (Rottländer and Schlichtherle 1979). Surveys could be directed specifically to bogs and other regions favoring preservation of plant foods. Microscopic use-wear analysis of microliths should certainly be pursued but in the future supported by experimentation with the gathering and processing of roots and other wild plant foods as well as other activities. In addition, spatial and temporal patterns of association and covariation of tools and activities should be given greater attention. Environmental reconstructions should include both animal and plant food potentials, perhaps separately. Regional surveys could then stratify according to each criterion and predictions about the relative importance of microliths in each stratum be generated, as has been done recently for southern England (Mellars and Reinhardt 1978). Situations with low probability of plant use, such as high elevations or winter camps, could then be examined with specific implications in mind. If microliths represent largely hunting equipment, then their varying frequency in relation to other hunting equipment, such as stone points and bone harpoons, could be examined for temporal patterns. Moreover, the varying size and spatial distribution of stone raw material should be examined for support of the assumptions for greater localization.

Early Neolithic Settlement Changes. A second problem concerns the change in residential and settlement patterns as an agricultural economy and population moved from southeast Europe toward the north and west. In simplified terms, Neolithic villages of small, single-family houses were replaced by settlements of fewer but larger houses as the Neolithic spread into central and western Europe. Interpretation of this change is hampered by the fact that the occupation floors of all known early Neolithic Linear Pottery houses in central Europe have disappeared through erosion, so that the reconstruction of the houses rests solely upon evidence of postholes.

Again, two simplified hypotheses about the function of these larger houses may be suggested (see Milisauskas 1978:99-105). The first is that nuclear families were still the major residential unit but that larger houses were necessary in the harsher central European climate to provide shelter for animals and storage for grain. This view places the change within the context solely of climatic differences between southeast and central Europe.

A second view is that the housing shift represents a change in economy and family units. That is, the larger houses are interpreted as reflecting extended family organization accompanying an economic transformation. This argument considers not just the climatic differences between the two regions but rather the greater environmental context. A number of cross-cultural ethnographic surveys have suggested some significant functional contexts favoring extended family organization, including the practice of pioneering slash-and-burn farming with labor-intensive forest clearance and a frontier situation with general labor shortages (Netting 1969; Pasternak et al. 1976; Thompson 1973). However poor our understanding of the Neolithic economies of southeast and central Europe, there are some indications that less sedentary agriculture and settlement characterized central Europe.

Unlike the first hypothesis, this second view examines the change in housing in relation to the complex interaction of environment, economy, and settlement. Changes in population density, land availability, and labor demand become important in understanding these interactions. Moreover, this second hypothesis, unlike the first, can address other changes in the archaeological record. The major domestic animals show a shift from sheep and goats in the southeast to cattle in central Europe. The latter require more land and perhaps more work and thus would increase the overall demand for labor, perhaps in conflict to the practice of agriculture, and thus favoring a larger economic unit. Furthermore, by comparison with the southeast, central Europe shows more evidence for joint activities in the form of communal drying pits and ovens, suggesting a change in the organization of economic units. The few true cemeteries outside of villages known for central Europe (and absent in the southeast) may represent one component of a communal system of land tenure in the context of shifting active farm plots.

Future archaeological research into this question should take a number of courses. The analysis of soil nitrogen within houses in an attempt to locate concentrations of livestock has been used sporadically with differing results (Milisauskas 1978:105); this approach could be pursued in an attempt to find patterns of concentration. The excavation of complete Linear Pottery sites as opposed to single houses and the survey of large regions should be given high priority. This is currently being done in a research program connected with brown coal strip mining in northwestern Germany (see, for example, Kuper et al. 1975). Building on such research, variation among Linear Pottery sites could be examined for systematic relationships between house size and variability and either climatic factors or population density, land availability, and the presence and distribution of storage pits and cemeteries.

The Localization of Paleolithic Cave Art. A third problem which can profitably be examined in an ecological context is the restricted geographical distribution of cave art in the Paleolithic. With few exceptions, painted caves of west and central Europe are confined to the region of northern Spain and southwestern France. Neither the suitable caves nor the practice of decorating smaller, portable objects shows such a limited distribution. Ignoring earlier interpretations based on assumptions of ethnic differences in artistic sophistication and appreciation, two suggestions may be offered which attempt to place this art in an ecological context. Both view the painted caves as fixed ritual spots, and both address the question of the functions of such ritual locations rather than the specific contents of the rituals themselves.

The first hypothesis stresses one well-documented aspect of the economy: hunting. In this view, some sort of ritual served to coordinate and integrate the normally dispersed and potentially competitive groups whose periodic cooperation was necessary for communal hunting (Hammond 1974). The painted caves, then, represent the locations of these rituals. Support is provided by the economic importance of reindeer and the small site sizes suggesting small labor pools in individual camps.

One major problem with this suggestion indicates one direction further work in this area might take. The importance of reindeer hunting extends beyond the region of painted caves to areas such as southern Germany with many cave sites but no decorated walls (Hahn 1979). Archaeologists must compare the two regions in terms of site densities, site locations, and faunal materials in an attempt to determine whether there existed significant differences in hunting techniques and work group size and distribution. If no such differences become clear, then a supplementary hypothesis might be proposed: that similar integrating rituals took a different form in Germany. For example, sites with impressive concentrations of portable art, such as have been excavated in the Rhineland (Bosinski _et al_. 1978), may represent functional alternatives to the French and Spanish painted caves as the locus of communal rituals, and the distribution of the two types of sites may be compared with similar patterns.

An alternative hypothesis may be offered, however, one which focuses on the interrelationships between _other_ economic activities, climatic and demographic changes, and patterns of land use (Jochim, in press). In short, this hypothesis views the painted caves as fixed ritual locations serving to assert land tenure and coordinate increasingly dense and sedentary populations associated with population influx and the growing importance of salmon. Southwestern

France is the most northerly part of central and west Europe to show any substantial, continuous occupation throughout the entire Upper Paleolithic. Despite the uncertainties involved in dating the cave paintings, it seems that they first appear at about the beginning of the last glacial maximum (Leroi-Gourhan 1965). Beginning around the same time, much of the surrounding areas are progressively abandoned, including Britain, northern France, the Low Countries, and much of Germany. Little attention has been given to the fate of these regional populations. Southwestern France has long been recognized as a refuge area for plants and animals during the last glaciation; it may well have been a refuge for humans as well.

Such a population influx may have led to increased population densities, greater land scarcity, decreased human mobility, and an increased use of more abundant and secure resources such as fish. In this connection, the archaeologically documented utilization of salmon in the French and Spanish Upper Paleolithic deserves emphasis, and the greater use of screening and flotation techniques during excavation becomes critical in ascertaining the degree of economic significance of this resource. Environmental reconstructions of the European Paleolithic could profitably be based not only on terrestrial data but also on such information as the recent CLIMAP simulations of glacial ocean surface temperatures (CLIMAP 1976) which, combined with studies of modern salmon distribution, suggest that it was precisely northern Spain and southwestern France that held the spawning grounds for the majority of Atlantic salmon during the last glaciation.

In other words, the region of painted caves can be distinguished by being a refuge zone of great biotic diversity, a region of continuous occupation and possibly demographic compression, and the habitat of an abundant and secure anadramous fish resource. All of these characteristics set this area apart from other parts of Europe, and it is in this context that the painted caves developed.

Future research should be directed, as mentioned, to the determination of both reindeer hunting techniques and salmon utilization, as these vary among regions. In addition, the spatial distribution of the painted caves within their region of occurrence must be examined, and for this, the catalog recently assembled by archaeologists at the University of Bonn will become useful since it attempts to document all Paleolithic painted caves and thereby includes many not previously counted with the more dramatic finds (Naber _et al._

1976). Environmental reconstructions could be based alternatively on reindeer habitat and behavior and on probable salmon abundance, and the distribution of caves examined in relation to each. The spatial relationships of the caves to one another and to other contemporary sites should also be studied since both hypotheses imply certain regularities in these patterns. Regional assessments of site sizes and densities should be attempted and compared among areas in order to assess the nature of demographic shifts. Finally, the complex array of changes during the late glacial when the cave art ceases must be given more attention. Not only do reindeer decrease and eventually disappear, for example, but also there is a rapid out-migration and reoccupation of Central and Northern Europe. Attention should also be given to southeastern Europe since it, too, may represent a potential refuge area during the glacial maximum and might show functionally similar responses to a demographic influx.

Obviously, the problems, the alternative interpretations, the available evidence, and the possibilities for future research have, in each example, been presented only superficially and simplistically. These topics were chosen, however, for a number of specific reasons.

1) They all demonstrate the necessity for dealing with complex ecosystemic interrelationships and patterns of spatial and temporal variation, both in hypothesis formulation and in research designed to test them.

2) They all demonstrate the value of recent methodological developments, such as techniques of chemical analysis, programs of extensive regional survey, and precise compilation of existing data.

3) They demonstrate the wide scope of ecological approaches in archaeology whereby technology, settlement behavior, and even art can be examined in systematic environmental contexts.

4) They all demonstrate the utility of having contrasting working hypotheses, even though oversimplified, in order to isolate critical factors for study.

5) They all suggest the need for multiple environmental reconstructions in ecological

research, depending on the problem and factors of interest.

Archaeological Problems in Ecological Research

Despite the promise of these new research approaches, it must be realized that archaeology faces a number of problems in trying to examine prehistoric ecosystemic relationships. First of all, reconstructions of prehistoric environments depend largely upon two approaches: 1) the gathering of information about plant and animal resources from particular sites and 2) the analysis of pollen diagrams. Neither of these is especially suitable for reconstructing the spatial patterns of environmental features. Materials derived from sites represent a biased sample of only those resources of economic importance from a surrounding region of unknown size. The selectivity of human interaction with the environment cannot be evaluated. Pollen diagrams give a representation of vegetational composition from an area of uncertain relationship to the region of economic importance and, moreover, provide no information about the spatial distribution of the vegetational components. The relative patchiness of prehistoric environments is difficult to assess. Thus, we can identify only coarse-grained, major biotic zones and must depend upon analogy with modern habitats to estimate the spatial distribution of the plant and animal constituents.

Secondly, our control of fine-scale temporal variations is poor. We rely largely on stratigraphic and pollen evidence to reconstruct temporal changes in the environment. As a result, we can reconstruct only major cycles of variation and largely miss briefer episodes and shorter cycles. Consequently, we miss much environmental variability and uncertainty, which is unfortunate, given the growing emphasis on these factors in explaining some aspects of behavior. People do not adapt to average conditions, yet our environmental reconstructions tend to produce just such an average. One can imagine two hypothetical environments, for example, with the same average conditions but with one more variable than the other. Assuming that people would behave differently in the two, we would see archaeologically two adaptations to the "same" environment and have difficult explaining these differences. The degree of environmental variability is of great significance in ecological theory but difficult to reconstruct archaeologically.

Different patterns of environmental variability are also important and should produce different adaptations. Two environments may be equally variable but not equally predictable. One area might have a drought every five years with great regularity, whereas another may show droughts erratically but averaging one of every five years. These contexts should encourage different behaviors, which would be difficult to explain, given our inability to reconstruct patterns of variability on such a fine scale.

Furthermore, given our poor control of fine time differences, our reconstructions of behavior tend to be aggregates of behavior over uncertain lengths of time. In some cases these reconstructions may resemble a type of average: if a region had nine good years and one drought year, the evidence for behavior during good years might be nine times more abundant than that of drought years. In other cases, however, the extraordinary behavior, such as population aggregation or a major ceremonial event, might have high archaeological visibility, and we would wrongly consider it as either the most important behavior or part of each year's behavior. Such problems of spatial and temporal resolution present major obstacles to the reconstruction of dynamic ecological relationships in the past.

New Directions in Ecological Research

Despite such obstacles, there are a number of directions future ecological research in archaeology might profitably take. We might take various properties of ecosystems such as the flow of energy, materials, and information, or the patterns of species abundance diversity and stability, and attempt to reconstruct or estimate these for past human ecosystems in order to determine specific problems facing various kinds of human behavior. In doing so, we must keep in mind the important dimensions of space and time and attempt to reconstruct the geometry of environmental interactions. Nutrient cycles help delineate boundaries in natural ecosystems. For cultural systems we need comparable studies not only of material exchanges but also of information transactions. Information needs that dictate certain spatial directions of interaction may direct other material interactions in this direction as well. For example, trade upstream (rather than downstream) by irrigation farmers might be inexplicable in material terms alone, whereas the need for information about flood levels may dictate this direction of interaction. Similarly, salmon fishermen may participate in downstream communications because of the need to monitor oncoming runs. Energy flows may influence the direction of information flow, and exchange of materials may be used to maintain the necessary channels of communication.

We must also take the ecosystemic processes of interest, such as the distribution and diversity of biotic components, the flow of materials and energy, and the temporal variability of different factors, and examine the implications for archaeological data gathering. We have rightly broadened our focus from sites to larger regions, but we must rethink our techniques of environmental classification in regional surveys. Currently, regional survey techniques often stratify the region according to present environmental variation. Such attention to environmental differences is necessary for the goals of ecological research, but there are some problems which must be recognized. Past and present vegetational zones, for example, may not have coincided, and small differences in environmental patterning may be of enormous significance. The shifts of vegetational zones during glacial periods, for instance, may not simply have resulted in unique low-latitude tundras but also have created much steeper latitudinal gradients in vegetation than is seen at present, providing access to a great variety of resources within a small region (see, for example, Stein and Wright 1978). In warm, arid regions slight variations in temperature or humidity may have had profound effects on vegetational distributions. For example, by converting patchy, mosaic forests and grasslands into more homogeneous woodland-savannas, such climatic changes might have led to great changes in animal and human distributions. In assessing climatic changes, therefore, archaeologists must recognize both quantitative and qualitative distributional changes.

A second problem with current techniques of regional stratification and survey is that the reasons for selecting criteria for stratification are frequently not clear. Often a few obvious environmental characteristics are used, such as elevation, vegetation, or proximity to water, without consideration of their relevance to the research topic (see Moran, in this volume, for a discussion of how this has affected systems ecology as well). It is doubtful that a single environmental reconstruction and classification will be suitable for all interests. Attention to large-scale elevational variation may be sufficient for discussions of transportation routes, geographic isolation, or altitudinal effects of climatic conditions on different crops, whereas small-scale topographic investigations may be necessary for examinations of drainage problems and field distributions. Archaeologists must specify the necessary environmental information to be collected, with the realization that different research topics may demand different criteria, so that the environmental variables used in one valley survey may be of little value to another study.

Finally, perhaps the most important focus of future research should be the differences in scale of temporal resolution in archaeological and modern studies. As mentioned earlier, archaeological reconstructions of both natural environments and human behavior tend to produce only gross patterns which ignore fine-scale temporal variation. The study of tree-rings, varves, and microstratigraphy promise to increase our powers of resolution but may be applicable only in restricted contexts. Similarly, temporary hunter-gatherer sites may offer greater potential than permanent sites for the isolation of brief episodes of behavior, but the determination of the length of occupation and number of episodes is notoriously difficult for such sites (see, for example, the differences of opinion reflected in Andresen et al. 1981; Clark 1972; Pitts 1979). Our control of chronology is crude and our reconstructions of past ecosystemic relationships limited to the identification of relatively gross correlation of variables--a macro palaeoecology.

This situation is indeed unfortunate because our interpretations of such correlations derive largely from modern ethnographic studies. These studies monitor short-term behavior on a small scale; they are fine-grained studies of micro ecological relationships. Our vocabulary and entire mode of reasoning derive from such studies, and yet the archaeological data are not appropriate to such reasoning. If we derive hypotheses from such fine-grained studies, their implications may be archaeologically undetectable.

Clearly, we need to enlarge the scale for examining modern human ecological relationships. This is not to suggest that we leave human behavior behind and ascend to the rarified heights of a general systems perspective in which we view only system responses and assume adaptation on the system level. Such a perspective would change our focus in terms of the organizational unit but would not produce data more comparable to the archaeological record. Rather, we need to maintain a focus on ecosystemic components, including human behavior, but to monitor these components over long periods and to study the gross patterns of their interrelationships. In short, we need to turn to the historical past as well as the ethnographic present (see Ellen, Adams and Kasakoff, and Netting, in this volume). We might sample the past at intervals and attempt to reconstruct an interrupted "archaeological" picture of changing ecological relationships. The underlying dynamic causes of observed changes could then be suggested on the basis of additional, more detailed historical and ethnographic evidence. Such an approach might help us bridge the gap between fine-scale processes and large-scale patterns, between a micro- and macro-ecology of human behavior.

References Cited

Andresen, J.M. et al.
1981 The Deer Hunters: Star Carr Reconsidered. World Archaeology 13:31-46.

Bosinsky, K. (ed.)
1978 Geowissenschaftliche Untersuchungen. In Gonnersdorf. Wiesbaden: Franz Steiner Verlag.

Brown, A.
1973 Bone Strontium Content as a Dietary Indicator in Human Skeletal Populations. Ph.D. dissertation, University of Michigan, Ann Arbor.

Chard, C.
1969 Man in Prehistory. New York: McGraw-Hill.

Clark, G.
1967 The Stone Age Hunters. New York: McGraw-Hill.
1972 Star Carr: A Case Study in Bioarchaeology. Addison-Wesley Modular Publications 10. Menlo Park: Cummings Publishing Co.

Clarke, D.
1976 Mesolithic Europe: The Economic Basis. In Problems in Economic and Social Archaeology. G. Sieveking, I. Longworth, and K. Wilson (eds.). London: Duckworth. pp. 449-481.

CLIMAP Project Members
1976 The Surface of the Ice-Age Earth. Science 191:1131-1137.

Hahn, J.
1979 Essai sur l'ecologie du Magdalenien dans le jura souabe. In La Fin des Temps Glaciaires en Europe. D. de Sonneville-Bordes, ed. Paris: CNRS. pp. 203-213.

Hammond, N.
1974 Palaeolithic Mammalian Faunas and Parietal Art in Cantabria: A Comment on Freeman. American Antiquity 39:618-619.

Isbell, W.H.
1978 Environmental Perturbations and the Origin of the Andean State. In Social Archaeology: Beyond

Subsistence and Dating. C. Redman et al. (ed.). New York: Academic Press. pp. 303-313.

Jochim, M.A.
in press Palaeolithic Cave Art in Ecological Perspective. In Pleistocene Hunters and Gatherers in Europe. G. Bailey, ed. Cambridge: University Press.

Jorde, L.B.
1977 Precipitation Cycles and Cultural Buffering in the Prehistoric Southwest. In For Theory Building in Archaeology. L.R. Binford, ed. New York: Academic Press. pp. 385-396.

Kuper, R. et al.
1975 Untersuchungen zur neolithischen Besiedlung der Aldenhovener Platte. Bonner Jahrbucher 175:191-229.

Leroi-Gourhan, A.
1965 Treasures of Prehistoric Art. New York: Abrams.

Mellars, P. and Reinhardt, S.
1978 Patterns of Mesolithic Land-Use in Southern England: A Geological Perspective. In The Early Postglacial Settlement of Northern Europe. P. Mellars, ed. London: Duckworth. pp. 243-294.

Milisauskas, S
1978 European Prehistory. New York: Academic Press.

Naber, F., D. Berenger, and C. Zalles-Flossbach
1976 L'Art Parietal Paléolithique en Europe Romane. Bonner Hefte zur Vorgeschichte 14-16.

Netting. R.
1969 Ecosystems in Process: A Comparative Study of Change in Two West African Societies. In Ecological Essays. D. Damas, ed. Ottawa: National Museums of Canada Bulletin No. 230. pp. 102-112.

Pasternak, B., C. Ember, and M. Ember
1976 On the Conditions Favoring Extended Family Households. Journal of Anthropological Research 32:109-123.

Pitts, M.
1979 Hides and Antlers: A New Look at the Gatherer-

Hunter Site at Star Carr, North Yorkshire, England. World Archaeology 11:32-42.

Rottlander, R. and H. Schlichtherle
1979 Food Identification of Samples from Archaeological Sites. Archaeophysika 10:260-267.

Stein, J. and H.E. Wright, Jr.
1978 Review of Amerinds and Their Paleoenvironments in Northeastern North America. Science 200:306-307.

Thompson, S.I.
1973 Pioneer Colonization: A Cross-Cultural View. Addison-Wesley Modular Publications 33. Menlo Park: Cummings Publishing Co.

Michael A. Little, Neville Dyson-Hudson, Rada Dyson-Hudson, James E. Ellis, David M. Swift

5. Human Biology and the Development of an Ecosystem Approach

Ecological Studies in Human Biology[1]

Introduction and History

The disciplinary origins of human biology or biological anthropology are quite diverse and cross-cut the social and biological sciences. Today, the field is unified by the theoretical framework of human evolution and the concept that behavior and biology interact within human cultures and societies to facilitate adaptation to the environment.

"Adaptation" as a concept in human population biology preceded the interest in ecological systems as the context of adaptation. Research on human adaptation to the environment in the early 1950's centered on narrowly defined climatic characteristics (Coon, Garn and Birdsell 1950; Newman and

---

[1]Scientific collaborators on the South Turkana Ecosystem Project are Professors Geoffrey M.O. Maloiy and Mutuma Mugambi of the University of Nairobi, Terrence McCabe and Kathleen Galvin of the State University of New York, Layne Coppock of the Colorado State University, and Jan Wienpahl of the University of Arizona. Their contributions as members of the research team are acknowledged with thanks. We are grateful also to the Beijer Institute of the Royal Swedish Academy of Sciences and the International Livestock Centre for Africa for logistic support. Several of us owe a great deal to Dr. Philip O'Keefe for his warm hospitality at Kuni Kastle in Nairobi. Funding was provided by the National Science Foundation under NSF Grants BNS 78-15923, BNS 80-107800 and DEB 80-04182.

Munro 1955; Roberts 1953). In the 1950's, too, the ecologist and epidemiologist Marston Bates argued persuasively for the development of a field of "human ecology" in which ecological principles were to be applied to the study of human populations (1953, 1960). Bates played an influential role during this period because he was one of the few scientists who was willing to consider humans as simply another species subject to evolutionary and ecological processes while at the same time he recognized some of the unique properties of our species.

Despite Bates' exhortations, much of the research conducted throughout the 1950's was biogeographical in scope and emphasized adaptation of human morphological features to climatic extremes. However, other trends were under way at this time that were to strengthen the research foundations of human biology. First, demographic studies on tribal societies (Birdsell 1953; Roberts 1956; Spuhler 1959) underlined the need to consider populations and population variation rather than the individual as the unit of investigation. Second, work in environmental physiology (Brown and Page 1952; Scholander *et al*. 1957, 1958) stimulated research in areas other than just morphology (Baker 1958; Roberts 1952). Third, in addition to climate, other environmental elements were seen as imposing stress on humans (Newman 1960).

By the 1960's pioneering human biologists on both sides of the Atlantic were developing ecological approaches to the study of human adaptation (Baker 1962; Newman 1962; Weiner 1964). Such ecological approaches, or perspectives, arose from the evolutionary traditions of physical anthropology, which were centered fundamentally on the concept of "adaptation to the environment" (Little 1982). These trends were reinforced by the initiation of the *International Biological Program* and its *Human Adaptability* component during the mid-1960's.

International Biological Program

Planning for the International Biological Program (IBP) began in 1961 and the program was initiated by the International Council of Scientific Unions in July 1964. The IBP extended over a period of ten years and was divided into the three phases of planning, research and synthesis. In the United States, the IBP became operational in 1967 and was administered through the National Academy of Sciences.

The objectives of the IBP were clearly ecological in scope with stated goals of furthering basic scientific research on biological productivity, natural resource management, biological systems, and human adaptation. IBP research in the U.S. was divided into two components: 1) environmental management, which was dominated by several large "analysis of ecosystems" projects (grassland, desert, tundra, coniferous forest and deciduous forest) and 2) human adaptability, which was constituted of three major and numerous minor projects (National Academy of Sciences 1974). Although the U.S. involvement in the IBP was limited at the beginning, by the end of the synthesis period in 1974 its contributions had been substantial. The analysis-of-ecosystems program was instrumental in developing sophisticated computer-based models to characterize the properties and processes of ecosystems as integrated units. Such comprehensive tasks required hundreds of personnel working at various levels of research design, field organization, technical assistance, data collection, analysis, modeling, and management of the research organization. It is certain that a major contribution to the IBP by the U.S. was the development of the ecosystem paradigm (Johnson 1977), a synthesis of population and evolutionary biology with systems and ecological theory.

Many of the human adaptability projects in the U.S. and abroad were initiated at a conference in Austria in July, 1964 (The Wenner-Gren Foundation's Burg Wartenstein Conference; see Baker and Weiner 1966). At this conference, papers were presented that dealt with planned research and research synopses of human adaptation on all of the major continents of the earth. Although the human adaptability projects were much more modest in scope than the ecosystem projects, there were, however, marked similarities. The approach taken to investigate the patterns of adaptation of a single population was multidisciplinary; that is, investigators from many different sciences worked together on an integrated project designed to solve a series of scientific problems and to gain an understanding of the whole human-environment system. Projects were also multinational with scientists drawn from host nations and the United States. There were strong ecological interests in several of the human adaptability projects, but for a variety of reasons, including lack of involvement of ecologists and lack of funds, ecological research never became well-integrated within these major projects. In fact, among the human adaptability projects, "ecology" was really translated to mean "environment," and the emphasis was placed on human adaptation to the environment or to environment stress.

Attempts were made to bring about further integration between ecological research and human adaptability research.

A conference was held on "Man in the Ecosystem" (Little and Friedman 1973) in which the theme was "to incorporate humans as an integral component of ecosystem studies." Following three days of close contact between ecologists and human biobehavioral scientists, it became clear that collaborative ecosystem research incorporating humans was most readily accepted when technologically simple populations within relatively intact or only slightly modified natural ecosystems were considered for investigation. It was observed, further, that in more technologically advanced societies, political, trade and communication networks transcended ecosystem boundaries and magnified the complexity of the analysis.

The conceptual differences among social scientists, human biologists, and ecologists on how they view ecosystems, i.e., as relatively "open" or "closed" ecosystems, was a serious barrier to exchange of ideas at this conference (Little and Friedman 1973). Definition of boundaries, to many, is an exercise in taxonomy, and it continues to constrain interdisciplinary communication. Ethnic (Barth 1969; Ross 1975), human population (Brues 1972), and ecosystem (Terborgh 1971) boundaries can each be delineated by different criteria. Ethnic boundaries may be defined by non-transfer of shared values or certain cultural practices and limited interaction (Barth 1969:11); population boundaries may be defined by mating practices and social barriers (Harrison and Boyce 1972); ecosystem boundaries may be defined by marked change in the abiotic environment (steep environmental gradients), by species competition, or by the identification of ecotones (Terborgh 1971). Collaborative efforts that involve the definition of intersecting boundaries of different systems introduce even more complex criteria for boundary definition. Finally, temporal boundaries are less often considered but add a further dimension of sublime complexity (Shugart 1978; Ellen, Adams and Kasakoff, and Netting, this volume).

One area identified by ecologists and biosocial scientists alike as fertile ground for collaborative work was energy and nutrient flow studies (Little and Friedman 1973). Accordingly, a workshop on "Energy Flow in Human Communities" (Jamison and Friedman 1974) was organized as a "means of integrating the study of human communities with the study of the surrounding ecosystems, . . . and to understand the implications of different patterns of energy usage for human populations." The overall recommendation from the workshop was that the most useful techniques for analyzing energy flow data were systems analysis and simulation models.

Although these and other recommendations concerning integration of humans into ecosystem studies came too late to affect the IBP human adaptability research, some progress was made toward a "human ecology" in population biology. Much of this progress occurred through human adaptability projects conducted within tundra, desert, tropical forest, coniferous forest and mountain ecosystems. A discussion of this research follows.

Multidisciplinary Studies in Human Adaptability

More than 200 human adaptability projects were completed throughout the world by the end of the IBP, although most were quite modest in scope with one or two investigators working on a narrowly-defined problem (Weiner 1977). Perhaps 10 percent or fewer of the projects were multidisciplinary, involved research teams with an integrated approach to learning how one or more populations had adapted to a specific environment, and had an organizational network designed for rapid information exchange. High mountain projects were conducted in: 1) the Pamirs of the Soviet Union, 2) the Simien mountains of Ethiopia, 3) the Nepalese Himalayas, and 4) the Peruvian Andes. Circumpolar and boreal forest studies were done of: 1) reindeer-herding Lapps in a joint Scandinavian project, 2) Eskimos from Alaska, Canada and Greenland in a four-nation cooperative venture, 3) Aleutian Islanders in Alaska, and 4) Ainu natives on the island of Hokkaido in Japan. Tropical humid forest projects included: 1) collaborative work on New Guinea natives by the United Kingdom and Australia, 2) studies of Congo Pygmies in the Central African Republic, Cameroon and Zaïre, and 3) a massive effort to study the Yanomama Indians of the Brazilian and Venezuelan Amazon. In addition to these single-ecosystem multidisciplinary projects, others were designed to explore the effects of environmental change through migration. Studies were carried out on migrants to Israel, Japanese migrants to Hawaii and California, migration of Venda Bantu to cities in South Africa, and migration of Andean Indians in Peru to the lowland tropical forest and to the semi-arid Pacific coast. Three of these projects will be discussed briefly to outline the extent to which ecosystem studies played a role in their formulation and outcome.

There were many human adaptability projects completed by U.S. scientists, but several large, multidisciplinary research programs exemplified the U.S. contribution to the IBP. Each project reflected a single frame of reference that was environmentally (but <u>not</u> ecosystematically) oriented: that of investigating the adaptive mechanisms of populations living under some form of environmental stress (National

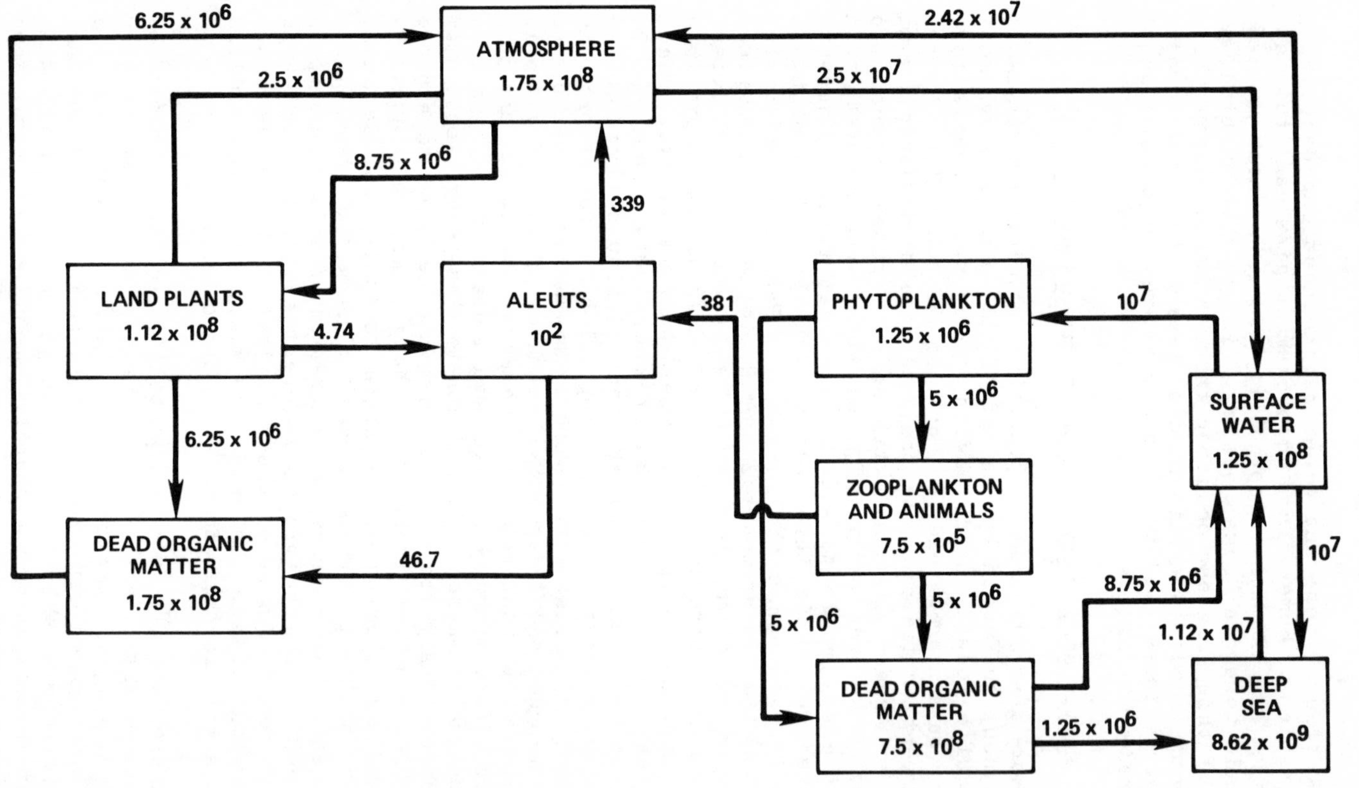

Figure 5.1 An Aleutian ecosystem model of carbon flow. Terrestrial components are to the left in the diagram and marine components are to the right. Values are in kilograms of carbon. (after Hett and O'Neill 1974)

Academy of Sciences 1974:69). The multidisciplinary projects were: (1) The International Study of Circumpolar Peoples with Eskimos (Jamison et al. 1978) and Aleut (Laughlin 1970; Laughlin and Harper 1979) subprojects; (2) the Population genetics of Native Americans (largely Amazon Yanomama) (Neel et al. 1977); (3) the Biology of Human Populations at High Altitude (Baker and Little 1976). These projects will be discussed briefly to outline the extent to which ecosystem studies played a role in their formulation and outcome.

Alaskan Eskimo and Aleut Population in Biology

The northern Alaskan Eskimo and Aleut studies were independent sub-projects on peoples who were living within quite different ecosystems and exploiting different kinds of food resources. Coastal Eskimos depended on sea mammals and caribou in the frigid northern tundra and sea-ice, while Aleut were dependent on shellfish, fish, birds, and sea mammals that flourish as the result of the nutrient-rich upwelling systems around the more temperate Aleutian Islands (Laughlin 1970). Both sub-projects were interested in population biology, including food resource exploitation, nutrition, general health, and ecosystem constraints on population growth.

As noted above, the Alaskan Eskimo project was part of a four-nation effort to study Eskimos around the Arctic Circle. U.S. investigators were responsible for the north coast and inland areas of Alaska; Canadians worked at Igloolik; the French studied Eskimos on the east coast of Greenland; and Danish scientists worked on the west coast of Greenland. Since comparable methods were employed in studies of health, disease, growth, demography, nutrition, genetics, and acculturation, it was possible to compare Eskimos from widely diverse environments (Milan 1980).

Very little modeling was done on either the tundra ecosystems with Eskimos as a component or the island ecosystem including Aleuts, with the notable exception of Hett and O'Neill's (1974) model of carbon flow. This model is illustrated in Figure 5.1.

The model was based upon data from the literature on the amount of carbon in each state variable and estimates of early Aleut population size (16,000), human biomass (mean weight by sex and age classes), and food inputs. An assumption in the model was that Aleuts derive 95 percent of their food from sea animals and five percent from land plants. However, analysis indicated a sensitivity to changes in the marine subsystem of 10,000:1, rather than 20:1, as expected. The marine subsystem is much less subject to seasonal change than the terrestrial subsystem, and thus the "sea appears to offer a more 'dependable' source of food." Also, the model suggested that the rate of ecosystem recovery from disturbance showed little dependence on Aleut activities. A number of other interesting hypotheses concerning Aleut origins and the human carrying capacity of the Aleutian ecosystem were generated by the carbon-flow model.

Some modeling of energy flow through an Eskimo system was done by Kemp (1971) based on data from two hunting families from Baffin Island, Canada. There were, however, no successful attempts to coordinate the extensive IBP tundra ecosystem project at Barrow, Alaska (Brown *et al.* 1980) with any of the Alaskan Eskimo human adaptability studies (Jamison *et al.* 1978; Milan 1980).

Yanomama Indian Population Biology

The Yanomama project was an integrated research program with a focus on population genetics, tribal structure, environmental pressures, and human evolution in a population of Amazon lowland natives (Neel *et al.* 1977). The research team was constituted of a social anthropologist (Chagnon 1968) and numerous population geneticists and biomedical scientists from the United States, Venezuela and Brazil. Although the investigators were very much interested in the wet tropical forest environment and Yanomama techniques of survival and resource exploitation, the project was not oriented toward systems ecology *per se*. However, considerable effort was devoted to innovative genetic and demographic modeling of the Yanomama (MacCluer *et al.* 1971). Indeed, there are no comparably detailed demographic and genetic studies of a tribal population anywhere in the world as those conducted among the Yanomama.

Andean Indian Population Biology

Investigations of the biological and cultural patterns of adaptation of a high-altitude Quechua population were centered in Nuñoa in southern Peru at elevations ranging from 3800 to 5000 meters above sea level (Baker and Little 1976). Abiotic characteristics of this *puna* ecosystem included low atmospheric and oxygen pressure, broad diurnal temperature variation with cold nights, low humidity and seasonal aridity, and high levels of solar radiation. In addition to these severe climatic conditions, highland peoples are faced with limited nutritional and energy resources as well as problems associated with altitude-aggravated and altitude-induced diseased states.

The approach of the project was both ecological and evolutionary, with the major goal being to define how Andean natives had adapted genetically, developmentally, physiologically, and behaviorally to life under these environmental stresses. Research included comparative laboratory tests, field studies, population comparisons in relation to migration, studies of the relationships between sociocultural practices and biological attributes, and energy flow analysis. It was in the area of energy flow analysis that some very important insights were gained about the human population and the managed puna system. Figure 5.2 is an energy-flow diagram developed by Thomas (1976) based on H.T. Odum's (1971) modeling framework.

Energy values in the diagram represent thousands of kilocalories (kcal) utilized annually by a Quechua Indian family of two adults and four children. This approach led Thomas to several conclusions about the energetic efficiency of the mixed subsistence system of herding and cultivation. Comparing food energy production (outputs) with labor expenditures (inputs), cultivation of plant foods yields more than a 10:1 return. Livestock herding in the absence of trade provides for only a 2:1 return. However, because animal products are highly valued at lower elevations where sheep and camelid livestock cannot be kept easily, the net gain with trade of animal products (meat, hides, wool) for plant foods increases the ratio to more than 7:1.

These relationships demonstrated the utility of a mixed subsistence pattern in this area of the Andes. Cultivation yields alone are insufficient to meet all of the human food requirements under the present subsistence system and demographic structure. Livestock provide a relatively stable protein resource, dung for cultivation and for cooking fuel and valuable trade commodities.

The human adaptability studies reviewed here demonstrate the potential value of investigating human populations within an ecosystem framework. However, these projects focused largely on human adaptive responses to the extant ecosystem. There was little consideration of the influence of the human population on ecosystem dynamics and development. Only patterns of energy flow were followed, whereas recent ecosystem studies have emphasized the influential role of, and limitations imposed by, nutrients such as nitrogen and phosphorus (Gorham et al. 1979; Odum 1969; Woodmansee 1978).

The remaining section of this paper will outline the conceptual framework and objectives of an ecosystem-human ecology project currently underway in northwest Kenya. The research is multidisciplinary, and modeling is a central analytical process.

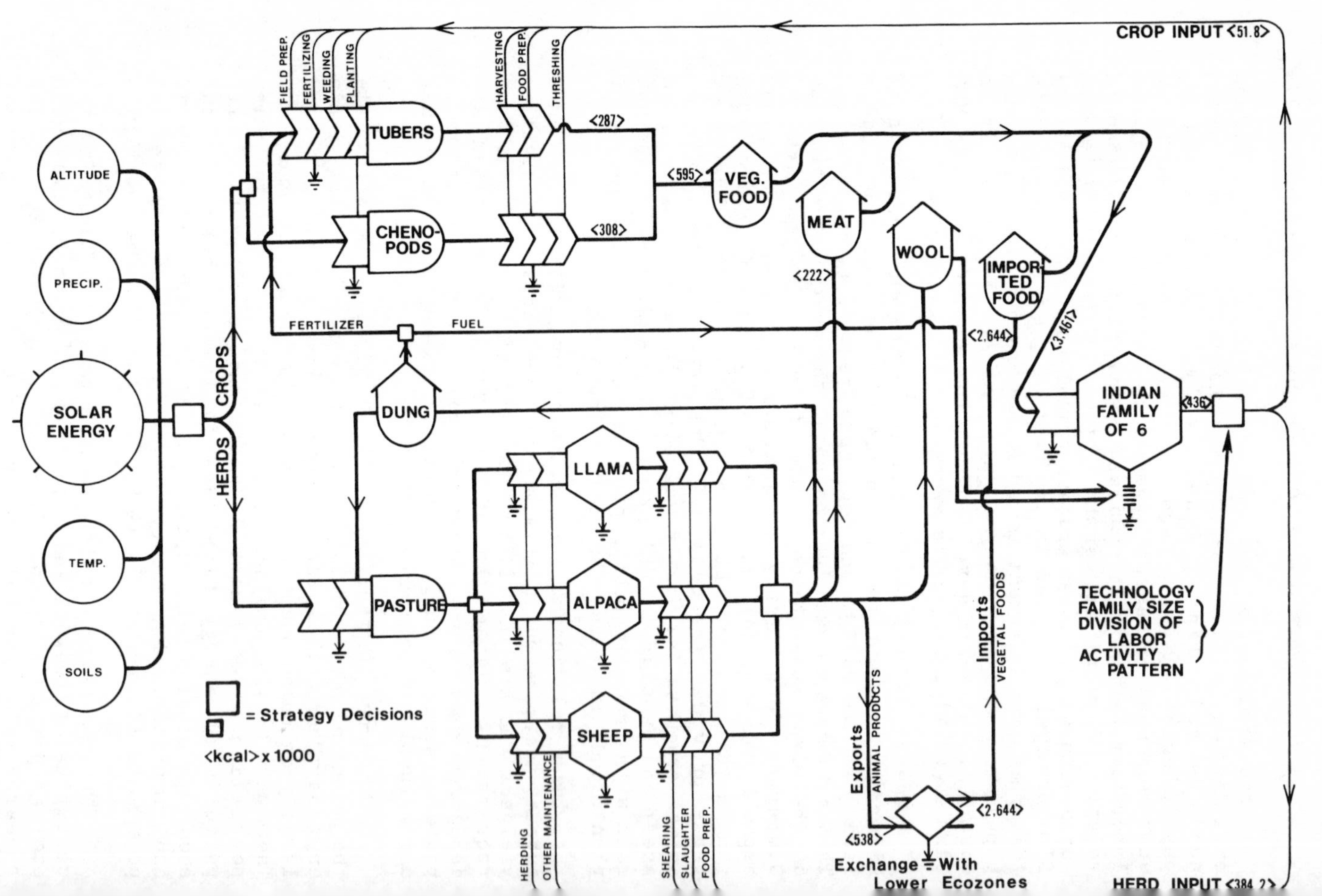
CROP INPUT <51.8>
FIELD PREP.
FERTILIZING
WEEDING
PLANTING
HARVESTING
FOOD PREP.
THRESHING
ALTITUDE
PRECIP.
SOLAR ENERGY
TEMP.
SOILS
CROPS
HERDS
TUBERS
CHENO-PODS
<287>
<308>
<595>
VEG. FOOD
MEAT
<222>
WOOL
IMPOR-TED FOOD
<2.644>
<3.461>
FERTILIZER
FUEL
DUNG
INDIAN FAMILY OF 6
<436>
LLAMA
ALPACA
SHEEP
PASTURE
HERDING
OTHER MAINTENANCE
SHEARING
SLAUGHTER
FOOD PREP.
Exports
ANIMAL PRODUCTS
Imports
VEGETAL FOODS
<538>
<2.644>
Exchange With Lower Ecozones
TECHNOLOGY
FAMILY SIZE
DIVISION OF LABOR
ACTIVITY PATTERN
= Strategy Decisions
<kcal> x 1000
HERD INPUT <384.2>

South Turkana Ecosystem Project

Background

The South Turkana Ecosystem Project has as its major objective the analysis of the role of human populations in a dry savanna ecosystem. Ecological anthropology and plant, animal and soil ecology have been incorporated within an ecosystems framework in which the research design focuses: 1) on the influence of pastoralists and their livestock on the energy and nutrient dynamics in an arid savanna ecosystem and 2) on the patterns of adaptation of the human populations enabling them to survive and persist in this ecosystem.

South Turkana is a region of northwest Kenya characterized as semi-arid--or at the xeric end of the East African savanna moisture gradient (see Figure 5.3). The topography of the region is rugged and soils are largely coarse sandy alluvium or thin stony lithosols with lava outcrops. Ambient temperatures are uniformly high throughout the year which, when combined with a low annual rainfall that is concentrated into only a few months (March to May) and a high evapotranspiration rate, leads to a marked moisture deficit. Vegetation is xerophytic and dominated by *Acacia* spp. and *Commiphora* spp. trees, a variety of shrubs, and annual grasses and forbs. The South Turkana region is inhabited by a southern branch of the Turkana tribe, a group of migratory or nomadic pastoralists who herd cattle, camels, goats, sheep and donkeys, and who live under relatively traditional conditions.

Figure 5.4 (pp. 116-117) is a simplified model of the state variables, material flows and controls in the Turkana ecosystem. Basically, plant biomass is consumed by livestock (cattle, camels, goats, sheep and donkeys), and the products of the livestock (milk, blood, meat, hides) are either consumed by the Turkana or traded for food and other items. In order to maintain the output of livestock products, the Turkana must manage the livestock in specific ways. The impact of their management alters photosynthesis rates, respiration rates, species composition, total plant biomass, and soil nutrient conditions.

Figure 5.2 (left) Energy flow in a highland Andean *puna* ecosystem. Values are in thousands of kilocalories annual flow with reference to a Quechua Indian family of two adults and four children. (adapted from Thomas 1976)

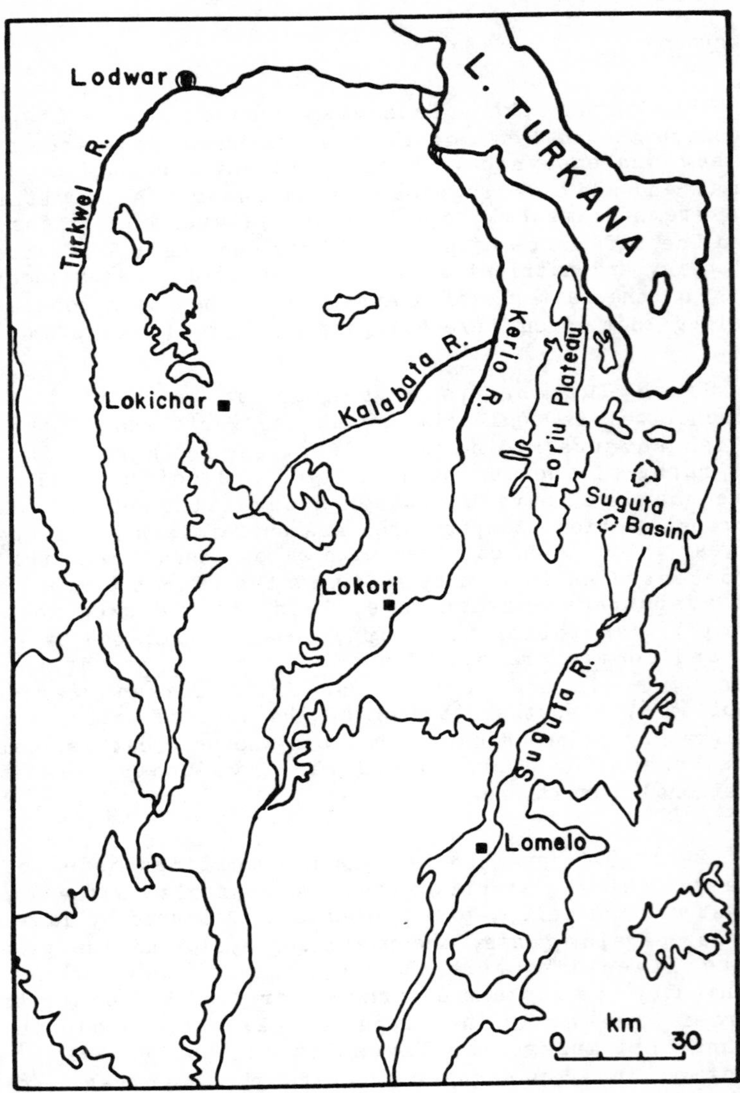

Figure 5.3 Map of South Turkana. The study area of the South Turkana Ecosystem Project is bounded by the Turkwel and Kerio Rivers and the towns of Lokichar and Lokori.

The project has three principal and many lesser components that reflect both the project objectives and the capabilities of the research personnel. The principal components are: 1) savanna ecosystem analysis; 2) human behavior and sociocultural anthropology analysis; and 3) human health, biology and adaptability analysis. There is considerable complementarity in these components. For example, livestock are of interest to the ecologists in terms of their impact on the ecosystem and their consumption of plant productivity, while sociocultural anthropologists are concerned with livestock management strategies and how the cultural system facilitates or constrains the implementation of these strategies. Human biologists, on the other hand, are concerned with the physical effort required to manage the livestock, the dietary products derived from the animals, and the adequacy of these products as measurable in child growth, nutritional status and health status of the Turkana. All components of the project are similarly linked via the modeling efforts. Simulation models will play an important role in at least two ways: 1) to assist in data interpretation and to test hypotheses and 2) to extrapolate results and make predictions about unmeasured effects in the South Turkana ecosystem. Existing subsystem models developed by scientists at the Natural Resource Ecology Laboratory of Colorado State University, as well as the human energy and nitrogen balance model under development, will be integrated into an ecosystem-level model to deal with processes and regulation within the system.

Description of the study area[2]

We have been working with a "neighborhood" community of Turkana of the Ngisonyoka tribal subsection. The whole community, which congregates during the wet season, numbers about 50 family production units or more than 1000 persons. Of these, we have close contact and excellent rapport with ten family units. The project area has been delimited by assessing the traditional region used by members of Ngisonyoka. It is approximately 8000 km^2 in size and consists of a central north-south massif with elevations up to 2500 m. The area is delimited by a broad alluvial dry-season bushland valley in the west, an alluvial wet-season plain in the northeast, and adjacent lava hills and plains in the southeast.

---

[2]Results from the work conducted to date are preliminary since many field operations were initiated in early 1981 and some subprojects have just begun.

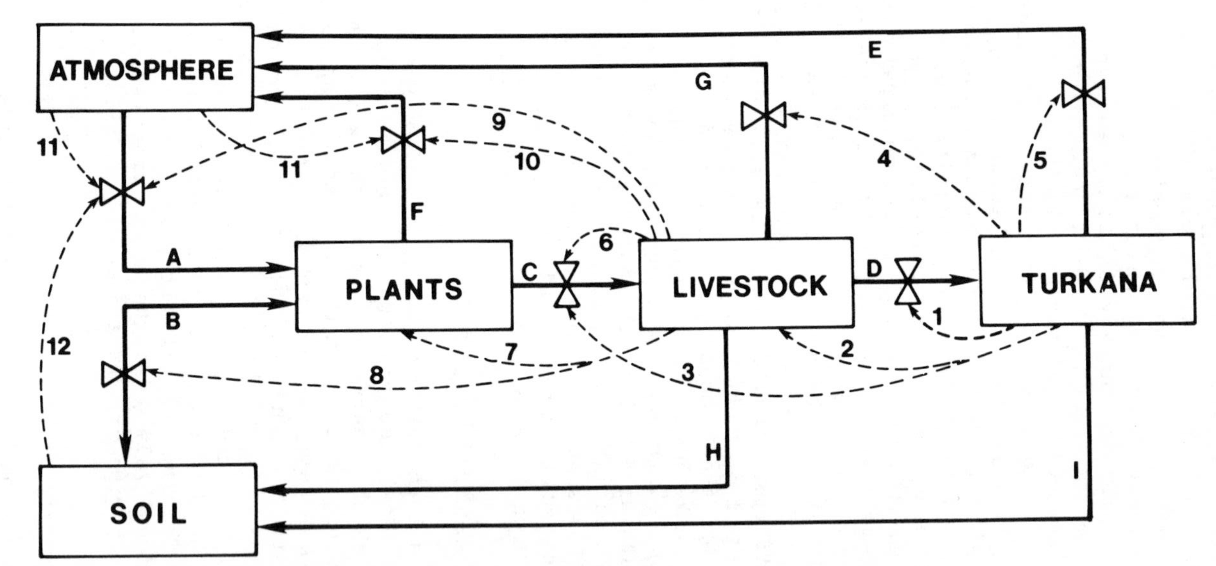
ATMOSPHERE
PLANTS
LIVESTOCK
TURKANA
SOIL
A
B
C
D
E
F
G
H
I
1
2
3
4
5
6
7
8
9
10
11
11
12

Figure 5.4 A control diagram representing system components, energy and material flows, and some controls for the South Turkana ecosystem.

ENERGY AND MATERIAL FLOWS

A – PHOTOSYNTHESIS

B – NUTRIENT UPTAKE AND DECOMPOSITION

C – CONSUMPTION BY LIVESTOCK

D – CONSUMPTION BY TURKANA

E – TURKANA ENERGY EXPENDITURE

F – PLANT RESPIRATION

G – LIVESTOCK ENERGY EXPENDITURE

H – LIVESTOCK NUTRIENT DECOMPOSITION AND RELEASE

I – TURKANA NUTRIENT DECOMPOSITION AND RELEASE

STATE VARIABLES

ATMOSPHERE – DRIVING VARIABLES

SOIL – SOIL NUTRIENTS AND SOIL ORGANIC MATTER

PLANTS – PLANT BIOMASS AND CHEMICAL CONTENT

LIVESTOCK – LIVESTOCK BIOMASS AND POPULATION STRUCTURE

TURKANA – TURKANA BIOMASS, POPULATION, SOCIAL AND SPATIAL ORGANIZATION, ETHNOECOLOGY, HEALTH AND ADAPTABILITY

SYSTEM CONTROLS

TURKANA GRAZING MANAGEMENT DECISIONS

1 – LIVESTOCK EXPLOITATION

2 – HERD COMPOSITION AND SIZE

3 – PASTURE SELECTION

4 – LIVESTOCK MOVEMENTS

5 – TURKANA LABOR ALLOCATIONS

LIVESTOCK GRAZING EFFECTS ON:

6 – DIET COMPOSITION

7 – SPECIES COMPOSITION AND BIOMASS

8 – SOIL NUTRIENTS

9 – PRIMARY PRODUCTION

10 – PLANT RESPIRATION

ABIOTIC EFFECTS ON:

11 – PHOTOSYNTHESIS AND PRIMARY PRODUCTION

NUTRIENT EFFECTS ON:

12 – PHOTOSYNTHESIS AND PRIMARY PRODUCTION

Vegetation and water availability are the major ecological factors determining livestock habitat use and human rangeland exploitation patterns. Accordingly, a general vegetation map of the ecosystem is being developed from on-ground surveys, aerial photographs, and LANDSAT imagery. We are also mapping all water-holes in South Turkana and recording their permanence, quality for different livestock species, and constraints on their use.

Livestock-plant-nutrient interactions

This subproject is concerned with: niche separation among livestock species; the specific components of the various vegetation communities consumed by each livestock species; the seasonal availability and quality of forage components; the resultant diet quality, nutritional condition and productivity of livestock; the impacts of livestock on soil nutrient status and plant associations in the ecosystem.

We have observed that the five livestock species feed on different forage components, their diets being separated on the basis of plant species, plant parts, and vegetation height. It is clear, also, that different vegetation canopy layers (herbaceous, dwarf shrub, tall shrub, tree) undergo quite different phenological sequences due, most likely, to variations in rooting depth. Thus, livestock diet quality, nutritional condition, and production of human food (including milk, blood and meat) vary greatly throughout the year among the livestock species. Turkana patterns of exploitation are sensitive to these variations in food production.

Livestock management and ecosystem utilization by Turkana

This subproject deals with the overall patterns of ecosystem exploitation by the Turkana. Of particular interest are the seasonal movements of the Turkana and their herds as they relate to changes in vegetation and water availability, and as they differ among livestock species. Equally important are the management strategies of Turkana herd owners (Dyson-Hudson 1980).

Through the contacts that we have established with family production units of various sizes, we have been able to begin to sort out a number of factors influencing adoption of given strategies. Small herd holdings and a small family unit allow for flexible responses and yet may require assistance from other families because of low livestock productivity. Large herds with all domestic species require detailed management operations and family labor allocation. One variable in the overall pastoral strategy that has played a very important role in structuring movement and settlement siting is external raiding by neighboring Pokot tribesmen and internal raiding by Turkana bandits or Ngingoroko. Hence, western Turkana border areas are avoided because of the danger of Pokot raids, while the area in proximity to the Loriu Plateau is avoided because of the risks of Ngingoroko. Some decision-making on movement is influenced by the pronouncements of a seer and clairvoyant (imuron). These and other phenomena are being studied in the context of movement and management strategies.

Livestock production and herd dynamics

Livestock production and the dynamics of herd size and composition are objective measures of pastoral ecosystem utilization. We are concerned here with: 1) the seasonal dynamics of livestock production and human offtake as they reflect ecosystem conditions and management tactics; 2) the size and composition of livestock herds as they relate to the pastoral exploitation strategy; 3) livestock numbers and biomass as they represent the major pathway of energy and nutrient flows to the human population.

Quantitative measures of milk, blood and meat production have been recorded for more than a year. The patterns of food utilization vary according to seasonal changes in livestock productivity. These patterns underline the utility of maintaining several species of livestock. Perhaps the most striking finding at variance with the literature (Gulliver 1951, 1955) is that Turkana consume large amounts of meat toward the end of the dry season (Jan.-Feb.) when milk production of all species is essentially nil and when some animals are dying. This pattern of meat consumption was reported by Turkana informants to be not unusual at this time of the year. Of course, meat consumption is considerably less at other times of the year when milk production is greater.

Human health and adaptation

The nutritional balance, health status, fitness level, child growth, and population dynamics of the Turkana people are largely the result of patterns of pastoral resource exploitation (Little 1980). Human knowledge, intelligence, and physical labor represent the human inputs into the system. In this subproject we are attempting to assess the labor or activity inputs as they relate to extraction levels (food energy and nutrients), and how the interaction of input

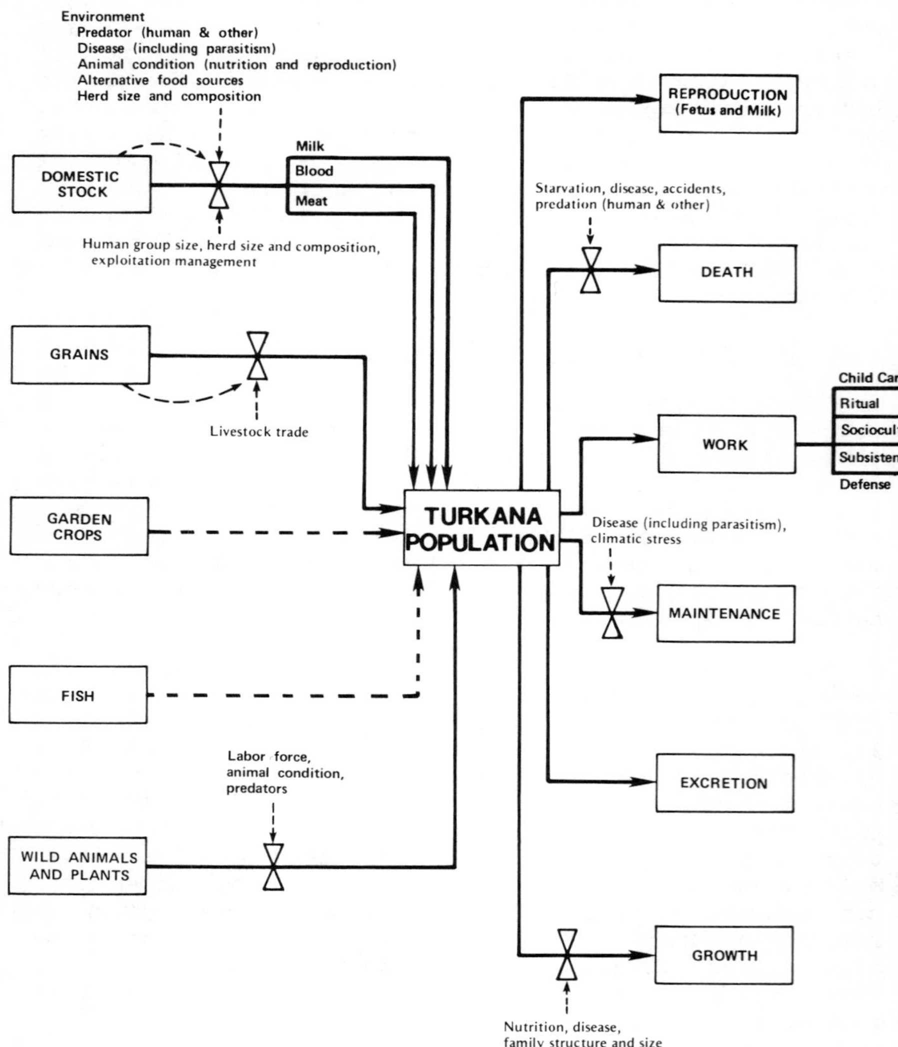

Figure 5.5 A model of energy and nutrient flows through the Turkana population. All flows are controlled in part by: age, sex, nutritional status, health status, size and body composition, physiological state, technology, required tasks, location, and other variables. Interrupted lines from garden crops and fish signify that South Turkana nomads rarely or never utilize these food resources.

and extraction or output influences the overall health status and adaptation of the Turkana.

A schematic energy and nutrient flow diagram for the Turkana population is presented in Figure 5.5. Basically, the diagram is a preliminary attempt to define the flows associated with energy and nutrient production (left side of Figure 5.5) and human expenditures (right side of Figure 5.5). The Turkana exploit the dry savanna ecosystem as primary (by gathering and, very rarely, cultivating plant foods) and secondary (by hunting and herding) consumers, and they draw energy through several kinds of food chains. In addition, they obtain food from outside of the immediate production unit through trade and by complex patterns of exchange with neighboring family production units. Human inputs of labor directly associated with food production include: 1) hunting and gathering; 2) management of livestock (herding, watering, moving); 3) harvesting livestock products (milking, bleeding, slaughtering, preparing hides, etc.); and 4) preparing food from plant and livestock products (drying, grinding, cooking). These inputs and other controls regulate the rates of energy and nutrient transfer between the designated state variables of the system.

A variety of different kinds of data must be gathered on members of the Turkana population in order to meet the dual objectives of a health and adaptability assessment and the construction of the human energy and nutrient flow submodel (Little 1980). Health assessment has begun with medical examinations of Turkana men, women and children. Preliminary results suggest that Turkana are reasonably healthy for a population with minimal health care. Clear signs of nutritional deficiencies were rare: among children, kwashiorkor was nonexistent although marasmus was present in one to two percent of children between three and six years of age. We interpret this as a general sign of nutritional adequacy for the population since these data represent the health status of the people following a particularly bad sequence of dry years. Despite these preliminary indications, full judgment on health and nutritional status should be reserved until more comprehensive results are available. For example, intensive dietary survey only began in August, 1981.

Most data collection efforts during the 1981 field season centered around defining the health, size, and body composition characteristics by age and sex of the human population. As noted above, these data are important for assessment of health and fitness and also provide data for the human submodel. Figure 5.6 illustrates curves for growth

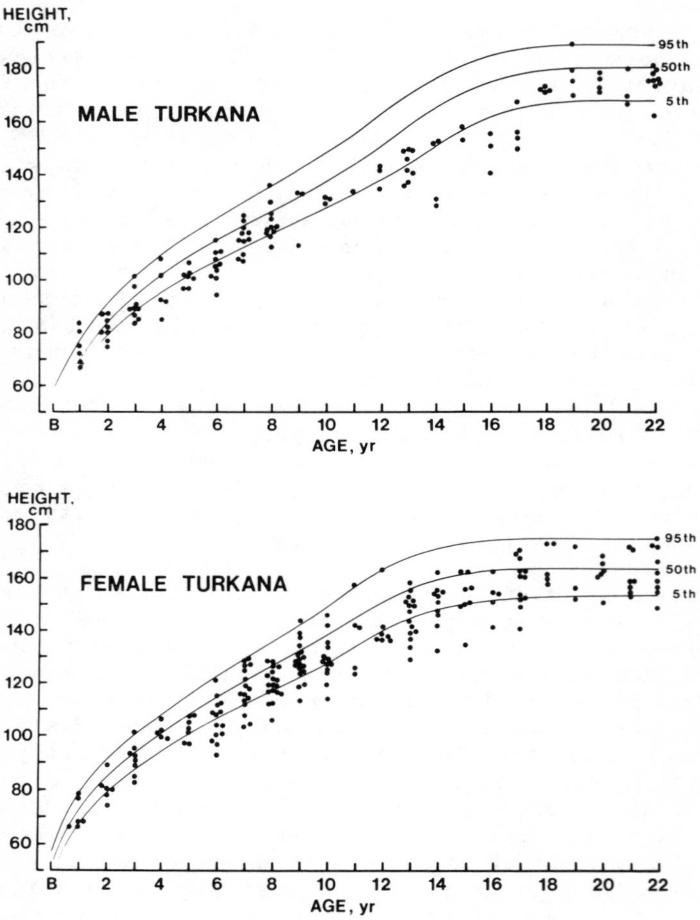

Figure 5.6(a) Growth in height of Turkana males and females. Curved lines are 95th, 50th, and 5th percentile rankings of growth based upon standards for the United States.

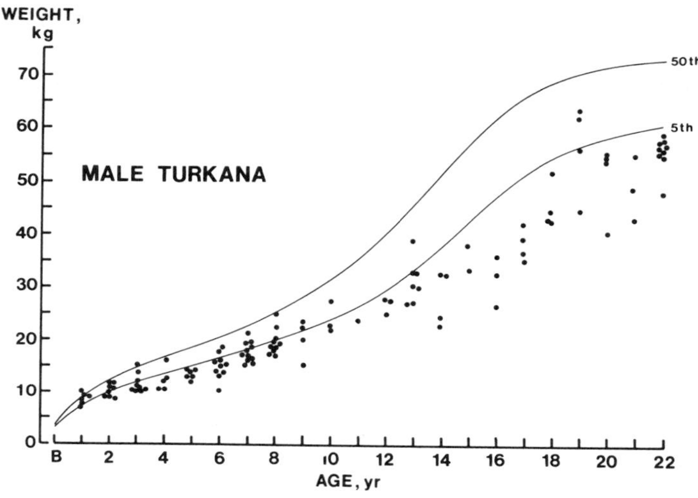

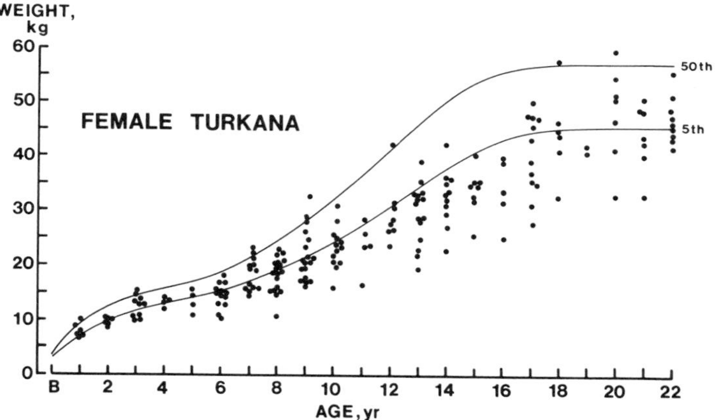

Figure 5.6(b) Growth in weight of Turkana males and females. Curved lines are 95th, 50th, and 5th percentile rankings of growth based upon standards for the United States.

in height and weight of Turkana. Most Turkana fall around or below the fifth percentile of weight for United States samples, yet are much closer to U.S. norms for height. This indicates that Turkana are extremely lean by U.S. and European standards. It also indicates that physical activities can be carried out at a lower energy cost than in comparable age- and sex-mates from western societies. Although sampling is not good in these age ranges, the adolescent growth spurt appears to be retarded and full maturity is not achieved until the early 20's.

Through the remainder of the study, we will increase the sampling for the growth study and conduct periodic anthropometric and health surveys to reveal seasonal trends as well as general patterns. Energy-activity budget analysis will continue in conjunction with the nutritional analysis. The combination of input (nutrition), output (activity), and status (body composition) analysis should provide us with information to assess the bio-behavioral adaptive patterns of the Turkana. The next step that needs to be taken is in the realm of demography. Modeling at the human population level is needed to simulate the effects on the ecosystem of changes in population structure, composition, distribution of numbers through time, and to predict how changes in ecosystem state variables will stimulate shifts in human population parameters.

Human social organization and resource exploitation

This subproject focuses on the ways in which the Turkana population exploits the natural environment principally via the livestock population. Our concern here is: 1) to define the Turkana perception of resources and their distribution; 2) to identify Turkana cognitive maps or ways of conceptualizing resources and places in space; and 3) to determine how the social organization and cultural system of the Turkana define access to rangeland, animals and water sources (Dyson-Hudson and Dyson-Hudson 1980).

The social organization of the Turkana has several structural levels and is characterized by some flexibility and individual variation. The largest unit with which we are working is the Ngisonyoka sub-tribal or socio-territorial group. This group has a spatially demarcated home range which is an area where Turkana expect to encounter the people so named and where they have priority of resource use. The smallest level of social organization is the family production unit represented by the family *awi* or settlement and satellite herding camps. Typically a production unit consists of an extended family, sometimes with other dependents, but in its basic form, including a family head/herd owner, his wives and their children. On occasion, the awi will include two or more herd owners tied by bonds of kinship or friendship. Intermediate between the socio-territorial and family production groups is the transientset of awis that form neighborhood associations or networks, called adakars. They constitute temporary common interest groups that form under a variety of conditions for defense as well as for social living, act as information networks, and provide a context of general insurance against emergencies in the small settlement groups which compose them.

Ngingoroko raids on Turkana family settlements influence social organization and settlement patterns. These raids were increasing during early 1981 to the point where several of the families with whom we had worked had suffered severe livestock losses. In response to this threat, about 50 herd owners decided to form a settlement cluster within an area of roughly ten km^2. This clustering of a neighborhood network was possible only because the rains had begun a month earlier, the plant growing season was well underway, and forage for the animals was abundant. Also at the family settlement level, there appeared a curious pattern of movement in which awis on the southern periphery of the neighborhood cluster were periodically moving into the center of the cluster. We are not certain, but this appeared to be for greater security and tended to move the cluster slowly to the north where raids were less common. Although not fully confirmed as well, it appears that the rainy season proceeds northward and the Turkana follow the green flush as it develops. Hence, the two variables that influence movement northward may reinforce one another.

Integration of Human Biology and Ecosystem Studies

Past studies of human biological adaptation to the environment suffered from two major shortcomings. The first is that very little information was gathered on the sociocultural patterns of the people under investigation. These data are important because in traditional subsistence societies the structure and organization of the society is at the same time (1) a reflection of behavioral adaptations to the ecosystem and (2) a sociocultural system with rules of behavior that regulate (in part) the exploitation of the ecosystem. Among the United States IBP human adaptability projects, sociocultural data links were weak in the Andean Indian (Baker and Little 1976), Alaskan Eskimo (Jamison *et al*. 1978), and Aleut (Laughlin and Harper 1979) projects. The Amazon basin Yanomama Indian project (Neel *et al*. 1977; Chagnon 1968) was a notable exception in its comprehensive cultural studies but was deficient in systems ecological aspects.

The second shortcoming of human adaptability studies has been in the limited amount of understanding sought about the ecosystem within which human adaptation takes place. If an environmental stress design is applied in biological adaptation research, then the dynamic attributes of the stresses arising from the ecosystem must be defined. In the case of the Turkana, limited dietary calorie intake could result from a poor milk production due to inadequate plant forage quality, e.g., low protein forage for livestock. The source of the low human calorie intake could only be defined by detailed work on the trophic relationships between primary productivity and the livestock. If modeling and simulation are principal analytical objectives, then ecosystems parameters are important input variables. Modeling of human energy and nutrient dynamics requires data on food webs and plant phenology and productivity, among other things.

It is our belief that the structure, dynamics, maintenance and evolution of human populations are controlled by the action of sociocultural, ecological and human biological factors. These controls are highly complex and interactive. Accordingly, an integrated ecosystem research approach is likely to be most productive in understanding these relationships.

References Cited

Baker, P.T.
1958 Racial Differences in Heat Tolerance. American Journal of Physical Anthropology 16:287-305.
1962 The Application of Ecological Theory to Anthropology. American Anthropologist 64:15-22.

Baker, P.T. and M.A. Little (eds.)
1976 Man in the Andes: A Multidisciplinary Study of High Altitude Quechua. Stroudsburg, Pa.: Dowden, Hutchinson and Ross.

Baker, P.T. and J.S. Weiner, eds.
1966 The Biology of Human Adaptability. Oxford: Clarendon Press.

Barth, F.
1969 Ethnic Groups and Boundaries: The Social Organization of Culture Difference. Boston: Little, Brown and Co.

Bates, M.
1953 Human Ecology. In Anthropology Today: An Encyclopedic Inventory. A.L. Kroeber, ed. Chicago: University of Chicago Press. Pp. 700-713.
1960 Ecology and Evolution. In Evolution After Darwin, Vol. I, The Evolution of Life. S. Tax, ed. Chicago: University of Chicago Press. Pp. 547-568.

Birdsell, J.B.
1953 Some Environmental and Cultural Factors Influencing the Structuring of Australian Aboriginal Populations. American Naturalist 87:171-207.

Brown, G.M. and J. Page
1952 The Effect of Chronic Exposure to Cold on Temperature and Blood Flow to the Hand. Journal of Applied Physiology 5:221-227.

Brown, J., P.C. Miller, L.L. Tieszen, and F.L. Bunnell
1980 An Arctic Ecosystem: The Coastal Tundra at Barrow, Alaska. Stroudsburg, Pa.: Dowden, Hutchinson, and Ross.

Brues, A.M.
1972 Models of Race and Cline. American Journal of Physical Anthropology 37:389-400.

Chagnon, N.A.
1968 Yanomamö: The Fierce People. New York: Holt, Rinehart and Winston.

Coon, C.S., S.M. Garn, and J.B. Birdsell
1950 Races: A Study of the Problems of Race Formation in Man. Springfield, Illinois: Thomas.

Dyson-Hudson, N.
1980 Strategies of Resource Exploitation Among East African Savanna Pastoralists. In Human Ecology in Savanna Environments. D.R. Harris, ed. London: Academic Press. Pp. 171-184.

Dyson-Hudson, R. and N. Dyson-Hudson
1980 Nomadic Pastoralism. Annual Review of Anthropology 9:15-61.

Gorham, E., P.M. Vitousek and W.A. Reiners
1979 The Regulation of Chemical Budgets over the Course of Terrestrial Ecosystem Succession. Annual Review of Ecology and Systematics 10:53-84.

Gulliver, P.H.
1951 A Preliminary Survey of the Turkana: A Report Compiled for the Government of Kenya. Communication from the School of African Studies, No. 26 (n.s.). University of Cape Town, South Africa.
1955 The Family Herds. London: Routledge and Kegan Paul.

Harrison, G.A. and A.J. Boyce
1972 Migration, Exchange and the Genetic Structure of Populations. In The Structure of Human Populations. G.A. Harrison and A.J. Boyce, eds. Oxford: Clarendon Press. Pp. 128-145.

Hett, J.M. and R.V. O'Neill
1974 Systems Analysis of the Aleut Ecosystem. Arctic Anthropology 11(1):31-40.

Jamison, P.L. and S.M. Friedman
1974 Energy Flow in Human Communities: Proceedings of a Workshop. University Park, Pa.: Human Adaptability Coordinating Office of the U.S./I.B.P.

Jamison, P.L., S.L. Zegura, and F.A. Milan (eds.)
1978 Eskimos of Northwestern Alaska: A Biological Perspective. Stroudsburg, Pa.: Dowden, Hutchinson, and Ross.

Johnson, P.L.
1977 An Ecosystem Paradigm for Ecology. Oak Ridge, Tennessee: Oak Ridge Associated Universities.

Kemp, W.B.
1971 The flow of energy in a hunting society. Scientific American 225(3):104-115.

Laughlin, W.S.
1970 Aleutian Ecosystem. Science 169:1107-1108.

Laughlin, W.S. and A.B. Harper (eds.)
1979 The First Americans: Origins, Affinities, and Adaptations. New York: Gustav Fischer.

Little, M.A.

1980 Designs for Human-Biological Research Among Savanna Pastoralists. In Human Ecology in Savanna Environments. D.R. Harris, ed. London: Academic Press. Pp. 479-503.

1982 The development of ideas on human ecology and adaptation. In A History of American Physical Anthropology, 1930-1980, ed. by F. Spencer. New York: Academic Press. Pp. 405-433.

Little, M.A. and S.M. Friedman

1973 Man in the Ecosystem: Proceedings of a Conference. University Park, Pa.: Human Adaptability Coordinating Office of the U.S./I.B.P.

MacCluer, J.W., J.V. Neel, and N.A. Chagnon

1971 Demographic Structure of a Primitive Population: A Simulation. American Journal of Physical Anthropology 35:193-207.

National Academy of Sciences

1974 U.S. Participation in the International Biological Program: Report No. 6 of the U.S. National Committee for the I.B.P. Washington, D.C.: National Academy of Sciences.

Neel, J.V., M. Layrisse, and F.M. Salzano

1977 Man in the Tropics: The Yanomama Indians. In Population Structure and Human Variation. G.A. Harrison, ed. London: Cambridge University Press. Pp. 109-142.

Newman, M.T.

1960 Adaptations in the Physique of American Aborigines to Nutritional Factors. Human Biology 32:288-313.

1962 Ecology and Nutritional Stress in Man. American Anthropologist 64:22-33.

Newman, R.W. and E.H. Munro

1955 The Relation of Climate and Body Size in U.S. Males. American Journal of Physical Anthropology 13:1-17.

Odum, H.T.

1971 Environment, Power and Society. New York: Wiley-Interscience.

Odum, E.P.
1969 The Strategy of Ecosystem Development. Science 164:262-270.

Roberts, D.F.
1952 Basal Metabolism, Race and Climate. Journal of the Royal Anthropological Institute 82:169-183.
1953 Body Weight, Race and Climate. American Journal of Physical Anthropology 11:533-558.
1956 A Demographic Study of a Dinka Village. Human Biology 28:323-349.

Ross, J.K.
1975 Social Borders: Definitions of Diversity. Current Anthropology 16:53-72.

Scholander, P.F., K.L. Anderson, J. Krog, F.V. Lorentzen, and J. Steen
1957 Critical Temperature in Lapps. Journal of Applied Physiology 10:231-234.

Scholander, P.F., H.T. Hammel, S.J. Hart, D.H. LeMessurier, and J. Steen
1958 Cold Adaptation in Australian Aborigines. Journal of Applied Physiology 13:211-218.

Shugart, H.H., Jr. (ed.)
1978 Time Series and Ecological Processes. Philadelphia, Pa.: Society for Industrial and Applied Mathematics.

Spuhler, J.N.
1959 Physical Anthropology and Demography. In The Study of Population. P.M. Hauser and O.D. Duncan, eds. Chicago: University of Chicago Press. Pp. 728-758.

Terborgh, J.
1971 Distribution on Environmental Gradients: Theory and a Preliminary Interpretation of Distributional Patterns in the Avifauna of the Cordillera Vilcabamba, Peru. Ecology 52:23-40.

Thomas, R.B.
1976 Energy Flow at High Altitude. In Man in the Andes: A Multidisciplinary Study of High-Altitude Quechua. P.T. Baker and M.A. Little, eds. Stroudsburg, Pa.: Dowden, Hutchinson, and Ross. Pp. 379-404.

Weiner, J.S.
1964 Part V. Human ecology. In Human Biology, by G.A. Harrison, J.S. Weiner, J.M. Tanner and N.A. Barnicot. Oxford: Oxford University Press. Pp. 399-508.
1977 The History of the Human Adaptability Section. In Human Adaptability: A History and Compendium of Research. K.J. Collins and J.S. Weiner, eds. London: Taylor and Francis. Pp. 1-23.

Woodmansee, R.G.
1978 Additions and Losses of Nitrogen in Grasslands Ecosystems. Bioscience 24:81-87.

Susan H. Lees, Daniel G. Bates

6. Environmental Events and the Ecology of Cumulative Change

Introduction

In 1968, A.P. Vayda and Roy Rappaport articulated a new approach for the study of human-environment interaction, representing a marked departure from previous anthropological approaches. Vayda and Rappaport's formulation advocated the adoption of "ecosystem" and component "populations" as conceptual analytical units in place of earlier conceptual units, namely "culture" and "environment." The advantages of their approach were immediately apparent to those who had become dissatisfied with the vague and ambiguous notion of culture when used to explicate human-environment interaction and who were impressed by the achievements of the emerging fields of systems theory, ethology, and ecology. This formulation was particularly attractive in that its treatment of humans as one population among many enabled anthropologists to use theoretical models developed in other fields. Among the ecosystemic models which were soon directed to questions of human behavior were those using optimal foraging strategy, population regulation and carrying capacity, and bioenergetics.

However, in the ensuing years a wide variety of shortcomings of the "ecosystemic" approach were discovered and expressed by critics outside and within the subfield of ecological anthropology (see Smith in this volume). Perhaps the most telling anthropological critique among these was that expressed by Vayda and Bonnie McCay (1975, 1977). The main challenge for human ecology, as Vayda and McCay saw it, was to discover and identify the actual problems people face and to delineate their ways of coping with these problems. In their opinion, ecosystemic approaches had so far fallen short of meeting this challenge. While an ecosystemic approach appeared to offer a practical means of modeling material transfers and flows of energy among populations, it did not address the questions of why these relationships were organized as they were or how people respond when they change. In focusing on the ecosystem as the object of study, the anthropologist was often led to confuse or misidentify problems which might threaten the defined parameters of the analytic unit, the ecosystem, with problems constituting a hazard to the human population itself (see also Bates and Lees, 1979).

We agree with Vayda and McCay that ecosystemic approaches used thus far for the study of human populations have serious limitations. In this paper we will try to take their arguments a step further and suggest one way of formulating research design or procedure which is particularly useful for identifying environmental problems and people's responses to them. We will review what we consider to be interesting and successful examples of studies which have taken this approach and discuss some of their general findings. We will contend, too, that there is a link between the shift in perspective that has resulted in these studies and the emergence of development and modernization research, and we will argue that even closer linkages between these two lines of research will be beneficial to both.

Shortcomings of Ecosystemic Approaches

The notion of ecosystem specifically incorporates the idea of self-regulation (Odum 1971). Even though it is often presented with suitable disclaimers, the ecosystem is almost inevitably utilized as a "superorganic" concept. It refers to a distinctive level of organization emergent from its organic and non-organic components. Ecosystem models assume that self-organization exists at the scale of the observer-delineated system and needs merely to be discovered. The literature is replete with organic analogies such as "the death" of an ecosystem, "maturity," "senescence," etc (see Golley in this volume). The inappropriateness of the organic analogy has been widely commented upon in the modern ecological literature, and the meagre theoretical results of the ecosystem concept are often noted (see, for instance, Colinvaux 1973, p. 229; and Smith, this volume).

To describe a human ecosystem is to describe the roles that humans play in the maintenance or mutual regulation of relationships between themselves, other living species, and non-organic elements with which they interact. Ecosystemic models involving humans organize description around an equilibrium or goal state defined as "carrying capacity" and interpret the structure of energy flows and the working of regulatory mechanisms in terms of dampening oscillation around this hypothetical point (see Bates and Lees, 1979, for a discussion). The habitat, in this view, is seen as the source of limiting factors, be they food items, water, disease or whatever. An objective of the analysis then is to see how the human population avoids coming up against these limitations.

It is possible, however, to describe human-environment relationships systemically without assuming the self-regulating properties inherent in the ecosystem concept. We might look for evidence of "self-regulation" but not find it. At times, what appears to be "self-regulation" is simply an artifact of the period of observation or of the boundaries delineated for the ecosystem (see Ellen, this volume). That is, while there is "organization" in the sense of systemic interrelationships, there is not necessarily a restoration of relationships built into the system itself. In human systems relationships are often not being restored in any sense but are undergoing continuous change. This probably has something to do with the character of human responses themselves. They are often cumulative because of our ability to organize ourselves in increasingly more comprehensive groups, to rapidly establish social and political hierarchies, and to subvert the material interests of many or those of a few. Humans have a unique ability to extend response devices through technological means and through effective communications.

Thus, our over-use of an essential environmental resource, such as locally available protein, water, or topsoil may not result in some mitigating response such as the reduction of the local human population but rather intensification of efforts to acquire the resource from alternative sources (see Bennett, this volume). Similarly, the effect of a local catastrophe such as a drought or a flood may not be the reduction of the local human population such that sufficient resources will be available over the long run to provide for those remaining. Rather, an increase in human population may result from increased demand for workers to supply labor for the technical means of averting the ill effects of the environmental hazard. Indeed, it appears that a common human response to the oft-perceived problem of "population pressure" is to increase population to provide labor for intensified resource extraction (see Boserup 1965). This can be described "systemically" but does not entail self-regulation.

Closely related to the problem of assuming self-regulation and treating what is essentially an analytic unit as a distinctive entity in nature (see Moran, this volume), is the over-reliance on explanations using "latent function." Explanations which rely on reference to latent function often implicitly assume a particular goal state or condition toward which change is directed. Often particular patterns of human behavior are explained not in terms of their ostensible or demonstrable objectives and effects but in terms of how such behaviors may maintain an ecosystem in some given state. An often cited example of this form of explanation is Rappaport's interpretation of ritual among the Tsembaga as serving to regulate a wide range of environmental relations (1968). Very few ecologists have gone as far as have human ecologists in utilizing this form of explanation although it is found in the earlier literature on biomes and succession. Explanations based on "latent function" usually involve ascribing teleological attributes to the analytic unit.

A final shortcoming of the "ecosystemic" approach, we feel, is an over-emphasis on constraints to the neglect of innovation on the part of organisms in general, and humans in particular. While it is valuable to recognize constraints affecting interactive systems, this must be derived from observing their effects. Individual actors are not simply subject to constraints, but they deal with them.

Changing Perspectives in the 1970's

Even more than an awareness of the theoretical shortcomings of an ecosystem approach, research on economic development has influenced anthropologists' perception of what constitutes an environmental problem and how such problems should be studied. Economic development studies focus attention on issues that are not usually emphasized or even readily accommodated in ecosystemic research (Barlett 1980a). These include: 1) the critical roles of external factors, including political ones; 2) the historical background to contemporary environmental circumstances; 3) the changes taking place in local systems; 4) the diversity and differentiation within local groups or populations; and 5) the various options that people have in their efforts to adjust to change. These issues have come to the fore in human ecological research in part as a consequence of growing awareness of the immediacy and acuteness of problems faced by local populations which are caught up in the political and economic transformations underway throughout the world.

Major geopolitical events of the 1970's fostered an atmosphere in which ecological models developed a decade earlier, emphasizing stability in closed systems, were found wanting. One such event of catastrophic dimensions brought to the attention of ecologists the world over the interrelationships between climatic and social factors: the Sahelian drought of 1968-1973. In the context of various emergency measures to relieve widespread famine in the Sahel, scientists had the opportunity to document both types of factors and to observe and to participate in responses to the pressures of change. It became clear that progressive alteration in human patterns of exploitation had interfered with the capacity of the affected human populations to cope successfully with drought conditions. The survival of many people had come to depend on outside intervention.

These events triggered intense concern and interest in the processes of desertification elsewhere. It has been suggested that some 9.1 million square kilometers of desert are the direct result of human activity and that the process of desertification is accelerating; an additional 30 million square kilometers in over 100 countries are threatened with desertification today, particularly in Africa, Asia, and Latin America (Babayev and Gerasimov 1980:137). These studies have also induced scholars to look into historical precedents for contemporary desertification processes. Zhao Sonqqiao (1980) points out that the process of desertification in the Mo-Usu Sandy Land of Eastern Mongolia, for example, has accelerated during certain historical periods. Adams (1965, 1981) similarly reports on long-term processes of desertification in Mesopotamia which involved periods of land reclamation as well as times of accelerated rates of loss of arable land. Such studies indicate the necessity of incorporating large temporal scale into environmental analyses (see Wobst 1979 for general discussion of this problem; also Netting, Adams and Kasakoff, and Ellen, in this volume).

Desertification is not simply a smooth and gradual process but proceeds at different rates, depending on climatic factors and human activities. Southern Africa, for example, has experienced several periods of above- and below-normal rainfall since the turn of the century (Tyson 1980). Major demographic and cultural changes have occurred in this region during the same period, but we have yet to learn about their interrelationships. Carmel Schrire (1980) has suggested that our understanding of the identity and adaptive responses of the !Kung San population of this region would be considerably enhanced were we to take their history and changing environment into account. Rather than viewing the San as "pristine relics of the Paleolithic," she argues that they shift from hunting/gathering to sedentary herders/cultivators and back, depending on environmental conditions favoring one or another life style. In this context, we would do well to ask when and why the San population, described by Richard Lee (1979) and others, came to settle where they did. The nature of San interactions with their immediate environment would be understood differently, Schrire argues, if two points were taken into account: 1) they sometimes leave it and 2) their opportunity to leave or stay depends at least in part on the immediate environmental circumstances of other groups, today namely White farmers and Bantu herders.

An event comparable in some respects to the Sahelian drought was the "oil crisis" of 1973-74. Although the source of the oil crisis was political rather than "natural," it had far-reaching environmental repercussions. In very short order, these consequences became a matter of public concern for ordinary citizens throughout the modern, industrial world. Despite the fact that the production, distribution and utilization of oil was the subject of detailed study for some time, the actual effects of an oil shortage were largely unanticipated. This is partly because the "event" was without precedent, so there were no clear-cut patterns for people to follow in dealing with the effects of locally experienced fuel shortages. Scholars were led to examine carefully the historical background to the current situation and the ways that prior commitments of technology and social organization structured options for adjustment. Attention was rapidly drawn to such factors as the duration and intensity of the problem and, accordingly, to changes in strategies of response by groups differentially affected by problems related both to oil shortages and measures taken to relieve them.

Connected with the energy crisis was a global concern with food production and the chancy outcome of what is sometimes called the "Green Revolution." A fair number of studies have examined the nutritional, demographic and health related effects of agricultural development, yet at least one anthropologist (Miller 1977) has claimed that the Green Revolution *per se* has been surprisingly neglected by human ecologists. Be that as it may, the concern of policy makers and the public over food production has stimulated problem-oriented research involving subsistence as well as consumer agriculture (see Farmer 1977).

As a consequence of their involvement in these issues, human ecologists have come to view environmental change as common, often inevitable, and interesting for its own sake. The questions that current human ecological researchers are most concerned about today are connected with the impact of linkages between local and extralocal factors in human-environment interaction. The theory that predominates is characteristically drawn from one or another version of dependency theory which emphasizes the loss of local autonomy and its detrimental outcomes as a result of capitalist exploitation of rural resources (see Oxaal, Barnett and Booth 1975). The historical process generally observed is one of rural impoverishment and increasingly unequal access to resources (see, for example, Ehrlich 1974; Gross and Underwood 1971; Wisner and Mbithi 1974; and Wisner 1982).

Studies of human adaptive strategies have increasingly focused on decisions and choices made by individuals faced with new or changing circumstances (Barlett 1980b; Orlove 1980). Moreover, researchers no longer are positing that it is "the group," "population," or "culture" that is the basic adaptive unit (see Irons 1979; also Bates and Lees 1979). Many have abandoned the idea of cultural adaptation in favor of behavioral approaches to human adaptive responses in which group or population characteristics are simply viewed as the outcome of individual action (Vayda and McCay 1975, 1977; Orlove 1980). In fact, there has been a wholesale shift away from approaches in which the ecosystem is treated as a discrete level of integration and toward particularistic studies of response patterns of individual actors (Orlove 1980). This move is in keeping with the prevalent dissatisfaction in both biology and anthropology with the use of superorganic concepts.

Looking at Environmental "Events"

One important outcome of the new directions in ecological study has been an increased focus on human adaptability (cf. Moran 1982). In the context of time-specific development studies, researchers have come to document the diverse and sometimes unexpected or unpredictable innovations devised by individuals acting alone or in groups to cope with new or different situations (Moran 1981).

Environmental change is a vague and too inclusive a term for the purpose of defining a research strategy. We said at the outset of this paper that a major concern of human ecology today is to identify the problems to which people respond as part of the larger study of the evolutionary process of adaptation. Vayda and McCay (1975) urged human ecologists to focus on life-threatening hazards which are actually experienced, not just potentially faced, by the group under study. Such hazards might be, for example, recurrent frost-induced crop failure, drought, or a disease for which there is no local resistance. Vayda and McCay (1975) argue that much effort in ecosystemic research has been misdirected to the identification of non-problems--for instance, the question of protein availability in populations who are apparently well nourished. This has occurred to the neglect of problems which are regularly being experienced and which do require some adjustment in the behavior of people. There are, in this view, no universal problems, not even those as seemingly basic as energy constraints, but rather different populations are seen as experiencing different hazards or constraints which can be only empirically discovered. Protein scarcity may, for example, be a significant problem for a particular group while an adjacent population may well have adjusted successfully to comparable levels of availability of protein and thus not experience any stress in this regard.

We find the "hazards approach" a useful one which reflects what in practice, if not in name, many researchers are actually doing as they conduct field research. But this approach still leaves the question of how one in practice differentiates among the many problems or hazards a group may face or links actual behavior to one or another of these. How does one evaluate the relative adequacy of coping strategies? We suggest that a useful alternative to efforts to evaluate a generalized problem or hazard is to look instead at the impact of particular events. That is, rather than attempting to show how the Kalahari San are adapted to desert life with scarce water resources, one would try to look at what they did in a particular drought and why. Or, instead of discussing the ways that New Guinea highland agriculture conserves soil fertility, describe instead what the highlanders did during the frost of 1972 in the context of prior events which shaped the responses observed.

Regardless of the level at which responses are studied, an event-focused approach to ecological study has numerous methodological advantages: it offers a convenient "point of entry" for the description of complex and changing relationships without an overburden of difficult assumptions. It leads the investigator to place the data collected in a diachronic perspective. It allows one to establish the spatial scope or range of the study according to the behavioral responses observed and to change the scope of the study quite readily as research progresses. Vayda (n.d.) calls this strategy "progressive contextualization."

An event-focused approach has significance for the development of theory as well. Just as Vayda and McCay (1975) noted in their argument for the hazards approach, looking at specific events and their consequences can facilitate generalization about response hierarchies and the ordering of human behavior in terms of costs and risks. More important, in our view, is the value of an event-oriented approach in framing and testing hypotheses about environmental change and human behavior. Events provide the circumstances for testing hypotheses having to do with immediate or proximate causality and thus take one beyond noting simple correlation or association.

In the examples which follow we have provided illustrations of "event-focused" approaches applied to extreme types of events--catastrophes or disasters. It should be emphasized that these cases represent one end of a continuum and are used here because extreme forms serve to demonstrate most clearly what can also be applied to less obvious cases as well.

Raymond Firth pointed out in 1959 that it is curious how little attention has been paid by anthropologists to natural disasters such as hurricanes. He could cite only one exception to his own study, a brief article about hurricanes on Yap by David Schneider (1957). Firth's own interest in such events was the result of his field experience in the context of a modernization study. He had returned to the Pacific Island of Tikopia in 1952 to do a re-study of the people he had visited in 1929. A month or so before his arrival a devastating hurricane had struck, destroying houses, facilities, and gardens; subsequently, there was a drought. During his stay in 1952, he witnessed the ensuing famine and period of recovery. Firth took pains to describe the course of these events, in sequence, and to analyze factors which contributed to that particular chain of events.

Firth described a wide variety of responses to food shortage. Household strategies involved changing diet, reducing and then eliminating hospitality, reducing ceremonies, using unripe crops, increasing labor to restore agricultural production, collective planning, and theft. Fallow was shortened, planting and collecting rights were restricted, and land boundaries were more clearly demarcated. Kinship obligations were reduced to a narrower sphere and their content was altered. Labor was pooled but food was not. In Firth's view, the success of the Tikopia in coping with famine rested in large part on social mechanisms for control of manpower, specifically the organization and control of movement and activity by the Tikopia chiefs. It was the chiefs who directed facility repairs, reduced opportunities for theft, enforced labor in planting rather than fishing, and recruited laborers to be sent abroad for wage work. Thus, while life in Tikopia became more "privatized" in the context of famine, the hierarchical social structure was sustained.

Although one could describe the presence of the chief-dominated hierarchy as a mechanism for "maintaining" or "restoring" equilibrium, this would tell one very little about how it actually worked, when it would be activated in a crisis, and through what processes. Firth's analysis, focused as it is on diverse individual strategies, rewards, and constraints, makes it clear how the chiefs exercised control, what they gained, and why people submitted to chiefly control.

Firth was also concerned to discover whether, and to what extent, the circumstances he witnessed were "abnormal." He found that such hurricanes were not unknown but apparently occurred on the average of once every 20 years, or about once a generation, and were often accompanied by famine. However, Firth suggests that because the population had increased over time the consequences may have become progressively worse. It was clear that hurricanes and famines did not reduce the population to pre-disaster levels; there was no mechanism to establish a population level at any point with regard to the available resources in times of stress.

For Firth the study of the events connected with hazard and disaster had critical value for understanding the "strengths and weaknesses" of a social system in that one was able to see a test of the extent to which the system could "withstand the strain of competing demands upon [its] agents" (1959:51). Indeed, Firth might have gone further and asked to what extent are patterns of social behavior and environmental interaction actually shaped by previous and anticipated hazardous events.

Eric Waddell (1975) asked these questions in his model study of how the Enga cope with frosts. He began with a specific event, the frost of 1972, and discussed previous adjustments to frosts of varying intensity and frequency among Enga groups in different locations. Their adjustments entailed varying levels of behavioral organization--individual, local, and regional, depending on the intensity and duration of the problem. The effectiveness of their strategies depended on their ability to take recourse to appropriate measures. In the 1972 instance, external intervention to relieve the local populations interfered with "normal" processes; in Waddell's view, this intervention was misguided and inappropriate. He believed, for example, that the provision of government relief would undermine the motivation of kin to help one another in future crises.

Many of the societies studied by human ecologists are situated in environments described as "harsh." Others, not so described, such as Tikopia and the New Guinea Highlands, are also subject to particular environmental conditions which pose serious problems for the health or well being of populations. In fact, for most populations these arise with considerable frequency. While sometimes mentioned in the anthropological literature, stressful events are usually treated as abnormal or aberrant conditions. Yet they have considerable evolutionary significance, as students of animal behavior have long noted. In the study of the characteristics of the members of non-human populations, not only the occurrence, frequency, and intensity of environmental events but their order of occurrence is of critical importance (Winterhalder 1980).

Two brief examples may serve to illustrate this. C.S. Holling, in describing the collapse of the Lake Michigan trout population, noted that it was not simply heavy human predation which suddenly precipitated the population crash but rather the fact that a year of heavy harvesting followed hard upon the effects of another predator, the lamprey eel (1973). A second case concerns the arid interior of northeastern Brazil. In the 1960's numerous small farmers adopted a new crop, sisal, in response (among other things) to a series of droughts. In the absence of the series of droughts, Gross and Underwood suggest, small farmers would not have undertaken this risky and ultimately deleterious shift in cropping strategy (1971). In both examples mentioned, the sequence or ordering of events is important in understanding the consequences.

As we have noted, some geographers and anthropologists, like Firth and Waddell, have paid close attention to disasters and their behavioral consequences, most notably earthquakes. Kates et al., for example, studied human response to the Managua earthquake of 1972, describing how people used social networks to avert the worst consequences of that disaster and various measures taken at different levels for recovery (1973). Anthony Oliver-Smith (1977) described the responses of urban residents in the city of Yunguay, North Central Peru, to the earthquake disaster of 1970, pointing out the rationality of their reluctance to relocate. The negative consequences of disaster relief are the topic of a study by William Torry (1978). He suggests that disaster relief nurtures long-term risks through short-term remedies by weakening local support structures and increasing dependence on "remote, unpredictable, and poorly devised bureaucratic solutions to disaster management" (p. 302).

But significant environmental events are not necessarily catastrophic. Thomas Rudel (1980) provides an example using a politically-induced resource shortage, the U.S. gasoline crisis of 1973-74, which resulted in changing response patterns as the intensity and duration of the problem increased. The order and range of responses, from individual to community to more inclusive units, parallels those of the Fringe Enga of New Guinea in response to frost, as described by Waddell (1975).

The events under study need not be as brief or discrete as an earthquake. Thomas McGovern (1980) provides an example in his study of the impact of a climatic shift on the viability of a socially stratified Medieval Norse Greenland colony. The colony had been in existence for several centuries. During the fourteenth century, the "Little Ice Age" occurred, indirectly leading to shifts in the distribution of land and sea game. This resulted in differential hardships for elites and commoners. While the "Little Ice Age" was not dramatically colder, difficulties in trade relationships arose due to stormier sea passages and more sea ice which reduced the availability of trade items. Adjustments in subsistence practices were rejected by elites whose dominance would thereby be threatened. Furthermore, the Norse appeared reluctant, perhaps for cultural reasons, to interact with Eskimo groups or adopt their hunting practices. Eventually the colony failed and vanished, leaving only archaeological traces behind.

The extinction of the Norse colony could be described in ecosystemic terms by detailing the constriction of vital food energy flows available to the human population as a result of failure of various regulatory mechanisms as embodied, for example, in elite status-marking activities. What McGovern's analysis offers, and which is not inherent in the ecosystemic approach, is a detailed statement about the sequence of events to which people had to respond and how their responses were shaped by previous experiences with similar problems. In this context, he pays close attention to the linkages joining the colony with other non-local economic systems.

A number of human ecologists have attempted to formulate generalizations with respect to human adaptations to hazards and other environmental events, drawn largely from theories formulated by L. Slobodkin, A. Rappaport, C.S. Holling, and G. Bateson (see McCay 1978; and Winterhalder 1980). These deal primarily with the "economics of flexibility," namely the adaptive advantages to an organism of having a structured sequence of responses available. Minimally costly responses are tried first so as not to overcommit the organism before it is necessary to do so. The direct application of this perspective to a study of the hazards of development is well illustrated by George Morren's study of the British drought of 1975-76. Morren (1980) shows how the operation of lower-order response mechanisms was gradually superceded through time as response to earlier hazards made permanent a condition that would otherwise have had limited duration. Population growth, urbanization, and industrialization resulted in increasing water shortage in Great Britain; in response to drought, control over water sources was increasingly centralized. By 1975-76, rural water users had few recourses to individual or local means of adjustment to water shortage and were forced to submit to the effects of shortages felt elsewhere from which they had previously been buffered.

Our final illustration is from a human ecological study specifically intended to inform and guide policy-makers in future development planning. Vayda et al. (1980) describe their study of the interactions between people and forests in East Kalimantan (Indonesia) with reference to rapid economic growth of the forestry sector after 1967. Their focus is on continuing human "responsiveness to changing conditions" and human "capability for situational adjustment." As such, their study emphasizes the kinds of continuous alterations that occur as different individuals and population sectors meet changing demands, constraints, and opportunities in their exploitation of forest resources. Among their various adjustments are: changing norms of labor exchange, population movements, and a variety of procedures to circumvent forestry laws and regulations. The scope of the study encompasses threads of influence beyond the spatial confines of East Kalimantan and a time dimension that traces historical precedents and causes of migration into the area.

In each of the case studies we have mentioned, research organized about the description and analysis of human responses to critical environmental events has led to a better understanding of how features of social and economic organization bear on environmental relations. Each study was able to describe the systems in question in terms of process and change, and to show the repercussions of human behavior for the immediate (sometimes longer-term) future of the local human populations under investigation. For these reasons, we believe that the approach they exemplify has considerably more descriptive and explanatory power than steady-state or equilibrium assumptions inherent in ecosystemic approaches.

Environmental Events, Ecology and Evolution

An important theoretical use of ecology is to shed light on evolutionary processes. One way to study these is to analyze behavioral and other responses to events. While this kind of study begins with the documentation of historical episodes, the ultimate goal is to discover the ways in which organisms respond to changes in the material conditions which affect their lives and the consequences of the responses themselves. This is not the only kind of approach to evolutionary process. Even studies of ecological succession can serve to document evolutionary change patterns. But given the cumulative and diverse character of human response devices, close attention to specific historical events is particularly enlightening.

Basic to evolutionary theory is the observation that members of populations are not uniform in their behavior but rather diverse in their means of coping with environmental exigencies. Thus, a specific environmental event, a change in material circumstances (such as a change in rainfall pattern or the opening of a new migration route), will elicit different responses from and have different repercussions for individual members of the affected group. In many respects it is best to regard even a major change in environmental circumstances from a neutral perspective as each event can be construed as a "problem" or an "opportunity," depending on who are involved and what happens to them. This is, perhaps, preferable to looking explicitly for hazards or problems, for to do so involves the assumption of group or population level threats and tends to obscure the diversity of actual costs and benefits incurred by affected individuals.

Viewed neutrally, changes in material circumstances or events provide a context for the observation of the different sorts of measures taken by members of a local group to meet new or different circumstances and of how well or poorly they deal with ensuing predicaments. Significant material changes often, if not invariably, result in some members of the group becoming materially more stressed, others less so. The researcher can study why and how this has happened and identify the most and least vulnerable members of the group with respect to a particular event. In short, the event-focused investigation can indicate who coped successfully and who failed to do so and why.

Evolutionary theory calls for some explicit measure of success or adequacy in coping. The Darwinian measure of reproductive fitness, while basic to evolutionary theory and indeed to theory in ecology, has limited immediate utility for most ecological anthropologists whose interests lie in relatively short-term behavioral change (see Chagnon and Irons 1979). More general (and readily verifiable) indicators such as nutritional adequacy, health, and material well being are ways to measure successful responses or coping strategies (see Moran 1982). They are directly or indirectly related to measures of Darwinian fitness in most instances, and they are easier to observe in the short run.

Responses to material changes occur at various levels of organization. While most of the studies we have mentioned in this paper discuss diversity of response at the individual level, they are more concerned with describing the mobilization of group-level responses. Concern with diversity at the individual-actor level is more evident in economic anthropology of the "formalist" variety and in some of the "natural hazards" literature of geography (see White 1974). While studies in the early 1970's tended to emphasize formal models of decision-making procedure sometimes without considering the ethnographic context and the limitations of choice (see Johnson 1980), increasing numbers of researchers have begun to empirically document variation in decision-making within populations. For example, researchers have examined differential adoption of "green revolution" technology (Farmer 1977) and cash-cropping (Chibnik 1980) in terms of the immediate costs and benefits of available choices. The implications of individual decisions and strategies for the study of ecological change are obvious. Looking at the environmental repercussions of behavioral continuity or change will tell us what happened but not why. Ecological analysis which takes into account people's perception of their varying interests allows for explanation of why they continue to act in a certain way or shift their behavior--though explanatory theories continue to be diverse.

Mobilized response at local group and more inclusive levels is the focus of a good deal of explanatory and descriptive generalization. Some of this work tries to look at the implications of higher-level response for flexibility and autonomy of response at lower levels (Morren 1980; Flannery 1972; Lees 1974a). Often, analysts seem to conclude that loss of local-level autonomy (re. increasing dependence) is detrimental to local-level groups in that they lose what control they once had over access to local resources and the means to use them for their own benefit. However, evidence that loss of local autonomy is detrimental to groups in terms of material well being remains inconclusive. Studies of the nutritional consequences of local involvement in market economies suggest that rural groups often suffer worse nutrition once they become dependent on a larger economic system (Fleuret and Fleuret 1980; Nietschman 1972), but demographic studies, particularly of infant mortality, seem to suggest that health care and conditions are often improved.

Development Research and Ecological Anthropology

We began this paper with a suggestion that certain changes in ecological anthropology were influenced by development research--research on economic "modernization" and change. In particular, we pointed out the influence on ecological research of a growing awareness of the inadequacy of ecosystemic models for dealing with the circumstances of certain major "environmental events" of the 1970's such as the Sahelian drought, which were the product of cumulative social, technological, and climatic change. These events brought home to many ecological anthropologists the importance of history, of viewing environmental problems in the context of very large-scale economic systems, and for considering the sources of disequilibrium and human material vulnerability in the study of even remote and small-scale societies. We suggest that the result of this awareness was a new focus on the problems or hazards people face in interacting with their environments, and that studying specific environmental events in their local settings was a useful way of organizing research on such problems.

We would like to look now at some aspects of "applied research" on development issues and the ways that they focus interest on specific types of "environmental events" and problems. Development agencies, such as the United States Agency for International Development (A.I.D.) and the World Bank, sponsor a considerable amount of research on human-environment interaction, and their policies shape both the character of this research and its practical application. The changes that affected the outlook of ecological anthropologists during the 1970's affected the various development agencies as well, albeit through different paths and in different ways. Worldwide criticism of the roles of "modernization" agents in increasing the hunger and material suffering of the Third World poor was one factor; pressure from some countries controlling essential raw materials, such as oil, was another. Many development agencies have responded to criticisms of the negative (or negligible) outcomes of their intervention in the development process by attempting to gear at least some of their efforts toward relieving the problems of the poor and needy rural masses of the less developed countries.

Since the mid-1970's, for example, A.I.D.'s policy has adjusted to a U.S. Congressional mandate which specifies by law that assistance to the poor shall take priority, and that emphasis shall be placed on helping the poor to help themselves by expanding access to the national economy by various means. The law specifies that A.I.D. agricultural research shall place a priority on the determination of the special needs of small (poor) farmers (Hoben 1980). In addition to a moral concern for the poor, there has also been a practical concern among all the development agencies for accountability. That is, agencies and their sponsors are requiring some sort of demonstration that their programs are having the desired effect of "development." For this reason, A.I.D., the World Bank, and others have launched major evaluation efforts to see what, if any, effects past programs have had and some effort to see how these evaluations can be put to use to improve future program design and implementation. Studies sponsored by international agencies of "environmental impact" as well as "social impact" are becoming increasingly common, as they have been with federally-funded and some state-funded projects within the U.S., thanks to the National Environmental Policy Act. While we might take issue with the actual implementation of such studies, the fact that many ecological researchers have become involved in them and that their existence is known to many others cannot but have influenced the course of ecological research in recent years.

In a very general sense, the "problem" an ecological anthropologist might be engaged by an agency to study is defined by the agency itself: a local population is identified as an appropriate target for "assistance" with respect to an area of intervention, such as transportation, water, or public health. But this "problem" needs to be clarified: in what respects are the target population doing well, and in what senses are they doing poorly, and how might they be helped to do better? Who needs this kind of help? In the context of the kind of study of hazards and how people cope with them as advocated by Vayda and McCay (1975, 1977), these sorts of questions might be addressed as a matter of course.

However, much anthropological research sponsored by development agencies is instigated after some problem in an assistance program has already occurred; the investigator is called upon to evaluate and often to determine what has "gone wrong." The literature of applied anthropology is replete with such cases. One classical example suffices to illustrate: a small Peruvian town's water supply was polluted by upstream wastes. A health-care worker was assigned the job of convincing the women of the town to boil their families' drinking water. After two years of her concerted effort, only 11 of the 200 households regularly boiled their drinking water. Why? Among the various impediments discovered by the anthropologist-investigator Edward Wellin was the difficulty of obtaining sufficient fuel. It was all the women could do, among their other chores, to gather enough fuel to cook meals for the day; the extra fuel for boiling water was too costly in effort (or cash), hence beyond their means. Was fuel shortage their "problem"? Not really. But the limited availability of fuel emerged as a "limitation" specifically in the context of a real problem, water pollution, and an effort to solve it by convincing women to boil their water (Wellin 1955).

The cases of "environmental events" we described above are mostly instances of disasters or hazards or clear-cut negative pressures on human populations. Development research adds another dimension to the study of environmental events: events generated by the human (social, economic, or political) environment which have environmental components and/or repercussions. Such events might include a change in the market price of a cash crop, or a land-reform law which alters land tenure, or relatively large-scale migration into or out of a locality or establishment of a quota on certain types of livestock (for a case involving imposition of restrictions on fishing, see McCay 1981), or a campaign to get women to boil water to improve health. As in events like droughts and hurricanes, explaining what people do in a response and why requires looking into past events, differentiation among the local population, and interactions between people and other environmental factors. Such events elicit changing response processes through time and sometimes call for shifts from individual to local or more inclusive responses (as in the "gasoline crisis" described by Rudel 1980). As in the case of "natural hazards," it is in the context of such events that real problems, limitations, and often strengths of local systems emerge.

An understanding of the tested strengths of a local system, it has been argued, is particularly important but largely neglected by development agencies (Wisner and Mbithi 1974; Waddell 1975; Lees 1980). Local groups which have experienced environmental hazards before sometimes develop regular and effective means of coping with them. The effect of external intervention by development and relief agencies is often interference with the utilization of these means and reduction of their effectiveness in the present and future. A major contribution that ecological anthropologists have to make to practical development research is to explain how local groups do cope with hazards and to help development planners either to enhance these coping devices or at least avoid interfering with them where possible (Wisner and Mbithi 1974; Waddell 1975; Lees 1980). One might assume, for example, based on Firth's analysis, that interference with the chief's power to control labor on Tikopia would reduce the effectiveness of that island's means of coping with such environmental hazards as hurricanes and drought. External assistance agencies would (hypothetically) be advised to avoid such interference and to provide support by way of helping chiefs to do their job.

We have pointed out that an important aspect of development research has been recognition and documentation of human adaptability. Development project evaluations repeatedly report that beneficiaries and other participants in such projects frequently do not behave as the planner, sponsors, and administrators expected. At times, the adaptiveness of this unexpected behavior by individuals affected by development activities is obscured, neglected, or misunderstood, but it surely deserves further study.

For example, Tony Barnett's study of the Gezira Scheme (1977), a very large irrigation project in Sudan, documents a variety of ways in which local irrigators both dealt with legal constraints of the Scheme and tried to achieve ends of their own which were not defined or recognized by the Scheme. All Scheme tenants were required to raise the cash-crop, cotton, on some land and to plant sorghum and other subsistence crops in rotation with cotton, all of which are irrigated by the Scheme. Tenants sold their cotton to the Scheme and shared the profits, but their subsistence crops were theirs alone. Because of this and because they found it more difficult to use cotton as a source of credit, tenants contrived with local field inspectors to divert irrigation water from cotton to sorghum whenever water was scarce. Both the reasons for this activity and the means by which it was carried out were embedded in a more complex adaptive system which applied directly to the problem of obtaining labor to work individual holdings. And both the labor problem and its resolution were specific to the way in which the Scheme was operated, that is, its constraints and opportunities. It seems clear that similar kinds of processes of adjustment occur in virtually every development project.

Conclusions: An Event-Focused Approach to Human Environmental Interactions

Many ecological anthropologists became disillusioned with the notion of ecosystem during the 1970's for a variety of different reasons. Other papers in this volume deal with problems of boundary definition, scale, and time depth, which limit the utility of ecosystemic modeling for describing human-environment interaction. Here we have been concerned with the problem of cumulative change, often described as "development" and the "development of underdevelopment." With Vayda, McCay and others, we have suggested that for those of us interested in the study of human adaptation our focus must be on human response to environmental "problems." We have argued that a useful way of organizing research on human response is to focus inquiry on specific environmental events. Studies of such responses suggest that their effects are often, if not invariably, cumulative.

An article by Margoh Maruyama (1963) brought to the attention of ecological anthropologists the notion of "deviation amplification" as a complementary systemic state to that of equilibrium. Some scholars who sought to apply this notion to human ecological systems have seen deviation amplification as a form of systemic pathology (Rappaport 1969; Flannery 1972) while equilibrium was seen as a form of health. However, "deviation amplification," another term for cumulative change, seems to be so regular and common a state of affairs for humans that the systems-based term "pathological" appears to us inappropriate. To paraphrase Vayda and McCay (1975, 1977), people (and other organisms) are sometimes obliged to abandon the "system" for the sake of their own survival and well being. While systemic terms used by Rappaport and Flannery such as "linearization" (the by-passing of lower order controls by higher-order controls) may be useful for conceptualizing a process of cumulative systemic change, they do not focus attention on the relative utility of the new arrangements for people coping with problems at hand.

McCay (1978) has argued for the replacement of "systems ecology" by "people ecology" in order to accomplish just this purpose. Many of the terms widely in use among ecological anthropologists such as "perturbation" assume the normative operation of a system which, in reality, may simply not occur because of continuous change. Looking at "events" rather than "perturbations" is a somewhat more neutral stance and retains a focus on situations occasioning material change.

If the people we study exist in a continuously changing context or even if they are relatively isolated and apparently stable, how do we select significant "events" about which to organize research? As in any type of research, this depends on our particular interests and, of course, opportunities. As ecological anthropologists, we are obviously interested in events which have environmental components and/or repercussions involving some sort of change in material circumstances. Most of us are also interested in particular forms of resource extraction or production such as fishing, hunting, irrigated agriculture, forestry, or livestock production; the "events" which interest us will most likely have some material bearing on these activities. Furthermore, we tend to do our research in specific localities whose environments are typified in part by characteristic "events" such as drought, floods, hurricanes, and frosts, of varying severity and duration. But the events in question need not be catastrophes nor need their genesis be, strictly speaking, "environmental." The events studied by Bernard Nietschman (1972) among the Miskito turtle hunters were generated by the appearance of an external market for turtle meat in the form of a new processing factory which increased the intensity of exploitation soon leading to the decreased availability of turtles.

By evaluating the impact of events and people's varying responses to them, we begin to relate our scientific interest to the needs of those whom we study and, perhaps not incidentally, of those who often sponsor our research. The practical utility of ecological research, while not the only consideration, is a matter that cannot be ignored. Indeed, some of the scientific benefits of these externally felt needs have already been demonstrated. Human ecological research has been brought into closer communication with other lines of anthropological inquiry, particularly areas related to history, political organization, and economics (Orlove 1980). The result has been, we believe, greater refinement and specificity in development theory and research and a better understanding of human adaptation and ecological change.

References Cited

Adams, Robert McC.

1965 Land Behind Baghdad: History of Settlement on the Diyala Plains. Chicago: University of Chicago Press.

1981 Heartland of Cities: Surveys of Ancient Settlement and Land Use on the Central Flood

Plains of the Euphrates. Chicago: University of Chicago Press.

Babayev, A.G. and I.P. Gerasimov
1980 The International UNEP-USSR Project on Combatting Desertification through Integrated Development. In The Threatened Drylands. J.A. Mabbutt and S.M. Berkowicz, eds. New South Wales: University of New South Wales.

Barlett, P.
1980a Adaptive Strategies in Peasant Agricultural Production. Annual Review of Anthropology 9:545-73.

Barlett, P. (ed.)
1980b Agricultural Decision-Making: Anthropological Contributions to Rural Development. New York: Academic Press.

Barnett, Tony
1977 The Gezira Scheme: An Illusion of Development. London: Frank Cass & Co.

Bates, D.G. and S.H. Lees
1979 The Myth of Population Regulation. In Humans in Evolutionary Perspective. N. Chagnon and W. Irons, eds. North Scituate, Massachusetts: Duxbury.

Bedoian, William H.
1978 Human Use of the Pre-Saharan Ecosystem and Its Impact on Desertification. In Social and Technological Management in Dry Lands. Nancie L. Gonzalez, ed. AAAS Selected Symposium 10. Boulder, Colo.: Westview Press.

Boserup, E.
1965 The Conditions of Agricultural Growth. Chicago: Aldine.

Chagnon, N.A. and W. Irons (eds.)
1979 Evolutionary Biology and Human Social Behavior: An Anthropological Perspective. North Scituate, Massachusetts: Duxbury.

Chibnik, M.
1980 The Statistical Behavior Approach: The Choice Between Wage Labor and Cash Cropping in Rural Belize. In Agricultural Decision-Making:

Anthropological Contributions to Rural Development. P. Barlett, ed. New York: Academic Press. Pp. 87-114.

Colinvaux, P.
1973 Introduction to Ecology. New York: John Wiley & Sons.

Ehrlich, A.S.
1974 Ecological Perception and Economic Adaptation in Jamaica. Human Organization 33(2):155-161.

Farmer, B.H. (ed.)
1977 Green Revolution?: Technology and Change in Rice-Growing Areas of Tamil Nadu and Sri Lanka. Boulder, Colo.: Westview Press.

Flannery, K.V.
1972 The Cultural Evolution of Civilizations. Annual Review of Ecology and Systematics 3:399-426.

Fleuret, P. and A. Fleuret
1980 Nutritional Implications of Staple Food Crop Successions in Usambara, Tanzania. Human Ecology 8:311-327.

Firth, Raymond
1959 Social Change in Tikopia. London: George Allen & Irwin Ltd.

Gross, Daniel and B. Underwood
1971 Technological Change and Caloric Costs: Sisal Agriculture in Northeastern Brazil. American Anthropologist 73(3):725-740.

Hoben, Allen
1980 Agricultural Decision-Making in Foreign Assistance: An Anthropological Analysis. In Agricultural Decision-Making: Anthropological Contributions to Rural Development. P. Barlett, ed. New York: Academic Press. Pp. 337-369.

Holling, C.S.
1973 Resilience and Stability of Ecological Systems. Annual Review of Ecology and Systemics 4:1-23.

Irons, William
1979 Natural Selection, Adaptation, and Human Social Behavior. In N. Chagnon and W. Irons, eds.

Evolutionary Biology and Human Social Behavior. N. Scituate, Mass.: Duxbury Press.

Johnson, A.
1980 The Limits of Formalism in Agricultural Decision Research. In Agricultural Decision-Making: Anthropological Contributions to Rural Development. P. Barlett, ed. New York: Academic Press. Pp. 19-44.

Kates, Robert W., J. Eugene Haas, Daniel J. Amaral, Robert A. Olson, Reyes Ramos, and Richard Olson
1973 Human Impact of the Managua Earthquake. Science 182:981-990.

Lee, Richard
1979 The !Kung San: Men, Women, and Work in a Foraging Society. New York: Cambridge University Press.

Lees, S.H.
1974a Hydraulic Development as a Process of Response. Human Ecology 2:159-75.
1974b The State's Use of Irrigation in Changing Peasant Society. In Irrigation's Impact on Society. T. Downing and M. Gibson, eds. Tucson: University of Arizona Press.
1980 The "Hazards" Approach to Development Research: Recommendations for Latin American Drylands. Human Organization 69:372-376.

Maruyama, M.
1963 The Second Cybernetics: Deviation-Amplifying Mutual Causal Processes. American Scientist 1:164-79.

McCay, Bonnie
1978 Systems Ecology, People Ecology, and the Anthropology of Fishing Communities. Human Ecology 6:397-422.
1981 Optimal Foragers or Political Actors? Ecological Analyses of a New Jersey Fishery. American Ethnologist 8:356-382.

McGovern, Thomas
1980 Cows, Harp Seals, and Churchbells: Adaptation and Extinction in Norse Greenland. Human Ecology 8:247-75.

Miller, F.C.
1977 Knowledge and Power: Anthropology, Policy Research, and the Green Revolution. American Ethnologist 4:190-198.

Moran, Emilio
1981 Developing the Amazon. Bloomington: Indiana University Press.
1982 Human Adaptability. Boulder, Colo.: Westview Press. Originally published in 1979 by Duxbury Press.

Morren, George
1980 The Rural Ecology of the British Drought 1975-1976. Human Ecology 8:33-63.

Nietschman, B.
1972 Hunting and Fishing Focus Among the Miskito Indians, Eastern Nicaragua. Human Ecology 1:41-67.

Odum, E.P.
1971 Fundamentals of Ecology. Third Edition. Philadelphia: Saunders.

Orlove, Benjamin
1980 Ecological Anthropology. Annual Review of Anthropology 9:235-73.

Oxaal, I., A.S. Barnett, and D. Booth (eds.)
1975 Beyond the Sociology of Development. London: Routledge & Kegan Paul.

Oliver-Smith, Anthony
1977 Traditional Agriculture, Central Places, and Post-disaster Urban Relocation in Peru. American Ethnologist 4:102-116.

Rappaport, R.A.
1968 Pigs for the Ancestors: Ritual in the Ecology of a New Guinea People. New Haven: Yale University Press.
1969 Sanctity and Adaptation in the Moral and Esthetic Structure of Human Adaptation. New York: Wenner-Gren Foundation.

Rudel, Thomas K.
1980 Social Responses to Commodity Shortages: The 1973-1974 Gasoline Crisis. Human Ecology 8:193-212.

Schneider, D.
1957 Typhoons on Yap. Human Organization 16:10-15.

Schrire, Carmel
1980 An Inquiry into the Evolutionary Status and Apparent Identity of the San Hunters-Gatherers. Human Ecology 8:1-32.

Torry, William
1978 Bureaucracy, Community, and National Disasters. Human Organization 37:302-8.

Tyson, P.D.
1980 Climate and Desertification in Southern Africa. In The Threatened Drylands. J.A. Mabbut and S.M. Berkowicz, eds. New South Wales: University of New South Wales.

Vayda, A.P. and R.A. Rappaport
1968 Ecology, Cultural and Non-Cultural. In Introduction to Cultural Anthropology. J.A. Clifton, ed. Boston: Houghton Mifflin.

Vayda, A.P. and McCay, B.
1975 New Directions in Ecology and Ecological Anthropology. Annual Review of Anthropology 4:293-306.
1977 Problems in the Identification of Environmental Problems. In Subsistence and Survival: Rural Ecology in the Pacific. T.P. Bayliss-Smith and R.G.A. Feachem, eds. New York/London: Academic.

Vayda, A.P., C. Colfer, J. Pierce, and M. Brotokusumo
1980 Interactions Between People and Forest in East Kalimantan. In Impact of Science on Society, Vol. 30, #3, UNESCO:179-190.

Waddell, Eric
1975 How the Enga Cope with Frost: Responses to Climatic Perturbations in the Central Highlands of New Guinea. Human Ecology 3:249-273.

Wellin, Edward
1955 Water Boiling in a Peruvian Town. In Health, Culture and Community. Benjamin D. Paul, ed. New York: The Russell Sage Foundation.

White, G.F. (ed.)
1974 Natural Hazards: Local, National and Global. New York: Oxford University Press.

Winterhalder, Bruce
1980 Environmental Analysis in Human Evolution and Adaptation Research. Human Ecology 8:135-170.

Wisner, B.
1982 MWEA Irrigation Scheme, Kenya: A Success Story for Whom? Boston: ARC Newsletter.

Wisner, B. and P.M. Mbithi
1974 Drought in Eastern Kenya: Nutritional Status and Farmer Activity. In Natural Hazards: Local, National and Global. G.F. White, ed. New York: Oxford. Pp. 87-97.

Wobst, Martin H.
1979 The Archaeo-ethnology of Hunter-Gatherers or The Tyranny of the Ethnographic Record in Archaeology. American Antiquity 43(2):303-309.

Zhao, Sonqqiao
1980 Desertification and "de-desertification" in China. In The Threatened Drylands. J.A. Mabbutt and S.M. Bekowicz, eds. Pp. 80-88.

Part 2

New Directions in Resolving the Problem of Time and of Boundary Definition in Ecosystems

Roy F. Ellen

7. Trade, Environment, and the Reproduction of Local Systems in the Moluccas

Introduction[1]

Theoretical objections to the ecosystem concept as applied to our understanding of social relations in human populations fall into two broad categories. The first stems from the very special character of the coded information which circulates in addition to matter, energy and other forms of non-cultural messages. The second arises from a fundamental ambiguity in the intentions of those biologists who originally developed and employed the concept. For, on the one hand, the notion of an ecosystem has permitted an emphasis on the relationship between variables otherwise considered separately, while on the other it has allowed the separation of a discrete universe for the purposes of analysis.

---

[1]I am grateful to the British Institute in Southeast Asia and the University of Kent at Canterbury who made possible the presentation of this paper at the January 1982 meeting of the American Association for the Advancement of Science in Washington, D.C. The empirical data referred to is derived largely from the pilot phase of a long-term project on 'Change and the social organisation of regional trading networks in the Moluccas, eastern Indonesia,' financed by the British Academy and the University of Kent at Canterbury under the auspices of Lembaga Ilmu Pengetahuan Indonesia (the Indonesian Academy of Sciences). I would like to thank Emilio Moran, C.W. Watson, and Nikki Goward for their comments on an earlier draft of this paper. Jane Shepherd has drawn the maps.

For a more extended discussion of the matters discussed in this and the following section see Ellen 1982, particularly chapters 4 and 8.

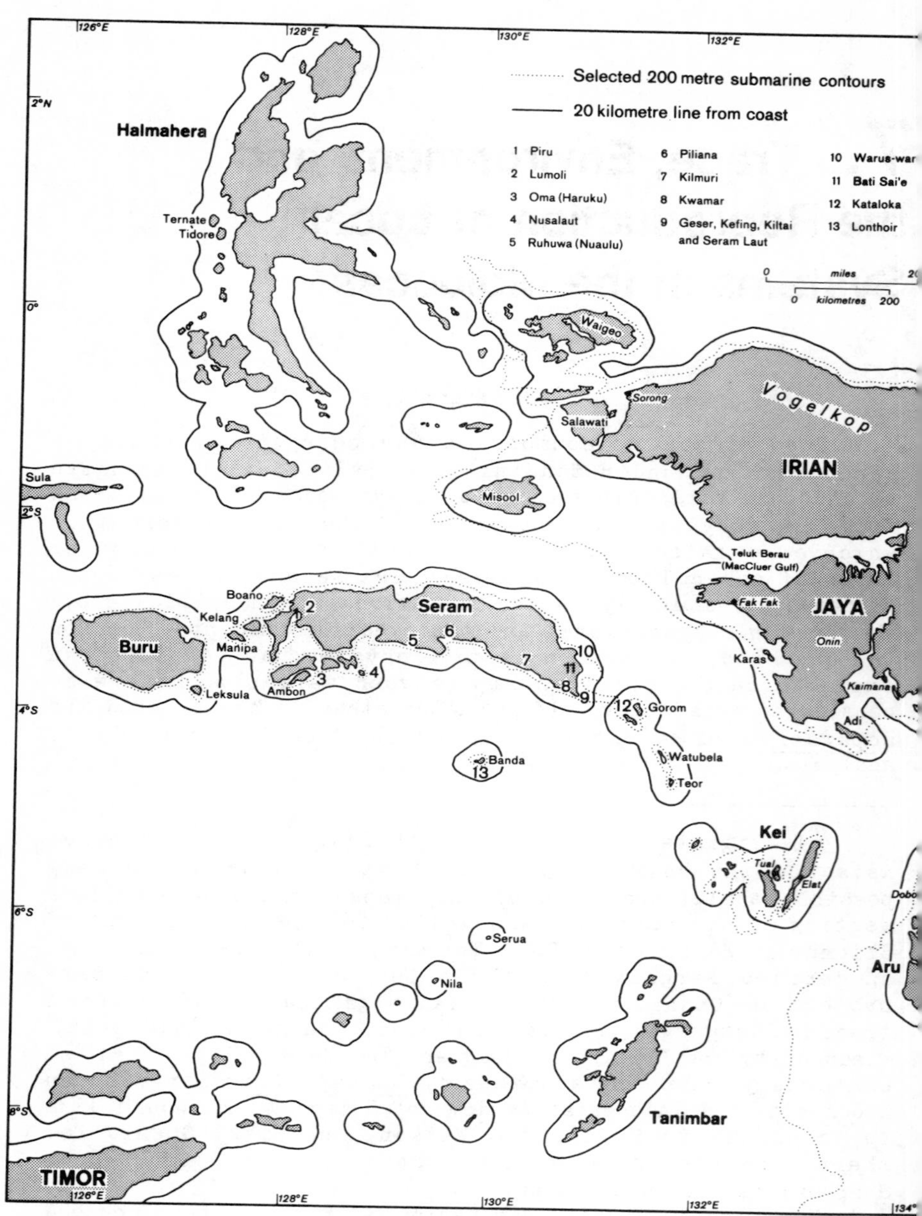

Figure 7.1 Some topographic aspects of the Moluccan region of eastern Indonesia, indicating localities mentioned in the text.

Yet while these objections are valid, and criticisms of the particular use of the ecosystem concept and its dangerous excesses often trenchant, it is difficult to deny the advantages which it has brought to scholarship. Some of these are worth repeating here. In empirical terms the new techniques and data associated with it have enabled us to correct mistaken notions about often unfamiliar subsistence regimes. In theoretical terms it has stressed the necessity for holism while focussing on specific relationships between human populations and features of their environment, and directed attention toward the existence of ramifications of particular relationships. It has shifted the emphasis away from the vulgar correlations of environmentalism, possibilism and cultural ecology toward more specific and integrated studies, and avoided simple-minded determinism by its stress not only on reciprocal causation, but also on complex networks of mutual causality. It has focused on the organisation and properties of systems, on the degrees and forms of stability which they may attain, and on the mechanisms which regulate their functioning and determine their evolution. By focussing on populations rather than on groups defined ethnically or socially it has provided a much more satisfactory basis for establishing conditions of analytical closure and for the exploration of the validity of the concept of adaptation.[2] More generally, it has provided a framework for description and analysis which accords due recognition to the complex and varied interactions of environmental and cultural variables. In so doing it has also paved the way for the introduction and development of further systems concepts, such as the idea of trophic exchanges, and has revived an interest (through parallelism) with Marxist dialectical theories of systems. While it has not escaped entirely from the constraints of disciplinary chauvinism, it has at least moderated them.

In this paper I restrict myself to the problem posed by the necessity for system closure, a matter which is not solely of interest to those concerned with ecological issues. I wish to examine the ways in which boundaries can be delineated (in both empirical and theoretical terms) for a series of populations interacting at different levels of intensity. These populations are situated in the south and central Moluccan islands of eastern Indonesia (Fig. 7.1). By showing how boundaries may be established so that such

---

[2] A notion of closure can only be effectively applied to discrete objects in a delineable field. Collectivities defined by cultural representations and particular social relationships do not easily meet this condition, even less so their reifications as 'cultures' and 'societies.'

populations can be seen as parts of systems on different scales of inclusiveness, I want to argue for the development of concepts of graded boundaries and a notion of system (and ecosystem) defined less in terms of absolute and discrete boundaries than in terms of centres, peripheries and structural focus. What I have to say is highly compressed, provisional and short on supporting data. As with an earlier piece (Ellen 1979), it is basically a theoretical exercise undertaken in connection with some long-term research on inter-island trade which has yet to be completed.

On Delineating Boundaries

It is becoming ever more difficult to argue that even the most isolated human population and its immediate environment can be treated as an unproblematic self-reproducing closed system (Bennett 1976:256; Friedman 1976; Langton 1973:133-135). Such systems are too empirically complicated to specify in terms of patterns and numbers of connections or intensity of flow. Moreover, it is rare for material exchanges suddenly to discontinue at a border, while systems are generally identified through subjective judgments as to what processes are critical to their functioning. Thus, it is usually necessary to demarcate or adjust boundaries according to research interests, models employed, and the patterns in emerging data.

However, it is empirically evident that some human systems do maintain a degree of integrity and are relatively well defined, while it is both practically and intuitively a relatively simple matter to isolate 'systems' which make sense of the data and which may be used in the investigation of a wide range of different problems. Those who most vociferously argue that we recognize the openness of human systems must at the same time employ some notion of closure themselves when determining what universe of variables to examine. If the search for "systemness" is to remain an important issue in the analysis of human social relations (and it is difficult to see how this could ever be otherwise), then it is better that this be done explicitly. The arbitrary and analytic character of most boundaries, together with the reality of exogenous intrusions of varying types, magnitudes and origins, should not compel us to accept a sloppy notion of receding causation, whereby the critical determinants always seem to lie outside the local system subjected to detailed analysis (cf. Mason and Langenheim 1957; Newcomer 1972:5). Neither should we infer the character and consequences of external influences entirely from specific local effects. That a small glass bead is recovered archaeologically in highland Papua New Guinea may well serve to represent the absolute frontier of the Portuguese mercantilist world system of the sixteenth century, but the systemic consequences of its appearance, compared with those of all other inflows of material, energy and information, were probably negligible. It may nevertheless be evidence for a kind of kick-on effect, of changes which have reverberated through a series of overlapping local systems geographically connecting the site in the New Guinea highlands with some putative point of origin in Portuguese adventurist activity in the Moluccas. Whatever the local consequences of this may have been in terms of Moluccan social formations, for highland New Guinea these will have been transformed into shifts in exchange and political relations, of which the occurrence of the bead is quite independent. The problem, therefore, is to recognize those empirical conditions necessary for assuming a particular degree of closure in the analysis of any one system, and to specify the magnitude and character of exogenous links in terms of their consequences for the effective reproduction of local social formations.

In order to do this it is useful to underline three axiomatic characteristics of human ecological systems. Few would now deny these, but in the past they have often been understressed or ignored in those studies to which the label 'ecological functionalism' is sometimes applied. The first is that subsistence areas associated with particular local human populations (and therefore ecological systems) generally overlap. Even among relatively self-sufficient groups where food production is technologically simple and where conditions for observing the functioning of the most isolated systems are best met, spatial distribution is preferably represented as a wide network of demes (Weiner 1964:401-2), where different groups and individuals are engaged in the mutual transfer of resources (personnel, genes, energy, materials and value). The subsistence and reproductive bases of such populations (whether designated ecologically or sociologically) are therefore not independent, and their boundaries might better be conceptualized as clines (Rappaport 1968:226).

It is unnecessary to labor this point by repeated ethnographic illustration, but the Nuaulu villages of the south coast of central Seram well exemplify the often complicated geographical relationships between the resource areas of nearby settlements in the Moluccas. These villages are part of a web of settlements of varying size, market integration and ethnolinguistic origin, which have for almost 100 years been in close political association as a result of events and population movements which took place between 1880 and about 1920. The land around Nuaulu villages constitutes a mosaic of cultivated plots: those owned and worked by the villagers themselves, those owned by Nuaulu from other villages, and those owned by Muslim and Christian outsiders (Ellen 1978:82). However, the resource base of the Nuaulu village is by no means limited to the area cultivated. That of the village of Ruhuwa amounts to some 214.75km^2 of forest and swampland at varying altitudes, from which are drawn a wide range of different food and non-food products (*ibid* 61-64). But this zone also overlaps the resource areas of perhaps 10 other major settlements. Although this kind of overlap is more unusual in upland and inland areas of Seram where population density is lower, the pattern must be quite common in all coastal areas of the Moluccas.

A second relevant characteristic of human ecological systems is that the environment upon which any one population subsists is seldom uniform. Ecosystems are not homogeneous but patterned, often in a way which is critical to an understanding of the functioning of the human populations within them. It has sometimes been useful to portray human groups as participating in several different relatively well-defined zones with varying food-getting potentials (e.g., Dornstreich 1977). Such discontinuities may affect the distribution of resources, yields and the selection of sites for cultivation, as well as emphasizing that human populations do not interact directly with *total* environments but only with particular fragments and species. Such spaces characterized by a particular biotic, geomorphologic and climatic composition are conventionally described as *biotopes*.[3] Table 7.1 shows the kind of biotopic pattern common for many parts of coastal Seram. This particular example is drawn from Nuaulu settlements in the Amahai sub-district.[4]

A third characteristic of human ecological systems i the Heraclitean one: that ecosystems and human populations (together with their various social and cultural representations) are in a constant condition of flux, coping with sudden or emergent environmental problems by

---

[3]Allee and Schmidt 1951; Coe and Flannery 1967. The term *biotope* is convenient in that it avoids some of the rather special theoretical and structural implications associated with *ecosystem*. However, I would not wish to reject entirely the notion of ecosystem or to suggest that biotopes do not also possess systemic properties.

[4]For a more detailed account of general environmental variation in the Nuaulu area see Ellen 1978:5-10, 22-6, 33, 43-6, 61-89, 108-18, 130-60.

'disturbing' rather than by maintaining balance. Emphasis must consequently be placed on types and rates of change. The recent interest in hazards research (Vayda and McCay 1977), the critique of negative feedback models and their replacement by amplification-deviation approaches (e.g., Bennett 1976; Ellen 1979) is ample indication that this point is now well taken.

Some Environmental Conditions for Closure

If closure is always a matter of degree, it becomes important to ascertain, in as precise terms as possible, what qualitative conditions might prevent the completely open flow of energy, materials and information for a particular human population. These can be grouped under three headings: geomorphologic (or physical), biogeographic, and cultural.

Geomorphologic closure is that which prevents the free flow of matter and its images between any two points through non-biological and non-cultural means. This may be achieved through altitude, distance, climate, terrain, seismic conditions, or any combination of these. As blocking mechanisms these rarely act independently of each other, or indeed of forms of closure under the remaining two headings. Thus, in eastern Indonesia, seismic disturbances may affect local weather by triggering-off torrential rain, while more regular patterns of precipitation are closely associated with the distinctive hydrological cycle of mature tropical forest (Kenworthy 1971). Moreover, the type and degree of closure possible in each case will vary. Altitude, distance and terrain must primarily be thought of in terms of spatial closure, while the immediate effects of seismic and climatic disasters are to induce temporal closure for particular localities. On the islands of the Banda arc, settlements have often been destroyed or severely damaged by tidal waves and earthquakes (Admiralty 1944:14, 16, 290; Kennedy 1955:147, 149, 150, 174), while the villages and nutmeg plantations of Banda itself have a long history of periodic destruction through volcanic eruption (Hanna 1978). The illustrations discussed here are confined to distance, terrain and the question of spatial closure.

Terrestrial distance in the Moluccas (whether measured orthographically, topographically or pherically) has important consequences for the closure of local systems. Although also affected by a range of other factors, distance is an important determinant of the distribution of Nuaulu cultivated plots. The relationship between village distance and both the number and total area of plots in hectares for the Ruhuwa Nuaulu is strongly inverse (Pearson's r = -0.89).

Table 7.1. The relationship of resource areas to food-getting activities among the Nuaulu of south central Seram.

Resource area (or biotope)	Altitude range (m above sea level)	Food-getting activities[1]										Total number of activities
		a	b	c	d	e	f	g	h	i	j	
1. Hamlet site - current	0 - 200				+		+		+			3
2. First year garden	0 - 400	+						+				2
3. Old garden - staple foods exhausted	0 - 200	+			+			+				3
4. Abandoned garden	0 - 200	+		+	+	+		+	+	+		7
5. Sago swamp and domesticated sago groves	0		+	+					+	+		4
6. Other groves	0 - 50				+				+	+		3
7. Mixed secondary forest	50 - 400				+	+		+	+	+		5
8. Mature rain forest	200 - 1000					+			+	+		3

Table 7.1 (continued)

Resource area (or biotope)	Altitude range (m above sea level)	Food-getting activities[1]										Total number of activities
		a	b	c	d	e	f	g	h	i	j	
9. Montane rain forest	1000 - 1400									+		1
10. Rivers	0 - 200								+		+	2
11. Streambank	0 - 400			+		+			+			3
12. Littoral	0								+		+	2
13. Sea	0										+	1
14. Total number of resource areas		3	1	3	5		1	4	9	6	3	

[1]a, swiddening; b, starch extraction from non-domesticated *Metroxylon* (sago) palms; c, starch extraction from domesticated *Metroxylon* palms; d, silviculture; e, gathering non-domesticated plant foods; f, animal husbandry; g, trapping; h, collecting non-domesticated animal foods; i, hunting; j, fishing. The mode of presentation adopted in this table (reproduced from Ellen 1982:167) broadly follows that employed by Dornstreich (1977:249-50) in his description of Gadio Enga subsistence.

This is so despite the amount of land under cultivation in 1970 (when this calculation was made) being almost equal for concentric zones of one kilometer width up to three kilometers from the village, and despite over 40 percent of the plots being more than two kilometers from the village. However, beyond the three kilometer radius the disadvantages of distance begin sharply to outweigh any advantages, as well as the disadvantages linked to the spatial constraints imposed by a preference for plots nearer to the settlement (Ellen 1978:133-8). However, the relationship between the amount of activity devoted to the extraction of non-domesticated resources and distance from a settlement does not show this strong correlation (Pearson's r = 0.1544; for data see ibid 63). This is in part due to an unevenness in the distribution of forest resources, and in particular to the tendency of exhausting resources nearer the settlement before moving further afield. Outside of subsistence, the effects of land distances can also be seen in the degree of social interaction, including spatially represented marriage relations (ibid 19-21).

Provided terrain and vegetation do not make routes impassable, land distances can be traversed without technical aids. This is not the case with maritime distances where some form of transport is unavoidable. However, as on land, the difficulties of communication increase in proportion to the distance involved, and short inshore movements are relatively common and straightforward.

In Figure 7.1 a continuous line has been drawn at a distance of 20 kilometers from the coast of all inhabited land-forms, a distance which corresponds approximately to the practical limit imposed by the use of small dug-out outrigger canoes by present-day Moluccans. This limit depends in part on the distance of the horizon, which may vary between 4.18 and 188.3 km, but is generally no more than 60 km. The physical demands of handling a small craft, the location of fishing grounds, the duration of journeys between nearby islands and perceived weather hazards also affect patterns of use. However, as a rule, small outrigger canoes keep well within sight of land. Traditional multiple-oared and long-hulled plank-built boats, as well as sailing boats of imported design, are not nearly so limiting. Their capabilities are well known (McKnight 1980), although it should be stressed that sub-types and individual craft are extremely variable in this respect. Much depends upon such factors as design and size. The dotted line on the same map marks the 200 metre depth contour. Both lines encompass island groups within which we might reasonably expect local settlements to be highly connected. If this is so--and I shall presently demonstrate in some fairly specific ways that it is--then the notion that islands necessarily provide us with convenient laboratories with a high degree of geographical closure (Thompson 1949; Fosberg 1963:5; Bayliss-Smith 1977:12) is misleading. This is so at least as far as human populations on geographically unremote islands are concerned.

The idea that small islands provide us with almost experimental conditions of closure is attractive, but in the Moluccas, and for large parts of insular southeast Asia and Melanesia, short sea-barriers are less limiting for humans than land barriers. The seas of the Indonesian archipelago are mostly warm, shallow and sunlit, with a rich and varied biomass. Although mud, shifting sand and submerged reefs sometimes provide navigational hazards, the seas are not subject to frequent bad storms or strong currents and are well suited for easy communication. Moreover, the main east and west monsoon winds are ideal for sailing craft moving between the mainland and various lateral points in the archipelago (See Urry 1981:2).[5] Even for populations at a low level of technical development using primitive vessels, small island groups are often better connected along coasts, across narrows and short stretches of open sea than coasts are with interiors divided by mountains, fast-flowing rivers, dense forest and difficult terrain. Moreover, lowland coastal regions draining large upland interiors are often swampy, and their foreshores covered with mangrove. In parts of the Moluccas (e.g., Nusalaut, parts of Haruku and Seram: see Figure 7.1), islands rise precipitously from the sea, and steep vegetation-covered slopes make coastal land travel awkward. In such areas, and also where forest, swamp, quagmirish paths, rocky and undulating surfaces prevent effective movement on firm land, intervillage travel may be along beaches. The littoral zone is particularly favored in this respect, but the availability of such routes depends on the tides. In the large islands to the west and in the Malay peninsula, estuaries and river networks provide access to the interior, but in the Moluccas such waterways are often shallow, full of rocks, liable to wet season flash floods and generally difficult to navigate.

---

[5]It was such considerations which led Coedes (1944:2) to develop his concept of an internal archipelagic sea as a powerful formative force in the history of southeast Asia, a notion which has been returned to in more recent writing on regional prehistory (Bellwood 1978; Urry 1981). In many ways, this role is similar to that attributed to the Mediterranean by Braudel (1949).

In the Moluccas the density of network connections has for a long time been infinitely greater along coasts and between small nearby islands than between the coast and the interior, and this has been closely linked to a high interdependency of local populations. By contrast, the most isolated and least dependent populations are those found in the interior and on highland peripheries. But while coastal connectivity within the small island groups of the Moluccas may well be high in terms of both human and non-human flows, as maritime distances increase beyond the 20 kilometer and 200 meter depth frontiers, so communication becomes technically more difficult and geographic barriers more resistant. As distance and sea-depth increase so separated land-masses become ecologically more closed and some potential lines of closure more apparent than others.

The second kind of closure to be considered is that between biotopes. Table 7.2 lists the main biotopes which can be usefully distinguished in the Moluccan area in the context of an essentially ethnographic examination. The table also indicates their degree of specialization, susceptibility to hazard and ability to sustain human populations. Six points about this table are worth noting.

1. The biotopes can be arranged according to their degree of ecological specialization, ranging from the most generalized (mature tropical rain forest, deep sea) to the most specialized (sago palm swamp, mangrove swamp).

2. The biotopes can be arranged according to their susceptibility to hazard. Generally speaking, more complex biotopes, such as mature rain forest, are the least affected by natural hazards, although the converse is not the case. While simple biotopes, such as sand bars, are certainly extremely fragile, the specialized conditions of the sago palm swamp are such that only the most severe disturbances are likely to alter its overall composition. If we order the biotopes according to their susceptibility to man-induced hazard in terms of known Moluccan history, then mature tropical forest must be seen as much more susceptible to hazard due to the continual firing and clearing of swiddens. On the other hand, the already stable conditions of the sago swamp are only enhanced by human husbandry which, while involving the periodic felling of stands, also ensures their vegetative propagation.

3. The boundaries between different biotopes vary in their degree of closure, fixity and clarity. Thus, mixed secondary rain forest merges imperceptibly into mature rain forest as it develops and increases in complexity. The break between sago swamp and mature forest is more abrupt: the circumstances in which one can develop into the other are rare and the overlap in species content negligible.

4. All biotopes listed may be used for human subsistence, although not all to the same degree. Both mature and mixed secondary forest is used by the Nuaulu for a wide variety of purposes (Table 7.1; Ellen 1978:61-80). By contrast, the extensive mangrove swamps of the extreme southeast of Seram are only used by inhabitants of the settlement at Kwamar as a source of firewood, palms (Nipa fruticans) and some minor marine foods (but see Dunn and Dunn 1977). However, although the range of products available from mangrove swamps is narrow, the economic significance of collecting firewood is considerable as the fuel depleted offshore islands of Geser and Kefing (Figure 7.1) have long been dependent upon it.

5. Biotopes vary in their ability to support human habitation and cater for the major part of their subsistence needs. Most of the more specialized biotopes are excluded on this basis, as are those which are entirely maritime. However, no Moluccan settlement is dependent upon only one (or even a few) biotopes for its subsistence. The Nuaulu example presented in Table 7.1 illustrates a particular case, although some idea of how the combination varies may be gained from an examination of Table 7.3. The overall stability of a particular resource base, its susceptibility to fluctuation and the predictability of its processes will depend on the combination of biotopes and the degree of subsistence dependence upon each. Crudely, the greater the number of different biotopes and the higher the ratio of generalized to specialized biotopes, the more stable a resource base is likely to be.

6. The degree to which these biotopes perpetuate themselves varies. All are dependent upon energy and materials from parts of a wider ecosystem.

Mature rain forest and other generalized systems can perpetuate themselves over a period of decades and centuries. Mixed secondary forest cannot maintain itself over the longer timescale since it is gradually moving toward climax rain forest. It can be maintained in a more immature condition, however, by periodic human intervention, through selective thinning and clearance. Though specialized, sago swamp is ecologically stable and can reproduce itself effectively over the 15 year life-span of the Metroxylon palm. Swiddens are highly unstable associations which are only prevented from changing into mixed secondary forest, grassland or bamboo scrub by constant horticultural attention. Groveland is more stable in this respect.

Resource Dependence and the Introduction of Asymmetry

Having examined some of the environmental preconditions which facilitate varying degrees of closure between Moluccan populations, we next turn to a comparison of these with the extent of cultural closure maintained in particular localities. All contemporary Moluccan populations are parts of wider trading systems. In Table 7.3 I have tried to indicate degree and type of closure for some of these. We must now investigate to what extent it is possible to ascertain the degree of functional independence of such populations at the present time or at some specified period in the past.

In an earlier publication (Ellen 1979a:47-52), I described the character of the most elementary Moluccan subsistence unit it is possible to conceive of in the light of available historical and ethnographic evidence. This, in part, is characterized by a critical dependence upon Metroxylon sago as a source of carbohydrate with a minimal use of domesticated resources, slight production for exchange and little reliance on other populations for food and materials. At the present time this condition is most closely approached by those populations listed in Table 7.3 as having the widest spread of food-getting activities over different terrestrial biotopes. Such populations also come nearest to fulfilling the maximum conditions of closure possible. Nevertheless, even when populations are capable of meeting their own food requirements in overall terms, periodic shortages of particular resources necessitate a degree of exchange with other similar populations. In many cases the resource areas of such populations may be almost

Table 7.2. Major biotopes distinguishable in the central and southeastern Moluccan region.

Biotope	Example	Degree of Specialization[1]	Susceptibility to hazard[2]	
			Man-Induced	Natural
1. Mature <u>Agathis</u> rain forest	extensive areas of the interiors of Seram and Buru below 1000 metres	1	1	3
2. Montane forest	highland areas of Seram and Buru over 1000 meters	2	1	1
3. Mixed secondary forest	extensive areas of Buru; on Seram mainly around human settlements	2	2	4
4. Bamboo scrub	lowland areas of Seram mainly around human settlements	7	3	3
5. Coconut palm and other groveland	extensive coastal areas of Kei Besar (coconut), Banda (nutmeg) and the Ambon group (clove)	7	3	3
6. Swiddens at different stages of development	within 4 km of most settlements on Seram and Buru	5	4	4

Table 7.2 (continued)

Biotope	Example	Degree of Specialization[1]	Susceptibility to hazard[2]	
			Man-Induced	Natural
7. Irrigated rice fields	rare: but some in transmigration areas of west Seram	10	5	5
8. <u>Metroxylon</u> palm swamp	lowland riverine areas of Seram: such as Nua-Ruatan confluence and Masiwang estuary	10	1	1
9. Mangrove swamp, muddy shores and estuaries	extreme southeast portion of mainland Seram between settlements of Kwamar and Kuwaos	10	2	2
10. <u>Imperata</u> grassland	coastal areas of Tanimbar and Kei Kecil; patches on all major islands	7	1	1
11. Savannah	southern parts of Aru group	6	2	2
12. Beach	all coastal areas	7	2	1
13. Intertidal (littoral) zone	all coastal areas	6	1	1
14. Lagoons	extensive in Kei archipelago	5	1	1

Table 7.2 (continued)

Biotope	Example	Degree of Specialization[1]	Susceptibility to hazard[2]	
			Man-Induced	Natural
15. Close in-shore waters and surf zone	all coastal areas	5	1	1
16. Banks and offshore shallows	Geser group	5	1	1
17. Cays - small coral islets	Geser-Gorom group; Kei archipelago	5	3	1
18. Coral shoals and reefs	Geser-Gorom group; kei archipelago	5	1	1

[1]A notional 10 point scale in which 1 represents the ecologically most generalized biotope and 10 the ecologically most specialized. Degree of specialization usually reflects species diversity.

[2]Two 5 point notional scales in which 1 represents a biotope least subjected to or affected by hazard and 5 that most subjected to or affected by hazard. Man-induced hazard may take the form of either intensification of disturbance or withdrawal of system-maintaining practices.

Table 7.3. Spread of food-getting activities for selected Moluccan settlements with some measures of their reproductive independence.[1]

	Local settlement and Population[2]	Basic subsistence pattern	Biotope combination[3]																		Trade dependence[4]						Degree of connectivity[5]
			1	2	3	4	5	6	7	8	9	10	11	12	13	14	15	16	17	18	a	b	c	d	e	f	
1.	Ruhwa (Nuaulu), south Seram - 100+	sago extraction, hunting and collecting, gathering, swiddening	+	(+)	+	+	+	+		+					+		(+)				1	2	1	2	0	0	1
2.	Piliana (Huaulu group), central Seram - 100+	sago extraction, hunting and collecting, gathering, swiddening	+	+	+	+	+	+		+											1	2	1	2	0	0	1
3.	Bati Sai'e, inland east Seram - 100+	sago-extraction, hunting and collecting, gathering, swiddening	+		+	+	+	+		+											1	2	1	3	0	0	1

Table 7.3 (continued)

Local settlement and Population[2]	Basic subsistence pattern	Biotope combination[3] 1	2	3	4	5	6	7	8	9	10	11	12	13	14	15	16	17	18	Trade dependence[4] a	b	c	d	e	f	Degree of connectivity[5]
4. Warus-warus, coastal east Seram - ±576	sago extraction, swiddening, fishing, cash-cropping			+	+	+	+		+					+		+	+			2	3	2	0	0	0	2
5. Sepa, south Seram - ±500	swiddening, cash-cropping, fishing, sago extraction			+	+	+	+		+					+		+				3	3	3	0	0	0	2
6. Oma, Haruku - ±2245	swiddening, cash-cropping, fishing, sago extraction				+	+	+		+					+		+				4	4	3	0	0	0	3
7. Lonthoir, Banda - ±1500	swiddening, cash-cropping, fishing					+	+							+		+				4	5	4	0	-	0	3

Table 7.3 (continued)

	Local settlement and Population[2]	Basic subsistence pattern	Biotope combination[3]																		Trade dependence[4]						Degree of connectivity[5]
			1	2	3	4	5	6	7	8	9	10	11	12	13	14	15	16	17	18	a	b	c	d	e	f	
8.	Kataloka, Gorom - ±1500	swiddening, cash-cropping, fishing, sago-extraction			+	+	+	+		+					+	+	+	+	+	+	4	4	3	0	0	0	4
9.	Blat, Kei Besar - 2000+	swiddening, cash-cropping, fishing, sago extraction				+	+	+		+					+		+	+			4	4	3	0	0	0	4
10.	Kefing, Geser group - ±500	fishing									+				+		+	+		+	5	5	5	0	5	5	4
11.	Gorogos, Gorom group - ±100	fishing												+	+		+	+	+	+	5	5	5	0	5	5	3

Table 7.3 (continued)

Local settlement and	Basic subsistence pattern	Biotope combination[3]																		Trade dependence[4]						Degree of connectivity[5]
		1	2	3	4	5	6	7	8	9	10	11	12	13	14	15	16	17	18	a	b	c	d	e	f	
12. Geser, Geser group - ±1230	fishing, trade													+		+	+	+	+	5	5	5	0	5	5	5

[1] The data upon which these schematic indices are based were collected in 1981, except for Piliana which were collected in 1975. In the cases of Ruhuwa and Sepa, the observations span 12 years from late 1969.

[2] Figures based on field data (1975-81) and annual statistical compendia available in relevant *kecamatan* (district) offices. These latter sources provide approximate figures only.

[3] Code refers to numbered biotopes in Table 2.

[4] Entries in column *a* are based on a notional 5 point scale of *overall* dependence on trade goods, where 1 represents minimal dependency. Entries in columns *b-c* indicate degree of dependence on non-food items, rice, fish, sago and vegetable foods respectively. In each case dependency is assumed to be theoretically measurable by dividing import subsidies (expressed by weight, calories, energy cost, time cost or economic value) by total population.

[5] Crude estimates expressed as a 5 point notional scale, where 1 represents minimal connectivity. However, the empirical information is available to construct graphs for local networks of which listed populations are parts. An 'accessibility index' for each interaction (or vertex) can then be calculated using standard techniques of network analysis (Haggett 1969).

identical or overlap extensively, but local demographic, ecological, subsistence and social variables give rise to imbalances in resource output per head which to some extent can be evened out through trade with immediate neighbors. Assuming a situation of basic exchange equality between populations, this kind of lateral trade has a mainly regulatory effect. We can say this without positing any preconditions for closure. It is enough to assume that all populations in the universe under observation are connected equally with each other and that ordinarily imbalances in local production are adjusted whenever possible by using connections nearest to the settlement concerned. The boundary of a system is never constant. No permanent frontier exists, only a gradation moving outward from a focus along which the limit defined at any one instance fluctuates. Moreover, such local systems overlap in proportion to the number of focal settlements.

It is now necessary to look at the ways in which asymmetry is introduced into trading relations, but before doing so I wish to make it clear that our working definition of asymmetry must be in terms of structural significance and not in terms of some convenient economic or ecological index which does not take into account the varying importance of particular resources in different localities. Thus, because a population is a specialized component in a world system does not automatically mean that it is a dependent component or that it need reduce its own generalized condition. For many centuries the highland villages of the larger Moluccan islands served as specialized suppliers of forest products which were of great significance in world markets, and they were able to do this while still maintaining a generalized subsistence base (cf. Dunn 1975). On the other hand, trade which may appear negligible measured by its bulk, calories, in terms of its external cash equivalent or the number of persons involved in its conduct, may involve products which have a high local value. Consequently, its role in an understanding of the functioning of indigenous social formations may be much greater. The value of shell bangles and pre-twentieth century trade porcelain and stoneware has always been much greater to the Nuaulu than to either the craftsmen of Gorom who made bangles or the traders who supplied the dishes. Now that both of these commodities are no longer available, their value has risen concomitantly. The value attributed by the Nuaulu to <u>kain berang</u>, a type of red cloth, has similarly been greater than that attributed to it by traders in Ambon from whom it was obtained or the factory owners in Java who manufactured it. However, unlike bangles and porcelain, red cloth has become more available not less. While shortages of the former items have had deflationary consequences, the increasing availability and circulation of red cloth has had inflationary consequences. Each of these categories of object obtain their local value through their role in ceremonial exchanges necessary for the social reproduction of clans, households, ritual houses, in the settlement of disputes, and so on. In some cases the inability to obtain new items at all (for example, patola cloths) to replace old ones generates crises for particular households or clans, which may herald a more dramatic breakdown of traditional social organization. The general loss of valuables over time (such as old Chinese porcelain) encourages either an unwillingness to participate in the exchanges at all or the switching to substitute articles (cheap trade plates, for example) which do not carry the symbolic load of traditional items and which in this way lead to a decline in the significance of the exchanges. Our notion of trade asymmetry must therefore always be one which takes into account differential structural significance.

Asymmetry may be introduced into trade relations either exogenously or endogenously. There is no doubt that the creation of asymmetry from exogenous links--that is, through Asian and European demand for forest products, marine products and spices--has been historically crucial. In terms of unequal exchange it accounts for the widest disparities and has had the greatest impact on changes in local social formations. However, I wish to focus here on asymmetry of endogenous origin. It will become clear that in the end we cannot consider one without reference to the other.

Endogenous asymmetry may arise through consistent shortfalls in particular resources. These may result from ecological disturbance, population fluctuations or socially determined changes in the pattern of extraction or demand. In such situations, local ties of dependency may arise in an otherwise symmetrical model. Asymmetry may also derive from the creation of demands which the local environment has never been able to supply, such as stone for the manufacture of implements or shell for ornaments. The historical and contemporary evidence for this kind of local trade in the Moluccas is considerable. Trochus shell for armbands is known to have been traded from the Gorom archipelago to highland Seram, while flint implements have been found in locations which suggest overland transport of raw materials (Glover and Ellen 1975) and pottery has been traded widely for many centuries (Ellen and Glover 1974; Spriggs and Miller 1979). At the present time much of the movement of sago into areas where it is deficient, and of fish from coastal to highland settlements, may be attributed to this kind of local endogenously-derived imbalance. In many places it takes the

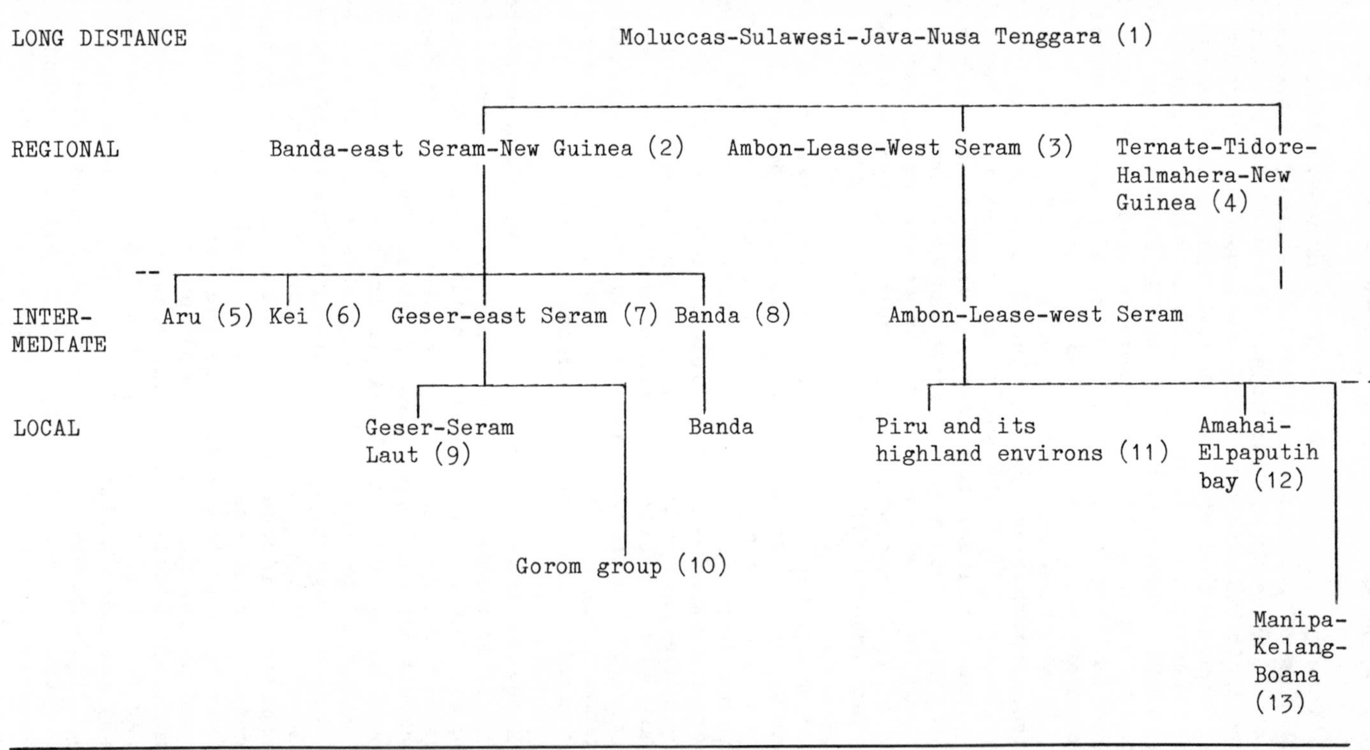

Figure 7.2. A hypothetical taxonomy of trading networks in the Moluccas.

classic 'fish for sago' (coastal-highland) pattern. The creation of this kind of continuing dependency provides permanent structural foci for a local trading network, which may grow asymmetrically through the incorporation of other specialist localities. Some of these networks may assume a degree of symmetry through circular linkages, of a kind exemplified by the kula in the New Guinea Massim. None of these developments are, of course, independent of other social relationships, which may well determine particular trading partnerships or patterns. A congruence between marital alliance and trading relationships is an obvious possibility. The final putative phase in the evolution of an endogenously-inspired trading network is, where conditions permit, the development of central places which become more important than other localities in the control of exchange within the network. It is at this level of development that exogenous links have proved most critical and have led to the development of more inclusive and highly structured local trading systems.

Networks and Nesting Trading Systems in the Moluccas

Moluccan trading networks can be reconstructed on the basis of both ethnographic and historical evidence. Figure 7.2 provides an outline taxonomy for those discussed here, indicating the four levels of spatial organization which I have found useful to identify: local, intermediate, regional and long-distance. Differences in scale between different networks may be judged in terms of distance, numbers of linkages, quantities of goods handled, size of populations integrated, and technological infrastructures, such as types of boat.

All networks have some systemic properties, but the degree of "systemness" varies between them. Conceptually, a trading system is composed of one or more networks and is characterized by a set of linkages which theoretically permit its reproduction over time through both a geographical and social division of labor. Most systems discussed here have a center and a periphery, connected by radial links. A center exhibits control over a periphery, although the extent of this control tends to diminish as we move further from the center. The center connects the system as a whole with the outside world, yet is dependent itself on the resources of the periphery. Settlements on the periphery which are points of production rather than simply nodes in a trading network, can be described as termini. The extent to which higher level systems absorb those at a lower level depends upon the degree and character of external commercial intrusion.

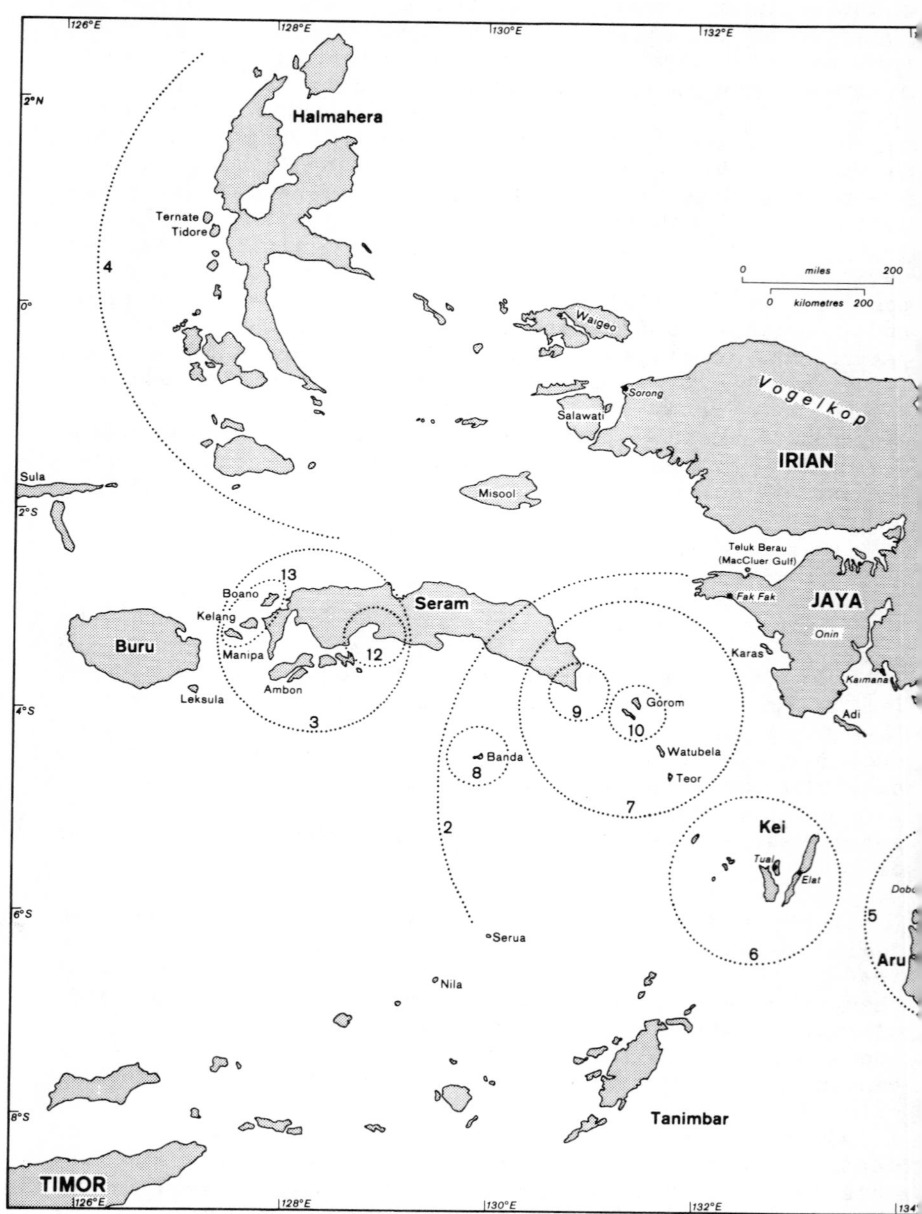

Figure 7.3 Spatial relationship between nesting Moluccan trading networks listed in Figure 7.2.

Membership of a higher level system may in turn redefine the structure and dynamics of lower level networks.

Local Trading Networks

In the Moluccas local trading networks tend to be confined to single islands, small island groups, and stretches of coast and hinterland. In Figure 7.3, the Gorom (10), Banda (8), and Geser (9) networks clearly illustrate this level of organization. In each case, local imbalances in the production of various subsistence crops are usually evened out within the area, and different villages within the zone provide certain specialized services, such as pottery manufacture, ironwork, sago production and fishing. The degree to which these zones overlap varies and affects their systemic character. The Banda group maintains a high degree of closure in terms of local trade, the Gorom group considerably less. Zones which include stretches of coastline, because of continuous habitation, tend to overlap much more. Some settlements may best be portrayed as simultaneously belonging to two or more local networks with different foci.

Intermediate Trading Networks

At a higher level, the central and southern Moluccan area can be seen as being composed of relatively discrete intermediate networks. At the hub of each of these is a small island (or number of small islands) serving as a redistributive center and point of articulation with the outside world: West Seram (3) is focussed on Ambon and the Lease islands, Aru (5) is focussed on Dobo, East Seram (7) on Geser, and so on (Figures 2 and 3). The trading centers, or foci, show varying degrees of dependency on their peripheries. The foci are generally very small islands which appear to owe their importance to their geographical centrality in the local trading area and because they provided intrusive traders or refugees with good harbors and safe havens in otherwise hostile territory.[6] Occasionally the reasons may have been environmental. For example, local

---

[6]For some comparative Melanesian studies of the role of small islands as crucial nodes in wider trading networks, see the following: Allen 1977a, 1977b (Motupure island in the vicinity of Port Moresby), Brookfield and Hart 1971:314-34 (general), Harding 1967 (Siassi islands in the Vitiaz straits), Harris 1979 (Torres Strait islands), Malinowski 1922 and Lauer 1970 (Tubetube, Amphletts and other islands in the *kula* area), Sahlins 1972 (general) and Schwartz 1963

inhabitants on Kefing claim that it was first inhabited to avoid the mangrove swamps along the southeastern coastline of Seram. But in this case one might ask why not settle at that point on the mainland where the mangrove ends. The real reason is more complicated and is probably largely political and economic in character: that an island among banks and shoals provided ready access to desirable sea products, that land elsewhere was politically inaccessible, that anchorages were convenient and safe, and that Kefing lay in the immediate vicinity of what was already an important trading center (the Seram Laut archipelago). The reasons for settling on such small islands must have been strong since the disadvantages were often severe. Small islands such as Geser, Kiltai and Kefing are flat, tiny and exposed coral islets, subject to frequent flooding, vulnerable to tidal waves, with virtually no possibilities for cultivation and with only brackish drinking water. There is oral and written evidence, as well as that of contemporary administrative boundaries, that in the past local political domains rivalled for control of these small strategic islands (Kolff 1840:287-8). Islands with so little natural wealth, with the possible exception of sea produce, must be contrasted with powerful political domains such as Kataloka on Gorom (Gorong, Goram) which also exported locally-grown spices and had opportunities for subsistence cultivation.

This play-off between precarious environmental conditions and supreme economic advantage does not only apply to minute islands whose entire livelihood depends on the transhipment rather than production of commodities. We have already mentioned that access to exotic sea produce may have been an important locational feature for some of these centers, at least since the eighteenth century (Urry 1980). The same is true for certain settlements on the periphery, either populated reefs subject to storms (Gorogos) or islands vulnerable to seismic disturbances (Nila) (see Figure 7.1). Banda has had a continuous and violent history of seismic disturbance (Hanna 1978), and much the same may be true of Ternate and Tidore. But in these cases, we are not only dealing with ideal centers for transhipment but with primary

---

(Admiralty archipelago). Such systems might be regarded as pristine in evolutionary terms. Similar systems in which the nodal points have their origin as settlements for exogeneous trade are also well known if not analyzed. Consider, for example, the role of Zanzibar, Pemba, and the Comores in Arabic commerce along the east coast of Africa, or Fernando Po in the Spanish-consolidated trading links across the Bight of Biafra.

locations for the production of nutmeg (Banda) and clove (Ternate/Tidore).

Very small islands with no possibilities for cultivation are entirely dependent on the import of basic foods and materials: rice and manufactured goods from outside the Moluccas and other starch staples (largely sago), vegetables, fruit and constructional and craft materials from other islands in the immediate vicinity. Such needs in a hypothetically pristine world might initially have been met through highly local trade, such as between Geser and Seram Laut. Geser, Kiltai and Kefing are still very dependent on the vegetable produce of nearby Seram Laut, and the economic significance of this island is reflected politically in the division between the polity (now *pemerintah negeri*) of Kelu on Kefing and Kiltai. But long-term requirements for trade objects to exchange for rice and manufactured goods and the increasing scale of such trade and home consumption has led to the growth of a much larger periphery. In the case of Geser, Kiltai and Kefing, it meant the incorporation of the eastern part of mainland Seram and parts of Teluk Berau and the Onin peninsula of New Guinea.

Trade in locally produced commodities falls into two categories: goods which are consumed within the network (or perhaps in adjacent ones) and those which are part of long-distance trade to Sulawesi, Java, or elsewhere. Commodities consumed within the network include sago, pottery, vegetables, fish, red sugar, timber, firewood and alcoholic liquors. Within each zone different localities specialize in different products for trade and the local circulation of these products, either radially through the center or laterally within the periphery, serves to integrate a complex social and economic *system*. Thus, the Banda islands as a whole are self-sufficient in red sugar, firewood, vegetables and fish, although no one settlement within the group is self-sufficient. But while the circulation of commodities maintains integral systemic properties within each trade zone, trade also occurs between zones. Thus, timber (and previously large quantities of sago) is generally imported into Banda from southeast Seram and Gorom (Kolff 1840:287), whereas Kei pottery was exported (after 1621) both to Seram and Banda. The circulation of such commodities serves to integrate Kei, Banda and S.E. Seram into a wider intermediate system, both laterally (between localities of more-or-less equal political and economic significance) and radially (focussing on secondary and primary centers).

Trade in commodities of the second kind--nutmeg, clove, exotic forest products such as edible birds' nests, trepang, pearls, tortoise-shell, and so on--only serve to integrate center with periphery (Seram Laut with Geser, Geser with Banda, etc.) or various points on the periphery _through_ the center since the demand is not local and is only mediated through traders operating from central places.

Termini are of two kinds. First of all there are those which are generally self-sufficient but which are the source of products desired elsewhere, in local centers, other parts of Indonesia, Asia and Europe. Prior to 1900 all interior mountain villages would have fallen into this category. Thus, Lumoli in West Seram has traditionally exported _damar_ resin (_Agathis alba_) to Piru, while Kilmuri on the southeast coast of Seram has traditionally exported sago to Geser. Other highland termini could have been involved in the export of timber, rattan, medicinal barks (_kayu manis, kayu lawan_), dried meat, antler, bird plumage and wild clove (_cengkeh hutan_). Because such termini were self-sufficient in a material sense, this is not to deny that the objects which they received in exchange (red cloth, _patola, ikat_, porcelain) represented a form of concealed value very necessary for the maintenance of local exchange and ritual cycles (Ellen 1979; Elmberg 1968). I have already made a point of emphasizing this. The second kind of terminus is one whose very existence is dependent on a wider trading network, secondary rather than pristine. An example of this would be the Gorogos reef, a fishing settlement exporting fish, trepang, _lola_ and _batu laga_ via Kataloka and Geser. Despite having to import all of its vegetable food, starch staples, and timber, Gorogos has grown from a temporary to a permanent settlement in the course of the last 20 years.

Secondary and primary centers can also be classified into those which are basically self-sufficient and those which are utterly dependent upon others. Examples are found in Kataloka (on Gorom) and Geser respectively. They can also be distinguished according to whether or not they are also centers for spice production. It now appears that spice cultivation at such centers may have been secondary to their emergence as centers of trade, as local trading communities dealing in spices produced elsewhere attempted to exercise more control over the production of the commodity. This at least appears to be the case for the east Seram network and Banda. We know that for many centuries wild nutmeg (_pala panjang_) had been coming from the forests of New Guinea via the trading polities of east Seram. It is possible that the emergence of Gorom as an important trading and political center was linked to the planting of nutmeg (_pala panjang_ and _pala bundar_) brought from New Guinea. In turn, it is equally possible that the first nutmeg grown on Banda (_pala bundar_) was brought from Gorom. Thus a wider Banda-focused system (Figure 7.2) may have been a rational outgrowth and extension of an east Seram system (Figure 7.2), linked to the planting of nutmeg in the Banda archipelago, the growth of the islands as a general primary trading center for incoming traders from the west and the consequent re-focussing of other radial supply links. But in any case, the principal Banda-east Seram artery remained for good geographical, navigational and economic reasons.

Regional Trading Networks

There is some historical evidence for the existence of three reasonably distinct regional trading nexuses located in the present-day Indonesian province of the Moluccas and adjacent areas of the New Guinea coast (Figures 7.2 and 7.3). Each is focused on a densely-populated spice-producing center, dependent upon an extensive sago-producing periphery. The three spice-producing foci are Ternate/Tidore, Ambon-Lease and Banda; the major sago-producing peripheries are, primarily and respectively, Halmahera, west Seram and east Seram-Kei-Aru-New Guinea.[7] These trading nexuses did not all emerge at the same time, and the conditions of their emergence were in each case significantly different. However, by the early part of the seventeenth century their simultaneous existence is quite well documented, while the consequences of the interaction of external factors with their internal dynamics are evident over the subsequent 300 year period. In the past they have shown strong systemic properties.

I shall confine myself here to the Ambon and Banda systems. However, these two systems differ in one important structural respect quite apart from the many detailed historical and ethnographic differences between them. The Ambon system (Figure 7.3) is a network without obvious intermediate level components, despite certain sub-systemic local tendencies (e.g., in the Elpaputih bay and Boano-Kelang-Manipa areas). On the other hand, the Banda system (Figure 7.3) is composed of at least four separate and identifiable intermediate networks plus some less clearly attached networks. The four major intermediate level components are the Banda, Kei and Aru groups and the network connecting the Geser-Teor chain with the mainland of east Seram. The attachments are the New Guinea (Irianese) coast

---

[7] In an earlier paper (Ellen 1979:70) I have described the peripheries of the Ambon and Banda systems as 'Seram and Aru-Kei-New Guinea' respectively.

from Teluk Berau southeastward to Mimika and the extreme southeastern islands focused on Tanimbar. The systemic properties of the Banda regional nexus derive almost entirely from intrusive long distance trade. The incorporation of various intermediate networks has depended on the importance of their products outside the Moluccas and, to a lesser extent, demand elsewhere in the system. With the drop in external demand for their products, some intermediate (and local) networks regain something of their earlier autonomy. Thus, strong local sub-systemic properties have continually threatened the integrity of the system as a whole.

Connected with this important structural difference between the Ambon and Banda systems is the question of distance, and the appropriate boat technology in each case. While in the past the Ambon system could reproduce itself internally by relying on small coastal craft, the Banda system involved major sea-crossings. Historically, this has meant the employment of much larger vessels, for the most part those belonging to intrusive trading groups such as the Buginese and Butongese.

It would be a mistake, however, to see the emergence of trading patterns in the Moluccas as simply the working out of some game-theoretic or market rationality under ideal Von Thünen and Christaller-Lösch conditions. Trade relations within any network were always constrained as well as facilitated by other social relations, such as inter-village *pela* alliances (in the Ambon-West Seram zone, or their functional equivalents elsewhere), marital alliances and ties of political subordination and control. Although it is difficult at this stage to make even intelligent guesses regarding the political organization of trade prior to the European period, the larger systems clearly brought together political entities of very different kinds: semi-dependent tribal groups (such as the Nuaulu), slave-based *kerajaan* (such as Kataloka) and class based traditional societies (such as Kei). From the seventeenth century onward, the number of different kinds of political entity and modes of production increased to include Dutch East India Company-run estates (Banda) and mercantilist control of peasant producers (Ambon group). It is quite clear that the Dutch period resulted not simply in changes in traditional trading patterns, but in some cases in their consolidation and the accentuation of some of their more distinctive properties. Thus, the geographical division of resources in the Banda archipelago after 1621 was administratively re-defined: firewood could only be taken from Gunung Api, and it was mandatory that vegetable gardens and nutmeg groves be located in different places. Clove cultivation was prohibited in large parts of Seram (e.g., the Huamoal peninsula) in order to maintain the Dutch monopoly, encouraging these localities to develop other trading specialties. But although Banda under the East India Company represented an entirely unique kind of social and cultural formation, the expansion and concentration of spice production not only connected Moluccan centers more closely with the world system but, paradoxically, made them more dependent on local trading links as well. The growth and specialization of centers of spice production and trade as the result of colonial policy had the effect of producing a more distinct and complex local division of labor and network of exchange relations. As land under spices and population increased, so also did the local trade in sago, root crops, vegetables and other products necessary to supply deficient spice-producing areas. When centers already important for trade were adopted as convenient administrative centers by the Dutch, bringing an increasing number of retail enterprises to cater for a growing number of wage earners and bureaucrats, trade routes became increasingly centralized, radiating to and from the administrative center.

Degree of Closure and Causality

Let me recapitulate the main points made in the previous section. Moluccan trading patterns may be conveniently represented as a series of nesting (and sometimes overlapping) zones of varying degrees of "systemness". Each local population may participate in up to four levels of trading organization: local, intermediate, regional and long-distance. Participation is defined minimally in terms of the destination of a population's exports and the origins of its imports. However, the structural significance of participation at any one level depends also on the types, proportions, range, value and volume of goods traded. For example, it may be important to know the scale of the trade in food products or the local significance of the trade in 'valuables.' Collectively, such factors determine the degree and kind of reproductive independence a local social formation maintains, and maintains at different levels of systemic inclusiveness. Table 7.4 illustrates how these patterns of participation at different levels of organization vary for six historically specified populations and between different kinds of functional components in wider systems. The patterns defined in these terms can help us to decide where we may legitimately draw boundaries in particular analyses, and what factors we can reasonably hold constant. Depending on the purpose of the analysis and the populations specified, we may decide to emphasize boundaries at the local, intermediate or regional level; but in all cases we

Table 7.4 Reproductive dependence of selected Moluccan populations at various levels of systemic inclusiveness.

Local population (functional component in system)	Incoming goods classified by level of origin[1]				Main exports and re-exports
	local	intermediate	regional	long-distance	
1. Ruhuwa (Nuaulu) south Seram (generalised terminus), 1969-1981	11. vegetable shortfalls, fish, certain	3. pottery, red sugar		1. CLOTH, PORCELAIN, salt, manufactured goods	cloves, copra
2. Bati Sai'e, inland east Seram (generalised terminus) 1981	8. FISH, pottery, ironwork	6. ←	2. pottery	1. CLOTH, manufactured goods	cloves
3. Bandaneira, Banda group (primary centre) 1797[2]	8. vegetable shortfalls, red sugar		2. TIMBER, thatch, coconut oil, SAGO, yams, slaves, pottery, TREPANG, pearls	1. CLOTH, porcelain RICE, ironwork	nutmeg, trepang, pearls
4. Kefing, Geser group (specialised terminus) 1825[3]	9. SAGO, ALL VEGETABLE FOODS	7. sago	2. edible birds nests, tortoise-shell, cloves, nutmeg, pottery	1. firearms, gunpowder, porcelain, cannon, CLOTH	trepang, edible birds nests, tortoise-shell, cloves, nutmeg
5. Gorogos, Gorou group (specialised terminis) 1981	10. SAGO, ALL VEGETABLE FOODS, TIMBER, thatch, ironwork	7. sago timber	2. pottery	1. CLOTH, manufactured goods, RICE	trepang, fish
6. Geser, Geser group (primary centre) 1981	9. sago, ALL VEGETABLE FOODS, TIMBER, thatch	7. sago pottery	2. pottery, tortoise shell, TREPANG, cloves, nutmeg	1. CLOTH, MANUFACTURED GOODS, RICE.	trepang, fish

[1]Those import items most crucial in structural terms are written in upper case letters. Numbers refer [illegible] [2]Source: Miller 1980. [3]Source: Kolff 1840.

must remember that boundaries are necessarily graded and determined by the structural foci of the systems they encompass.

We are now in a position to reinforce a number of observations about closure and the spatial character of causality:

1. We may agree with Faris (1975:239) that external causes only become effective through internal ones. Thus, growth in the spice trade accelerated local trade in sago, other food products, and basic resources. In turn, this changing pattern in purely local trade had repercussions elsewhere in the system. One cannot understand the spice trade in the Moluccas or the maintenance of trading centers without first tackling the dynamics of local trade. Even though the spice trade itself did not extend to the periphery, local trade in these areas did respond to its kick-on effects. For example, the increase in the east Seram sago trade was a response to the growth of a secondary trading center in Geser, which itself was the outcome of nutmeg cultivation and commercial activity in the Banda archipelago. Similarly, changes in local exchange relationships in the Vogelkop of western New Guinea (Elmberg 1968) following the introduction of increasing quantities of red cloth were an indirect spin-off of the central Moluccan trade in spices and international demand for maritime products, such as trepang and pearls, in the southeastern islands.

2. Although poorly connected systems may depend upon other levels of organization for their reproduction, this is not to reduce their overall dynamic to events at another level (Waddington 1970:180-3). While extrinsic factors may trigger changes in purely local trading arrangements, extrinsic factors alone are insufficient to explain the structural character of specific causation. One should no more expect to understand the spice trade in the Moluccas or the maintenance of trading centers without first tackling the dynamics of local trade than one should expect to understand local trade in isolation from external factors.

3. Few (if any) modern populations are engaged in trade which is confined to local networks. Where

this may have been the case historically, local patterns of trade had consequences for those populations participating in higher levels of organization. Moreover, even if a population does not handle materials produced within a system of which it is part, since objects must pass through any intermediate level, that trade must have some affect on participating populations.

4. While being part of a system does not in itself indicate dependence on that system, certain populations could not exist except as parts of wider systems. In some cases this is physically true, for example, in the case of Geser or Gorogos. The ethnography of Melanesia is full of examples of small offshore islands apparently developing as centers in endogenously pristine systems. But although this may provide us with a possible explanation for the origin and development of places such as Geser as centers, their subsequent development is no doubt closely bound-up with a role in regional systems and long-distance trade. Gorogos, on the other hand, we know to have developed in the last 20 years precisely to supply marine products in demand in the Asiatic and world systems.

Conclusion

Since ethnographers will continue to make assumptions about the boundaries of the systems which they investigate and about the degree of closure which they attribute to them, it is necessary to know with the greatest possible accuracy what criteria can be used to best establish the degree of reproductive autonomy of local populations (both ecologically and socially) under particular ethnographic conditions. It is also important to know to what extent legitimate and useful boundaries may be drawn at different levels of spatial or temporal inclusiveness since where boundaries are drawn determines the relationship between causes and effects.

I have shown that in order to ascertain the degree of dependence of particular Moluccan populations on wider systems we require information about:

(a) degree of physical isolation;

(b) spread of subsistence base;

(c) involvement in trade analyzed according to the destination of exports, the origin of imports and the general web of relations which connect local populations to wider systems; and information on the proportions, range, value and volume of goods traded.

But although this provides us with the basic preconditions for making realistic statements about the character and degree of reproductive independence, it is insufficient. It is not enough to know the extent to which a population is dependent or simply the items upon which this dependence lies; it is also important to understand the spatial position and function of a population in more inclusive local and regional systems (cf. Adams and Kasakoff, this volume). Once this information is available (and it implies a general understanding of the overall structural focus of superordinate systems), it then becomes possible to go beyond the explanation of a particular local change or pattern with reference to some general 'external' event(s) and specify in more detail how a cause has been transmitted from an imputed point of origin and transformed through intermediate variables, with varying and multiple consequences, to produce a particular local effect. It is then also possible to ascertain whether the population in which the effect is realized is simply a passive recipient of a set of consequences or whether it is itself an essential agent in the process which led to it being realized. I suspect that in most cases we will have to conclude that an effect is produced by an nexus of dependent factors which have their separate origins at different degrees of proximity.

References Cited

Admiralty
1944 Netherlands East Indies 1. Naval Intelligence.

Allee, W.C. and K.P. Schmidt
1951 Ecological Animal Geography. 2nd ed. New York: Wiley.

Allen, J.
1977a Fishing for Wallabies: Trade as a Mechanism for Social Interaction, Integration and Elaboration on the Central Papuan Coast. In The Evolution of Social Systems. J. Friedman and M.J. Rowlands, eds. London: Duckworth.
1977b Sea Traffic, Trade and Expanding Horizons. In Sunda and Sahul: Prehistoric Studies in Southeast Asia, Melanesia and Australia. J.

Allen, J. Golson, R. Jones, eds. London: Academic Press.

Bayliss-Smith, T.P.
1977 Human Ecology and Island Populations: The Problem of Change. In Subsistence and Survival: Rural Ecology in the Pacific. T.P. Bayliss-Smith and R.G.A. Feachem, eds. London: Academic Press.

Bellwood, P.
1978 Man's Conquest of the Pacific. Auckland: Collins.

Bennett, J.W.
1976 The Ecological Transition: Cultural Anthropology and Human Adaptation. New York: Pergamon Press.

Braudel, Fernand
1949 La Mediterranee et le Monde Mediterraneen a l'Epoque de Philippe II. Paris: Librairie Armand Colin.

Brookfield, M.C. with D. Hart
1971 Melanesia: A Geographical Interpretation of an Island World. London: Methuen.

Coe, M.D. and K. Flannery
1967 Early Cultures and Human Ecology in South Coastal Guatemala. Smithsonian Contributions to Anthropology 5. Washington, D.C.: Smithsonian Institution.

Coedes, G.
1944 The Empire of the South Seas. Journal of the Thailand Research Society 35(1):1-15.

Dornstreich, M.
1977 The Ecological Description and Analysis of Tropical Subsistence Patterns: An Example from New Guinea. In Subsistence and Survival: Rural Ecology in the Pacific. T.P. Bayliss-Smith and R.G.A. Feachem, eds. London: Academic Press.

Dunn, F.L.
1975 Rainforest Collectors and Traders: A Study of Resource Utilization in Modern and Ancient Malaya. Kuala Lumpur: Monographs of the

Malaysian Branch of the Royal Asiatic Society. No. 5.

Dunn, F.L. and D.F. Dunn
1977 Maritime Adaptations and Exploitation of Marine Resources in Sundaic Southeast Asian Prehistory. In Modern Quarternary Research in Southeast Asia. G.J. Bartstra, et. al. Rotterdam: A.A. Balkema.

Ellen, R.
1978 Nuaulu Settlement and Ecology: An Approach to the Environmental Relations of an Eastern Indonesian Community. (Verhandelingen van het Koninklijk Instituut voor Taal-, Land en Volkenkunde 83) The Hague: Martinus Nijhoff.
1979 Sago Subsistence and the Trade in Spices: A Provisional Model of Ecological Succession and Imbalance in Moluccan History. In Social and Ecological Systems. P. Burnham and R.F. Ellen, eds. (Association of Social Anthropologists Monograph 18) London: Academic Press.
1982 Environment, Subsistence and System. Cambridge: Cambridge University Press.

Ellen, R.F. and I.C. Glover
1974 Pottery Manufacture and Trade in the Central Moluccas, Indonesia: The Modern Situation and the Historical Implications. Man (N.S.) 9(3):353-379.

Elmberg, J.-E.
1968 Balance and Circulation: Aspects of Tradition and Change among the Mejprat of Irian Barat. Stockholm: Ethnographical Museum Monograph Series No. 12.

Faris, J.C.
1975 Social Evolution, Population and Production. In Population, Ecology and Social Evolution. S. Polgar, ed. The Hague: Mouton.

Fosberg, F.R. (ed.)
1963 Man's Place in the Island Ecosystem. Honolulu: Bernice P. Bishop Museum.

Friedman, J.
1976 Marxist Theory and Systems of Total Reproduction. Part I: Negative. Critique of Anthropology 2(7):3-16.

Glover, I.C. and R.F. Ellen
1975 Ethnographic and Archaeological Aspects of a Flaked Stone Collection from Seram, Eastern Indonesia. Asian Perspectives 18(1):51-61.

Haggett, P. and R. Chorley
1969 Network Analysis in Geography. London: Edward Arnold.

Hanna, W.
1978 Indonesian Banda: Colonialism and Its Aftermath in the Nutmeg Islands. Philadelphia: Institute for the Study of Human Issues.

Harding, T.G.
1967 Voyagers of the Vitiaz Strait: A Study of a New Guinea Trade System. Seattle: University of Washington Press.

Harris, D.R.
1979 Foragers and Farmers in the Western Torres Strait Islands: An Historical Analysis of Economic, Demographic and Spatial Differentiation. In Social and Ecological Systems. P. Burnham and Roy Ellen, eds. (Association of Social Anthropologists Monograph 18) London: Academic Press.

Kennedy, Raymond
1955 Field Notes on Indonesia 1949-1950. Harold C. Conklin, ed. New Haven, Connecticut: Human Relations Area Files.

Kenworthy, J.B.
1971 Water and Nutrient Cycling in a Tropical Rain Forest. In The Water Relations of Malasian Forests; Being the Transactions of the First Aberdeen-Hull Symposium on Malasian Ecology, Hull 1970. John Roger Flenley, ed. University of Hull, Department of Geography: misc. ser. 11.

Kolff, D.H.
1840 Voyages of the Dutch Brig of War Dourga - Through the Southern and Little-Known Parts of the Moluccan Archipelago and Along the Previously Unknown Southern Coast of New Guinea . . 1825-1826. London: Madden & Co.

Langton, J.
1973 Potentialities and Problems of Adopting a Systems Approach to the Study of Change in Human Geography. Progress in Geography: International Review of Current Research 4:125-79.

Lauer, P.K.
1970 Amphlett Islands Pottery Trade and the Kula. Mankind 7(3):165-76.

MacKnight, C.C.
1980 The Study of Praus in the Indonesian Archipelago. The Great Circle 2(2):117-128.

Malinowski, B.
1922 Argonauts of the Western Pacific. London: Routledge and Kegan Paul.

Mason, M.L. and J.H. Langenheim
1957 Language Analysis and the Concept Environment. Ecology 38:325-340.

Miller, W.G.
1980 An Account of Trade Patterns in the Banda Sea in 1797, from an Unpublished Manuscript in the India Office Library. Indonesia Circle 23:41-57.

Newcomer, P.H.
1972 The Nuer are Dinka. Man (N.S.) 7(1):5-11.

Rappaport, Roy A.
1968 Pigs for the Ancestors: Ritual in the Ecology of a New Guinea People. New Haven: Yale University Press.

Sahlins, M.
1972 Stone Age Economics. London: Aldine.

Schwartz, Theodore
1963 Systems of Areal Integration: Some Considerations Based on the Admiralty Islands of Northern Melanesia. Anthropological Forum 1:56-97.

Spriggs, M. and D. Miller
1979 Ambon-Lease: A Study of Contemporary Pottery Making and its Archaeological Relevance. In Pottery and the Archaeologist. M. Millet, ed.

London: Institute of Archaeology Occasional Paper.

Thompson, L.
1949 The Relations of Man, Animals and Plants in an Island Community (Fiji). American Anthropologist 51, 253-67.

Urry, James
1980 Goods for the Oriental Emporium: The Expansion of Trade in the Indonesian Archipelago and Its Impact on the Outer Periphery. Unpublished manuscript.
1981 A View from the West: Inland, Lowland and Islands in Indonesian Prehistory. Unpublished paper presented at Section 25A-Archaeology, 51st ANZAAS Congress, Brisbane, May.

Vayda, A.F. and B.J. McCay
1977 Problems in the Identification of Environmental Problems. In Subsistence and Survival: Rural Ecology in the Pacific. T.P. Bayliss-Smith and R.G.A. Feachem, eds. London: Academic Press.

Waddington, C.H.
1970 Towards a Theoretical Biology, 1. Edinburgh: Edinburgh University Press.

Weiner, J.S.
1964 The Biology of Social Man. Journal of the Royal Anthropological Institute 94:230-240.

John W. Adams, Alice Bee Kasakoff

8. Ecosystems over Time: The Study of Migration in "Long Run" Perspective

"When dealing with the entire world over four centuries, how does one organise such a file of facts and explanations? One has to choose. I chose to deal with long-term equilibriums and disequilibriums."

--Fernand Braudel

Introduction[1]

The study of cultural ecology has developed a great deal since the days when we could examine an isolated patch of terrain and feel confident about our ability to extrapolate from our findings to an entire region or ecotype. That these days, perhaps, are not so distant after all is witnessed by Moran's recent (1982) critique of this problem. Thanks to him, we will not neglect to sample in order to see how each particular patch of interest fits within the hierarchy of a region--and of a biome. Indeed, even in this volume, Ellen makes abundantly clear how misleading the local study can be when carried out in a region as diverse as the Moluccas: to isolate a locality as typical in such a situation misrepresents entirely the existing state of affairs.

---

[1]Our research on New England which underlies this paper was carried out thanks to a Faculty Research and Development Grant from the University of South Carolina, a fellowship from the National Endowment of the Humanities, administered by the Newberry Library of Chicago, and a grant from the National Science Foundation (Geography and Regional Science Program, SES #8016384).

Yet while these scholars address the facts of ecological complexity in space, another and equally salient dimension remains to be assessed--the dimension of time. That we realize the importance of knowing how our patches relate to each other at the moment of fieldwork should not permit us to remain content any longer with our "synchronic snapshots." Should we not also face up to the diversity which time presents?

Indeed, a standard criticism of the current approach to cultural ecology has been its lack of concern with processes over time (Orlove 1980; Netting 1977; Vayda and McKay 1975). Yet little thought has been given so far as to how this should be done, the units to be used, or the analytical framework to be employed. In our own research we have been forced to confront changes over time as a result of having to use materials which cover several hundred years of New England history; and in order to unfold something of the issue of time in ecological research, we present some of the problems we have faced and some of the ideas of historians we have found useful.

Migrations of New Englanders

Several years ago we began to investigate the topic of endogamy by trying to define the region from which spouses were chosen using a cross-cultural sample (Adams and Kasakoff 1973, 1976). To pursue this effectively, we needed substantial amounts of genealogical data covering a large geographical area. But such data are very rare in the current store of ethnographic cases, perhaps because the preferred unit of anthropologists has so often been the "village," conceived of as typical of a region full of similar villages, yet studied more or less in isolation from them. So after using (and using up) the data on Tikopia (Kasakoff and Adams 1977),[2] we felt that the best opportunity for broad genealogical coverage of a region lay in colonial New England.

We investigated the topic of migration at marriage among three families (1620-1775) and replicated what we had found elsewhere in the world, namely that local villages were

---

[2]Despite Ellen's observations (this volume) on the necessity for sampling a region, there are some research topics--endogamy is one--which nevertheless do allow greater degrees of "bounding" if we look at islands. On Tikopia there were two groups within which 80% of the people found spouses.

typically 50-60% endogamous, that there were no 100% endogamous groups, and a new finding, thanks to the excellent cartography, that 80% of spouses were found within a radius of 16 miles which included the intermediate surrounding villages (Adams and Kasakoff 1980).

To our surprise, however, historians had just completed a "new history" of New England which put various anthropological concepts to use on the data, notably our old idea of the "village study," and had finished by painting a picture of "closed corporate peasant communities" replete with "stem family households" isolated from their neighbors and "frozen in a world of timeless immobility!" (See Adams and Kasakoff 1980 for citations.) Yet as the first flush of the historians' enthusiasm wore off, various doubts were raised by their peers about this picture (Demos 1970; Prest 1976; Rutman 1977). Given our approach, it was easy for us to see that each village was embedded in a region of villages, that the marriage market was about 32 miles in diameter, and that the inhabitants were moving about the countryside from one village to the next at a much higher rate than historians thought likely. Indeed the supposed stability of the population was quite illusory, for once one looked at the <u>region</u> it was obvious that New Englanders had begun to move the moment they had landed (Breen and Foster 1973). Historians generally postulated a rapidly increasing and non-migrating population which could be contained within the original village land grant only so long as there was additional acreage to be distributed and which eventually "overflowed," forcing great numbers of sons to move away from their place of birth if they were to support a family in the proper style.

Part of the reason for our differences on this issue was a question of sources. We used published genealogies, whose basic feature was an attempt to link persons with the same surname wherever they happened to reside, and so preeminently concerned with migration, while the historians had practiced "family reconstitution," a method of constructing genealogies from vital records and church documents. Family reconstitution itself does not preclude migration--unless one limits oneself to the records of a single town as most of the New England historians have done. And this is precisely the crucial methodological point: whether to view New England from the vantage point of single isolated villages or to try to see the region as a whole. The two approaches result in quite basic differences on almost every issue which historians, anthropologists, or ecologists consider important. Not only do they affect the spatial units of analysis but the notion of what happened over time as well.

Thus a certain paradox appears in the different ways by which anthropologists and historians might characterize the data on Colonial New England. For historians the period between 1620 and 1691 was a kind of "Golden Age" replete with "community," a unity of purpose, and a time of relative equilibrium, a colony, as one historian put it, of "peaceable kingdoms": so long as there was enough land for families to remain together, no one needed to migrate. To an anthropologist aware of cultural ecology, however, the forest was not so primeval. Englishmen competed with Indians for the land, finally driving them West or killing them off. Demographic rates fluctuated considerably at first, and there was, in fact, a great deal of migration, more than in the immediately succeeding decades. But by the time the various parts of New England had lost colony status in 1691, they became in effect somewhat sleepy, "underdeveloped" outposts of the British empire. Migration slowed: demographic rates stabilized into a regime of high population growth. Historians, though, find this to be the beginning of a period of growing turbulence and instability--a prelude to the coming Revolution. Thus the whole issue of stability gets stood on its head to fit an idea of equilibrium still current among some historians: the Golden Age after which things get progressively worse.

Our concern in this paper, however, is not to question the sort of anthropology that historians of New England admire and practice--one of us has already done so elsewhere (Adams 1981). Instead we want to ask what sort of history anthropologists might pursue when their research leads them to the preserves of historians--a matter of relevance to many anthropologists in all sub-fields nowadays--as well as a matter of relevance to this volume. As it happens, many in the vanguard of historians actually utilize a sort of *ecological* approach.[3]

We are thinking of the kinds of history practiced by the *Annales* School in France, of whom Fernand Braudel and Le Roy Ladurie are most familiar; the Cambridge School of Laslett, Wrigley and Schofield; as well as the School of Wallerstein's "world capitalist economy" which is already in vogue among

---

[3]Of course, anthropologists have been taking account of history for generations now, yet "long-term study" means barely 40 years (Foster et al. 1979). It is even useful, moreover, for those regions which lack historical records to promote (or indulge) a kind of "as if": How would we now conceptualize them if we could pursue our data beyond the confines of the synchronic snapshot of a single village?

anthropologists today (J. Nash 1981). These writers offer valuable clues, we feel, about the nature of cultural-ecological systems over long time periods.

Braudel and the "Long Run"

We find in Braudel a division of history into three levels of time: on the surface, so to speak, is the instantaneous "event," l'histoire eventiellement. This is the special province of narrative history of the old school--and now, as well, of the "new Old School" (Stone 1979)--the history above all of political intrigue. Yet beneath this surface of events lies a longer time-frame, that of "conjunctures" (conjunctures) which last from roughly a decade to the 50 years of a full Kondratieff cycle (Braudel 1980:29; see also Braudel and Spooner 1967; Rostow et al. 1979; Thomas 1972). Then, finally, beneath these two temporal levels lies a third which underpins them something like the bass line of a musical composition, that of the "Long Run" or la longue duree, a time (or locus) of "structures," by which Braudel seems to mean something like Moran's levels of aggregation in the biome (1982), though because of the geographical extent of Braudel's interests, it is perhaps more like the concept of "ecosystem."[4] So, ironically, in our search for a useful way of treating the "historical" we come to a mirror in which we see ourselves, and a magic mirror at that, for it is one which reflects our youth.

Le Roy Ladurie (1981:1-27) has even extended Braudel's idea of the Long Run with his concept of a "history which stands still," l'histoire immobile. Treating the period from 1300 to 1730 as a whole, he notes that the population of France was virtually the same at the end as at the beginning--it had stood still, as it were--yet within that period--when looked at in terms of the smaller unit called conjuncture--there were sharp rises and falls in the population level--a fact not surprising given the occurrence then of the Black Death.

So the Long Run is a kind of "envelope" (Braudel 1980:31) within which there are striking fluctuations, but within which there are also continuities such as, in this instance, the Malthusian checks on population of war and plague. The subsequent Long Run, in which we live today,

---

[4]Braudel (1980:51) credits Marx with its discovery in a passage which refers to the social composition of the Capitalist mode of production.

began about 1720-30 (Le Roy Ladurie 1981:1-27) or 1750 (Braudel 1980:32) and is characterized by preventive population checks, such as increasing age at marriage and birth control as well as cyclical economic depressions rather than by inflations of the prices of food and land. Yet our current Long Run appears to be terminating according to Le Roy Ladurie (1981:270-89). The growing shortage of oil, he predicts, will bring about the return of Ricardian (and Malthusian) checks in the future. We are at a moment of transition, then, between two Long Runs, each with its characteristic structure.

Change as such, which we might innocently suppose to be the historian's concern, is reduced to a fleeting moment between "Long Runs" metaphorically likened to the occurrence of an earthquake (Le Roy Ladurie 1981:288). Thus the Long Run looks rather like a "demographic regime" (Nugent 1981) if we read between the lines of Le Roy Ladurie's writings (1981:28-83) about the plague. These units therefore are analagous to, though not precisely interchangeable with, the "stages" of cultural evolution.[5]

Middle-Size Units of Time in Social Anthropology

It is clear from the work of both the Cambridge and the Annales Schools that the systems they studied existed for much of the time out of equilibrium. Whether characterized by positive or preventive checks on population, the systems are not very finely tuned. The Cambridge School (Wrigley and Schofield 1982) has found a 40 year time lag between economic cycles and the birth rates that respond to them; Ladurie has focussed on a period when an equal amount of time was spent in crisis--plagues or war--to that spent out. In good times populations expanded to the very limits of capacity and beyond, preparing the way for the crises which were so severe as to wipe out a large proportion of the population (Postan and Hatcher 1978; Le Roy Ladurie 1978).

Yet we are terribly impoverished in social anthropology for lack of the long time span needed to observe so many processes, a span far longer than the traditional term of anthropological fieldwork or even of long-term restudies. In

---

[5]Timpanaro (1975) notes the difficulty which the concept of Long Run poses for many Marxists who worry that acceptance of such long periods of unchangingness might foster an unwitting acceptance of unchangingness itself as part of the "human condition."

fact, the time lag which Wrigley and Schofield find between changes in prices and changes in demographic rates--40 years--corresponds exactly to the length of time between our most widely spaced restudies (Foster et al. 1979) and this suggests that even over that long a span we may be unable to observe equilibrium. Nevertheless, we are fortunate to have several cycles reported in the literature: the periodic recurrences of the Tsav complex among the Tiv (Bohannon 1958), the 20 year cycle of peace and war among the Tsembaga (Rappaport 1968), the alternation of Gumsa and Gumlao phases of political organization in the Burmese highlands (Leach 1954), and the 50 year cycles of Lugbara lineage fission (Middleton 1960).[6] Their lengths fall somewhere in between the "event" and the "Long Run" and thus would seem to be the equivalent of "conjuncture."

It is to be expected that the cultures with which anthropologists customarily deal would have different kinds of cycles and that they would be of different lengths than those visible in the pre-modern state.[7] And it is probably not enough to gather traditional sorts of ethnographic data since most of that is very much influenced by the world system at the time they were gathered. We will have to analyze the underlying causes of cycles and their magnitude and compare them with what we know about population regulation in order to deduce the kinds of demographic perturbations that were likely to have existed. Here the data from the premodern state will be useful if only as an example of one type of system. At first guess, however, it looks as though our Long Runs are considerably longer than those of historians. In some places, at least, what seems to be "the same culture" has lasted for some 40,000 years, the length of time _Homo sapiens_ is known to have existed, although such examples are cultural backwaters away from the main roads of human development.

Historians help us see that the units of time in ecological systems are linked with internal instability and fluctuation of different parameters (cf. Vayda and McCay 1975) and that such fluctuation often has its source outside

---

[6]The full extent to which some of these cycles are basically demographic in nature remains to be studied. Age sets create a regular cycle but one which seems relatively independent of natural ones.

[7]The extent to which such cycles could be moderated by population controls needs to be studied but here again it is well not to expect one answer for the whole human race.

the system itself. Though they define their systems so as to be extremely large spatially, the ultimate source of changes is often outside: plague from Asia and Africa or silver and gold from the New World. Anthropologists often study contemporary crises of this sort but they usually try to imagine them away in order to visualize the system as it must have looked just before "contact" with outsiders destroyed it. However, it is quite likely that continual interaction with outsiders was a feature of such systems at all times and an increasingly important one the more we attempt to deal with time.

The Importance of Multiple Localities in the System

Spatially, these historians study extremely large units, the Mediterranean, for example, even the entire world. The units are bounded on the basis of the similarities in process which occur within them as well as contact between individuals and communities through trade and migration. Their systems contain several cultures, as anthropologists understand them. A local situation, therefore, represents a "choice" within a larger system because each locality is part of a cultural tradition which comes to it from outside and, as such, each locality operates within a larger institutional framework. Granted that each may be said to rework this tradition or to carve out its own "niche" in the larger system, it nevertheless starts within a system, not *de novo*, even when, as in America, it is a pioneering situation.

In fact, such frameworks are being found at levels above that of the individual culture: for example, Hajnal's (1965) contrast between European and Asian marriage patterns. More recently Wrigley and Schofield (1982) proposed that the English pattern of population control was based upon preventive checks in comparison to Europe where positive checks were more important. There is also an "African style" of population control based on postpartum abstinence (Saucier 1972; Whiting 1964), while in India a prohibition on widow remarriage was important (Reining 1981). Similarly, though in a different sub-field, Murdock et al. (1978) were recently surprised to find super-regional disease philosophies.

This is not meant to raise the ghost of "culture areas" but to point out that quite contemporary analyses of processes basic to human adaptation have found continuities over very large areas, continuities which unite not only the tiny communities anthropologists and ecologists study but even the larger units with which they deal, the cultures themselves. These "philosophies" are on a spatial scale while the Long Run is on a temporal scale.[8] They indicate continuities in time as well as space.

The pitfalls of looking at only one locality are quite apparent in the study of New England. Historians of that region have recently used two ecological models, though whether they would all recognize them as such is hard to say. These treat basically the same process, either from the vantage of the locality or of the larger system. The process is one of the filling up of the landscape over time resulting in overflow from the local community once it is filled. Lockridge (1970), Greven (1970) and Rutman (1977) all share this view though Rutman develops it more explicitly using comparative data from different towns. A complementary view (Lockridge 1968) is the idea of two segments of the population, one mobile and poor, the other sedentary and wealthy. The former pool is being fed from the latter for it consists of sons who must leave the locality due to overflow. This dichotomy does not become apparent until the initial period of filling up is over (G. Nash 1970). The very basic question is how much of this overflow became sedentary in a new locality, possibly on the frontier.[9] To answer this, one must study the region as a whole.

In our view, there was a constant process of moving in and out of towns rather than a "golden age" of filling up and a subsequent period of "spilling over" once towns were filled. Forces external to the local community offered important inducements to movement and thus we do not assume that under "normal" conditions everyone wanted to stay put. Even when a local community is not full--even in early Massachusetts--there may be outside attractions which result in mobility.

The rising price of land itself results in mobility since there will always be cheaper land elsewhere in the system so long as there is a frontier. If some event external to the local community such as war or a change in Indian policy opens up new land, and transportation is cheap enough, people will be apt to leave regardless of whether the community is full. Ultimately one would need to include such

---

[8]We must reluctantly postpone for another occasion the fascinating question of the relationship of these "philosophies" to the historians' concept of mentalité.

[9]Kearl et al.'s paper (1980) underscores the mechanism whereby this situation occurs on the Utah frontier. That is, the rise in land prices as an area ages, makes it difficult for sons to buy land in the towns where they grew up.

external variables as England, and suppliers, balance of payments and business cycles.

The Issue of Overpopulation

Studies of towns and communities show a loss of people regularly, for when a person leaves the town he leaves the study! Therefore, because the "new history" of New England is written from such a local perspective, its authors see mainly "overpopulation" and consider only a push type of migration.[10] Indeed, if we are to believe them, New Englanders were never enticed to leave home because of cheap land. Yet this overpopulation disappears when the scope of the analysis is enlarged. Labor was actually the most expensive factor of production in New England despite one of the highest rates of population growth ever recorded (Smith 1972)! This is enough to suggest that "community" (and "family") no longer serve as useful units of analysis unless they are considered in a field of like units. The act of bounding an inquiry in this way overlooks the fact that these units are themselves attempts to bound off a part of the field of interaction which actually consists of many such units.

A sense of when the old area was full is, in any case, a relative notion because intensification made the same geographical unit capable of sustaining more people. But intensification was delayed for generations in most areas due to the availability of cheap land and lack of access to markets. A third response to overpopulation could have been population regulation, an alternative which has been stressed in the American context by Easterlin (1976). But if it was practiced, it was long in coming. Greven (1970) and Lockridge (1966, 1970) suggest that the effects of land shortage were being felt by the second quarter of the eighteenth century, yet the earliest evidence of population regulation occurs 50 years later--approximately the same time lag which Wrigley and Schofield (1982) find for England. Here again we see the enticement of cheap land for some if not all of the population. So if cheap land had once before retarded the decline, why didn't it work to do so once again, especially since the beginning of the decline coincides with

---

[10]Yet there were times when certain social classes in New England such as the roving poor experienced push and pull. Why they stayed in the old areas rather than colonize new ones, we do not yet know. Presumably they were too poor to travel the considerable distances involved at this period and to pay the prices demanded for new land.

the opening up of New York and other areas after the Revolution?

In short, not only the definition of overpopulation but the "solutions" to it in New England varied over time, as well as space, in ways which make it impossible to study, except on a scale which is larger than anthropologists, and indeed many historians are accustomed to. In periods when cheap land was available people apparently migrated unless they were too poor to find the wherewithall to do so. But at some point they did begin to reduce their fertility and to intensify their agricultural production apparently because of the easier transportation available to markets which led to the commercialization of agriculture. Changes in the costs of new land were also important: after the Revolution people were offered land simply for serving and this led to a peak in migration. Prior to this it was more expensive to move and a class of "roving poor" had developed in the older areas.

New England in "Long Run" Perspective

Our source of data is a set of genealogies, so our unit of analysis is a population. Further, it is a population which migrates. We see one long period from 1620 to 1850 (and beyond) with fluctuating rates of migration due to the relative availability of cheaper opportunities. In our view, the so-called Golden Age of stability was caused by lack of land for expansion on the periphery due to continued warfare with Indians and the French, not because there was still plenty of land in the old towns. Moreover, the strategy of intensifying agricultural production was familiar to them, though it was apparently not practiced until after the Revolution (Bidwell and Falconer 1925). We therefore see overflow as a constant feature of the model and that some of the overflow became a stable portion of new communities over time. The rate at which this occurred varied with fluctuations in external cycles and events.

In sum, our perspective differs from that of historians and, we think, from the usual anthropological one, in ways which are important for cultural ecology to consider. Like Braudel and Ladurie, we see only a single "Long Run" in this seemingly jumbled period. A principal feature was mobility, and this mobility, moreover, was not a signal of breakdown in the system but rather a feature which characterized this particular Run and which, furthermore, united several localities. Our model, therefore, is of a system which is spatially larger than a local community. Indeed, it includes the entire New England region. We define it this way because of the substantial movement of the population within New England (and not to other regions), the fact that all its communities were subject to roughly similar external forces which impinged on them from the world system, such as the availability of land and markets, and because communities in the region had a similar demographic history, namely a high rate of growth.

As such, the major parameters were set by forces acting on the region as a whole (or which the region as a whole initiated) such as the legal impediments and/or inducements to migration, as well as warfare, the increasing availability of land and so on. Within this structure there were fluctuations over the Long Run--"conjunctures," to use Braudel's term for them--in the rates of migration, and these fluctuations corresponded to shifts in the balance of opportunities within the system.

Migration in Human Ecosystems

Until recently most ecologists have ignored the effects of demography on the local situation even though most of their models include assumptions about whether or not the population was expanding or stable. Indeed, on closer analysis these demographic regimes often assume the status of "prime mover" without being either adequately described or explained. The historical data we have is preeminently demographic, and this allows us to incorporate demography into ecosystemic explanations.

When demography is systematically incorporated into ecological models, it will be necessary to incorporate migration as well since demographic inequalities between local groups foster population redistribution even when populations are not growing (see Netting, this volume). Of course, when they do grow the system must react by creating new opportunities which may lead to migration as well. The way in which the system responds to demographic changes will create temporal cycles. In some cases these will be synchronized across local communities; in others they will be more localized. But changes in the fortunes of one community will lead to population redistribution affecting large areas. Entire regions or "cultures" may have different roles in the larger demographic system. Thus Braudel (1973:60-82) speaks of the mountains sending people to the coasts, which he calls those "demographic sinks of Europe" because they were malarial.

How did the "migration system" in New England operate and change over time? What do we mean by "system"? We mean a framework which will include both localization of people and their dispersion. The question is not: Why did people leave one place and enter another?--which is how it is often posed by persons who look at localities--but rather, What was the larger system of opportunities like?

Conclusions

At a time when anthropologists have been trying to make their models of ecological adaptation more dynamic (Orlove 1980), it has been particularly exciting to read the work of historians who have taken a decidedly ecological turn in their studies while making use, at times, of an anthropological vocabulary and systemic approach.

But these historians are doing a sort of cultural ecology which is very different from the sort usually done in anthropology. Instead of using tiny local communities which are in equilibrium with their environment (Rappaport 1967; Baker and Little 1976), their spatial units are entire world regions; their temporal units are hundreds of years. Periods of equilibrium alternate with those of pronounced disequilibrium; indeed, only a view over the Long Run can disclose any equilibrium at all! Large as their systems are spatially, these historians are always looking beyond their borders for sources of change to the extent that the entire globe is sometimes seen as a single theater (Le Roy Ladurie 1981:28-83; Wallerstein 1974, 1980).[11]

---

[11]The new look in ecology has been to develop the idea of adaptive strategy (Jochim 1981; Orlove 1980; Bennett 1969). The result seems to us overly psychological and too dependent on the analysis of the decision-making process. Often it substitutes a description of the process for an analysis of the determinants of it. Of course, it is exactly on the point of motivation that an analysis based upon historical documents falters. Yet, should we not ask if such an approach really is necessary? Aren't the advocates of adaptive strategy finding their dynamics in the wrong place, in the minds of individuals, rather than in the changes occurring in the "environment" of the systems they are studying? Or in those systems themselves?

When one breaks away from the time lock of the traditional anthropological field study, one can find dynamics where they most surely belong--"out there"--whether that be located inside the system itself, the inexorable effect of the persistence of a system over time--"filling up"--or located outside the system, in its impingement upon other units in the form of cultural borrowings, new crops,

In any reformulation of the interlocking hierarchy of spatial and social units in cultural ecology, we feel it necessary to include the propensity of humans to move about. The time has come to abandon the "rootedness" notion of the past--as well as the present. The idea that people stay put no matter what, or more precisely until a terrible crisis drives them away, does not apply to New England, Old England, and probably would not have characterized the primitive cultures we usually study had records been kept of their comings and goings.[12] Certainly it is an important empirical question to find out when rootedness does exist--as it assuredly does in some times and places--but it is not a universal attribute of a species which is so often said to be distinguished by its ability to live in all environments on the globe! This focus on migration highlights the poverty of our customary notion of community. We will be quite blunt: "community" is not the self-sufficient unit which anthropologists and historians continue to suppose. Understanding a single such unit requires understanding a field of time. One must also recognize that they are related to each other in space, as well as in time, historically, and subject to similar pressures from without.

A further attribute of this reformulation should be an awareness of, and emphasis on, factors usually considered external to local systems. To mention the idea of strategy, each individual has several choices: to stay in the community and change (e.g., intensify, reduce fertility) or to leave the community and join a new one, which can be either of the same kind or different. What his choices are do not depend solely on the little community but on the larger system. Moreover, the inducement to change often comes from outside the local community.

But while the historians whose work we admire offer the promise of releasing anthropologists from their "slice of time" approach into a longer and more useful temporal unit, they have, in a sense, only pushed the real problem farther into the past or future. In making the Long Run the largest unit of analysis, historians have not addressed the question of how one Long Run changes into another, though in an important essay Le Roy Ladurie (1981:270-89) has discussed

---

diseases, and the like, or its changing place within a larger system depending on the size unit preferred.

[12] Actually certain ethnic groups, of whom the Athapaskans and the Bantu are typical, have seemed to force us to regard their migratory behavior as an essential part of their exemplary status in the record of human cultures.

the way in which crises did result in the development of infrastructure which slowly presaged a new Long Run. We wonder if the effect of being new disappears so quickly that anthropologists could see it only rarely. Or is there a regular ecological sequence that might be visible at almost any stage in the development of a community? In terms of the old world where colonization is not the issue, what is the meaning ecologically of the various temporal watersheds sketched by the Annales School in their notion of the Long Run? Do these really bound (divide) ecosystems? What is an ecosystem in this very large sense?

It is particularly striking that the Annales School uses ecology to mean the very biggest, most universal forces acting on a system. In this they are like the biologists who originally developed and used the concept (see Golley, this volume). These always transcend the local community and include such forces as disease, climate, warfare, in which the existence of the modern state has had a hand. These are unifying experiences for a region if not for the human race. While history, writ large, in this sense, is certainly not "complete," it is a perspective which we feel is very much needed in ecology today to counterbalance the extreme particularism and isolating perspective of local units which has prevailed. In brief, many historians are telling us that we should not look for equilibria, but look instead for long periods in which there are characteristic fluctuations in the rates which typify the system and that only observation of large areas, over "the Long Run," will reveal these to us. We agree.

References Cited

Adams, John W.

1981 Consensus, Community and Exoticism. Journal of Interdisciplinary History 12(2):253-65.

Adams, John W. and Alice B. Kasakoff

1973 Factors Affecting Endogamous Group Size. In Population and Social Structure. Moni Nag, ed. The Hague: Mouton.

1976 Central Place Theory and Endogamy in China. In Regional Analysis. Vol. 2. Carol Smith, ed. New York: Academic Press.

1980 Migration at Marriage in Colonial New England: A Comparison of Rates Derived from Genealogies with Rates from Vital Records. In Genealogical Demography. Bennett Dyke and Warren Morrill, eds. New York: Academic Press.

Baker, P.T. and M. Little, eds.
1976 Man in the Andes. Stroudsburg, Pa.: Dowden, Hutchinson and Ross.

Bennett, John
1969 Northern Plainesmen. Chicago: Aldine.

Bidwell, Percy W. and John I. Falconer
1925 History of Agriculture in the Northern United States. Washington, DC: The Carnegie Institute.

Bohannon, Paul
1958 Extra-Processual Events in Tiv Political Institutions. American Anthropologist 60:1-12.

Braudel, Fernand
1973 The Mediterranean World in the Age of Phillip II. Vol. 1. New York: Harper and Row.
1980 On History. Chicago: University of Chicago Press.

Braudel, Fernand and Frank Spooner
1967 Prices in Europe from 1450 to 1750. In Cambridge Economic History of Europe. Vol. 4. E.E. Rich and C.H. Wilson, eds. Cambridge: Cambridge University Press.

Breen, Timothy and Stephen Foster
1973 Moving to the New World: The Character of Early Massachusetts Immigration. William and Mary Quarterly 30:189-222.

Demos, John
1970 A Little Commonwealth: Family Life in Plymouth Colony. New York: Oxford.

Easterlin, Richard A.
1976 Factors in the Decline of Farm Family Fertility in the United States: Some Preliminary Results. Journal of American History 63:600-14.

Foster, George, Thayer Scudder, Elizabeth Colson and Rober V. Kemper
1979 Long-Term Field Research in Social Anthropology. New York: Academic Press.

Greven, Philip J., Jr.
1970 Four Generations: Population, Land, and Family in Colonial Andover, Massachusetts. Ithaca: Cornell University Press.

Hajnal, J.
1965 European Marriage Patterns in Perspective. In Population in History. D.V. Glass and D.E.C. Eversley, eds. Chicago: University of Chicago Press.

Jochim, Michael A.
1981 Strategies for Survival. New York: Academic Press.

Kasakoff, Alice B. and John W. Adams
1977 Spatial Location and Social Organisation: An Analysis of Tikopian Patterns. Man 12(1):48-64.

Kearl, J.R., Clayne Pope and Larry Wimmer
1980 Household Wealth in a Settlement Economy: Utah, 1850-1870. Journal of Economic History 40(3): 477-96.

Le Roy Ladurie, Emmanuel
1978 A Reply to Professor Brenner. Past and Present 79:55-59.
1981 The Mind and Method of the Historian. Chicago: University of Chicago Press.

Leach, Edmund
1954 Political Systems of Highland Burma. Cambridge: Harvard University Press.

Lockridge, Kenneth A.
1966 The Population of Dedham, Massachusetts, 1636-1736. Economic History Review Series 2, 19:318-44.
1968 Land, Population and the Evolution of New England Society, 1630-1790. Past and Present 39:62-80.
1970 A New England Town, the First Hundred Years: Dedham, Massachusetts, 1636-1736. New York: Norton.

Middleton, John
1960 Lugbara Religion. Oxford: Oxford University Press.

Moran, Emilio F.
1982 Anthropological Approaches to the Study of Human Impacts. Delivered at the symposium on "Human Impacts on Global Resources." Annual meetings of the American Association for the Advancement of Science, Washington, DC.

Murdock, George P., Suzanne F. Wilson and Violetta Frederick
1978 World Distribution of Theories of Illness. Ethnology 17(4):449-70.

Nash, Gary B.
1970 Class and Society in Early America. Englewood Cliffs, NJ: Prentice-Hall.

Nash, June
1981 Ethnographic Aspects of the World Capitalist System. Annual Review of Anthropology 10:393-423.

Netting, Robert
1977 Cultural Ecology. Menlo Park, CA: Cummings.

Nugent, Walter
1981 Structures of American Social History. Bloomington: Indiana University Press.

Orlove, Benjamin S.
1980 Ecological Anthropology. Annual Review of Anthropology 9:235-73.

Postan, M.M. and John Hatcher
1978 Population and Class Relations in Feudal Society. Past and Present 78:24-37.

Prest, W.R.
1976 Stability and Change in Old and New England: Clayworth and Dedham. The Journal of Interdisciplinary History 6(3):359-74.

Rappaport, Roy
1968 Pigs for the Ancestors. New Haven: Yale University Press.

Reining, Priscilla
1981 Anthropology of Fertility. Prepared for the Panel on Fertility Determinants, Committee on Population and Demography, National Academy of Science, Washington, DC (xeroxed).

Rostow, W.W., Michael Kennedy, assisted by Faisal Nasr
1979 A Simple Model of the Kondratieff Cycle. Research in Economic History 4: 1-36.

Rutman, Darrett
1977 People in Process: The New Hampshire Towns of the Eighteenth Century. In Family and Kin in

Urban Communities, 1700-1930. Tarama Hareven, ed. New York: New Viewpoints.

Saucier, J.F.
1972 Correlates of the Long Post-Partum Taboo: A Cross-Cultural Study. Current Anthropology 13:238-49.

Smith, Daniel Scott
1972 The Demographic History of Colonial New England. Journal of Economic History 32:165-83.

Stone, Lawrence
1979 The Revival of Narrative: Reflections on a New Old History. Past and Present 85:3-24.

Thomas, Brinley
1972 Migration and Urban Development. London: Methuen.

Timpanaro, Sebastiano
1975 On Materialism. London: NLB.

Vayda, Andrew P. and Bonnie J. McCay
1975 New Directions in Ecology and Ecological Anthropology. Annual Review of Anthropology 4:293-306.

Wallerstein, Immanuel
1974 The Modern World System I: Capitalistic Agriculture and the Origins of the European World-Economy in the Sixteenth Century. New York: Academic Press.
1980 The Modern World System II: Mercantilism and the Consolidation of the European World-Economy. New York: Academic Press.

Whiting, J.W.M.
1964 The Effects of Climate on Certain Cultural Practices. In Explorations in Cultural Anthropology. W.H. Goodenough, ed. New York: McGraw Hill.

Wrigley, E.A. and R.S. Schofield
1982 The Population History of England 1541-1871: A Reconstruction. Cambridge, Mass.: Harvard University Press.

Robert McC. Netting

9. Reflections on an Alpine Village as Ecosystem

In occasionally referring to the Swiss mountain village of Törbel as an "island in the sky" and describing the intricate economic and social means by which its inhabitants over the centuries struck a balance with their alpine environment (Netting 1981), I may well have been guilty of the ecosystematic fallacy. This common anthropological error involves an overemphasis on functional integration, stability, and regulatory mechanisms within the community and a relative neglect of disequilibrium, changes emanating from more inclusive political-economic systems, and instances of evolutionary maladaptation. The nature of long-term resident field research, our reverence for an holistic perspective, and the romantic mystique of the self-sufficient, autonomous, emotionally rewarding "little community" all perpetuate our proclivity to learn a lot about a very limited group.

Ecological anthropologists with their commitment to gathering a wider range of non-cultural data and organizing these variables into systems models often focus on small units of interaction for both practical and theoretical reasons. Biologists have told us comfortingly that ecosystem is an accordion concept, applying equally well to a drop of pond water or the entire biosphere. If indeed the ecosystem may be delimited at any magnitude appropriate for a particular investigation, and if natural boundaries are desirable but not essential (Fosberg, pers. comm.), we can continue to study those convenient social entities where we have always worked--the band, the village, or the tribe. The boundaries are, of course, recognized as artificial or drawn for "heuristic" purposes. We vigorously deny that we still labor in the expiring vineyard of neo-functionalism (Vayda and MacCay 1975; Orlove 1980). Nevertheless, we remain concerned with more or less closed systems whose internal processes are regulated by negative feedback loops, and we tend to make common cause with the biologists who stress the idea of ecosystems rather than of natural selection as an organizing concept (Richerson 1977). Distinguishing between local and regional ecosystems (Rappaport 1971a) recognizes part of the problem, but the sheer complexity of charting energy flows in local food production and consumption (Rappaport 1971b) may be so demanding that exchanges of goods, services, and people in the wider network over long periods of time cannot be adequately handled.

The appearance of biological orthodoxy and objective comparability that comes from selecting "populations" rather than "cultures" as units of investigation (Vayda and Rappaport 1968) is often illusory. Lacking species distinctiveness and geographical isolation, questions of where to bound a population as ecosystem may rely on endogamous groups or other ethnic bars to mating whose creation and effective maintenance are based on cultural rules of acceptable marriage (see Adams and Kasakoff, and Ellen, this volume). The fact is that human populations must be typified and analyzed by demographic means, but we necessarily begin with localized, co-resident, on-the-ground groups that identify themselves by name and tell us about the links of kinship, cooperation, and citizenship that bind their members together. Without hard information on such biosocial factors as diet and disease, warfare mortality and migration, and changing age-specific fertility (Buchbinder 1978; Morren 1977; Hassan 1978), ecological approaches to human cultures, populations, or ecosystems, however defined, can hardly rise above the level of explanatory sketches.

Jochim (1981:4) has pointed out that the boundary definition of human ecosystems is even harder than that of biological ones because of the more diverse interactions and because humans establish cultural boundaries that may or may not coincide with any natural ones. It seems to me now that I was led down the garden path of the independent population subsisting on its own resources in a clearly defined geographical area by the extraordinarily definite and enduring congruence between the Swiss folk model of the community and the historic realities of peasant village economy in the alps. But in the very process of finding out how orderly, effective, self-correcting, and responsive the local system had been in sustaining a self-conscious, corporate population through time in an unremittingly difficult mountain environment, I became aware of the often concealed interdependencies that sustained the system at its points of weakness and rectified its dangerous imbalances. We will consider some of the ways in which a culturally and materially defined local community ecosystem survived by means of significant economic and demographic flows back and forth across its boundaries.

Self-sufficiency and the Market

Anthropologists coming from technologically complex, occupationally specialized, economically interdependent societies may be attracted to groups where the entire labor process from raw natural resource to finished product and consumption is visible and comprehensible. We are devotees of mechanical solidarity for whom small has always been beautiful and ecological homeostasis in traditional societies is assumed until proven otherwise. It was with a sense of considerable satisfaction that I settled on the community of Törbel in the Visp valley of Valais Canton as a site for field research. Törbel seemed by all accounts a representative alpine village whose peasants had lived since at least the eleventh century A.D. on the returns of agro-pastoral subsistence pursuits carried on within their own demarcated territory. A contiguous area of 1545 ha. (including 967 ha. of field, meadow, and pasture, 455 ha. of forest, and 123 ha. of unproductive land in 1924) sloped from the Mattervispa river at 770 meters above sea level to the peak of Augsbordhorn at 2972 meters (Netting 1981:2). Various altitudinal zones were used for vineyards, hay meadows, grainfields, gardens, and summer grazing grounds (Netting 1972), so that almost the entire supply of wine, rye bread, dairy products, potatoes, vegetables, and meat were locally produced. Wood for building and fuel, slate for roofs, and wool for textiles also came from village lands, and the mountain stream powered grist mills, a saw mill, and a fulling mill. Every farm family had access to the various types of land and other means of production such as barns and livestock (Netting 1981:10-41). Climatic fluctuations were cushioned by the scatter of individually owned fields with various degrees of slope and sun exposure (Netting 1976), an extensive system of meadow irrigation (Netting 1974), and effective techniques for the storage of hay, grain, bread, cheese, and dried meat. The provision of adequate food, clothing, and shelter from within the village territory by subsistence methods that changed little from at least the fourteenth century does not appear to have degraded the local environment. Soil fertility was maintained by manuring, terracing and uphill transport of earth limited erosion, and carefully controlled timber cutting prevented deforestation (Netting 1981:46, 67). The localized ecosystem seemed to epitomize a well articulated, self-sustaining interdependence of physical environment, subsistence techniques, and human population.

Both the Swiss inhabitants of Törbel and the outsider ecologist are inclined to stress a peasant past in which comparative independence and autarchy distinguished the community from other European rural societies. But economic isolation was probably never the rule. A path through the Törbel hamlets of Burgen and Feld is part of the ancient trail connecting the Rhone valley with Italy. Roman coins found on the Theodul Pass indicate early connections, and a hill fort in Zeneggen near Törbel dates to the Iron Age (Netting 1981:8). Trails of this kind were perhaps less important than the Simplon or St. Bernard routes in linking northern Europe with the Mediterranean, but the alpine traffic could only be interrupted and the passes closed when a disaster like the bubonic plague caused medieval Valais to quarantine itself. Mountain agriculture is hardly imaginable without axes and other woodworking tools, hoes, and caldrons for cheese making. Metals have always necessarily been imported. Salt for the dairy cattle and for preserving cheeses had also to be brought in from a distance. Indeed the trade in salt from either France or Italy was a cantonal monopoly around which the late medieval international relations of the mountain districts revolved (Dubois 1965). Sixteenth century documents record an annual wagonload of salt delivered to Törbel, and in the nineteenth century it was estimated that an ordinary household with cattle used 70 kg. of salt per year (Franscini 1848:139).

From the time of the earliest parchment documents relating to the community, land sales have required money, and both churchly tithes and personal debts with interest are given cash values. Törbel had to participate in the market, but it is not completely clear how this was done. To this day, Törbel has a reputation for raising milk cows, and most families sell some breeding or slaughter stock every year. Animals were driven to the lower Rhone valley, across the passes into Italy, or disposed of at the annual markets in Visp and Stalden. Live sheep and goats as well as raw wool and cheese may also have been traded in former times, but the alpine herding pattern was more oriented to subsistence than exchange, and it seems likely that an appreciable surplus was not regularly produced. Cash income may have been dependent more on the export of labor than of agricultural goods. The trans-alpine trade required the seasonal work of drivers, mule skinners, and guards, and Törbel men may have taken such jobs as they did when the tourist industry began in the late nineteenth century. They also served for longer periods as mercenary soldiers in the armies of France, Spain, Naples, and the Pope (Netting 1981:54). If more recent accounts of wage labor outside the community as miners, craftsmen, and waitresses represent past practices, the earnings of such workers were returned in large part to parents or conjugal families in the village. The export of labor power allowed the community to meet its needs for commodities and manufactured goods, pay taxes, and conduct internal exchange on a cash basis. Though the typical farming village was something of a commercial cul de sac, its continued existence on the alpine margins has always required active exchange with the capitalist European centers of the world system.

Just how porous is the membrane separating the peasant economy from wider spheres is demonstrated by two processes. In the first place, self-sufficiency in food has been both aided and diminished by contact with external agricultural sources. There is evidence that mountain agriculture was made substantially more productive and dependable by the adoption of the potato in the late eighteenth century (Netting 1981:159-168). On the other hand, the purchase of cheap maize meal from Italian sources in the early 1900's decreased Törbel's reliance on its own rye crop. Construction of a road and daily bus service with valley towns more recently allowed the buying of bread made from imported wheat. Price and convenience of the white loaves spelled the quick demise of local grain Aecker, grist mills, and bake ovens.

In the course of our research, it also became clear that a model of village wealth built on inheritance of agricultural resources within a closed system did not adequately represent reality. If the major determinant of an individual's property in farm land and buildings was the holdings of his parents (and the parents of his spouse) to which he was heir, then there should have been an association between father's and son's wealth. Quantitative data from tax valuations between 1851 and 1915 failed to disclose significant correlations between father's and son's property measured by average wealth, maximum wealth, wealth at marriage, or wealth at age 40 (McGuire and Netting 1982). Even controlling for the number of siblings with whom the partible inheritance was shared brought no better prediction of the wealth of the son. This considerable mobility up and down the village wealth spectrum suggested that inherited resources were less of an influence than we had thought, and that differences resulting from cash earned outside the village context and then invested in agricultural property were substantial. The hard summer work on the mule train postal transport or on railway construction tapped funds from the national economy that allowed peasant households to prosper without leaving the land.

Population Growth and Self-Regulation

Ecological anthropologists have found it difficult to resist the attractions of an hypothesized human ecosystem in which population was somehow regulated without direct imposition of Malthusian sanctions, and growth rates, if present, were extremely low. Simple models of populations maintaining themselves below carrying capacity have been criticized (Street 1969, Brush 1975, Hayden 1975, Jochim 1981), and theoretical constructs of "group selection" in adjusting numbers so as to maintain local resource stability have been questioned (Lewontin 1970, Bates and Lees 1979, Orlove 1980). My choice of a Swiss village with adequate vital records and our major effort to reconstruct 300 years of local historical demography were motivated in part by the wish to determine (1) if population equilibrium with fixed resources had in fact been achieved and (2) what was the role of social factors in influencing population growth. The more extensive the quantitative data to be analyzed, the more complex and partial become the answers to simple questions. We have found that the population of Törbel went through periods of quite marked growth as well as times of relative stability (Netting 1981:90-108). These dynamics have been responsive to a variety of internal factors, both biological, such as life expectancy, seasonality of conception, lactation, and nutritional patterns, and socio-cultural, such as age of marriage, celibacy, and inheritance (Netting 1981:109-158). But at no time could the fluctuations of local population be understood in isolation from surrounding populations.

Törbel's demographic distinctiveness from its neighbors was due less to topographical barriers than to the conscious imposition of legal and political barriers that successfully barred most in-migration. Unlike the rapid turnover of population characteristic of most European rural settlements (Schofield 1970, Gaunt 1977, Macfarlane 1978), Törbel's family lines showed remarkable continuity over time, and no new family names took root in the village from before 1700 to 1970 (Netting 1981:70-89). Village citizenship descended in the male line, and local statutes first written down in 1483 prohibited outsiders from enjoying communal rights in the forests, the alp, or the irrigation system. Without such resources to supplement privately owned farm lands, alpine agro-pastoralism would not have been possible. Formulation and enforcement of these rules was explicitly an activity of the corporate community (Wiegandt 1978) which thereby "closed" itself and effectively resisted population expansion due to immigration.

Village boundaries were, however, permeable to the movement of people in the other direction. It is possible that mountain populations have long followed a type of gravity model--that is, flows set up by birth rates higher than the replacement level and a comparatively isolated and healthy situation have taken surplus people from the highlands down to the valleys and plains. Törbel citizens have always left their homes permanently as mercenaries, farm laborers, artisans, and clerics, but new opportunities such as the colonizing of the Argentine interior, hotel jobs, or the construction industry in Swiss cities led to increased departures (Netting 1981:101-107). Without this safety-value, local population would have outstripped the potential of the territory to provide viable household subsistence holdings. The late nineteenth century demographic growth would have resulted in both rapid impoverishment and even higher than observed rates of celibacy if everyone had been forced to remain within the village. As it was, Törbel's export of people was one means by which the creation of a landless proletariat was avoided.

Does the conception of a community rejecting settlement by outsiders and allowing its own excess bodies to migrate mean that Törbel remained a homogeneous isolate in biological terms? Again, the self-contained ecosystem proves a poor analogy. Analysis of 917 marriages since 1703 shows that 14% of these were with women from other villages who took up residence in Törbel (Hagaman, Elias, and Netting 1978). Though this represents a very low rate of exogamy (cf. Levine 1977:39), the comparison of genetic contributions show that in-migrants accounted for nearly 38% of the 1970 gene pool, while the more numerous Törbel ancestors were responsible for only 62% of the living population's genetic constitution. It appears that, for reasons not entirely clear, the fertility of children of in-migrants was significantly higher than that of Törbel natives. A high endogamy rate evidently does not create the conditions of a genetic isolate. The social and economic constraints on marriages between Törbel men and women from other villages have not prevented a substantial flow of "foreign" genetic materials into the local population.

Cultural Conception, Folk Model, and Ecosystem

In order to adequately conceptualize the ecological relationships of human groups, it may be necessary to treat them as if they were parts of a functionally integrated, persisting, homeostatic, isolatable ecosystem. Since Geertz (1963:9) cogently recommended the biologists' term ecosystem, ecological anthropologists have used it with characteristic alacrity and looseness. The danger was not so much in the flexible inclusiveness by which ecosystem could embrace a wide range of cultural, biological, and physical variables as in the tendency for heuristically-drawn boundaries to harden into the familiar shapes of geographical regions or self-conscious social groups. The tendency is strong for the anthropologist to accept the members of a peasant closed corporate community at their word and emphasize the historic identity, economic self-sufficiency, population continuity, and socio-political autonomy that they claim for their village. The direct reality of participant observation combines with the villagers' own behavioral spheres of kinship, neighborliness, farm labor, and religious participation to emphasize everything that is bounded, familiar, and parochial. Living in Törbel, the very mountains and streams and serpentine road to the valley became for me identified with 600-year-old log houses and parchment documents and peasant genealogies vanishing into medieval mists. The marvel that any people had lived so long and so well on these alpine slopes led me to see and describe Törbel as an ecosystem. But for all the intricate adaptive mechanisms and the balance between human needs and environmental potentials, the village was never encapsulated or cut off. Subtly variable flows of goods and money and people tied it to a wider world. The significance of these movements of salt, iron, cattle, soldiers, coins, New World migrants, and in-marrying wives was often hidden from me and from my Törbel friends. But without these surges and trickles of energy in both directions, the local system could never have survived. The concept of a human ecosystem, like the idea of a niche or a lineage or a community, does not help us to create an airtight case but to model a useful, well-wrought urn of the imagination.

References Cited

Bates, Daniel G. and Susan H. Lees
1979 The Myth of Population Regulation. In Evolutionary Biology and Human Social Behavior: An Anthropological Perspective. N.A. Chagnon and W. Irons, eds. North Scituate, Mass.: Duxbury, pp. 273-289.

Brush, S.B.
1975 The Concept of Carrying Capacity for Systems of Shifting Cultivation. American Anthropologist 77:799-811.

Buchbinder, Georgeda
1978 Nutritional Stress and Post-Contact Population Decline among the Maring of New Guinea. In Malnutrition, Behavior, and Social Organization. L.S. Greene, ed. New York: Academic.

Dubois, A.
1965 Die Salzversorgung des Wallis 1500-1610: Wirtschaft und Politik. Winterthur: P.G. Keller.

Franscini, Stephan
1848 Neue Statistik der Schweiz. Bern: Haller'schen.

Gaunt, David
1977 Pre-Industrial Economy and Population Structure. Scandanavian Journal of History 2:183-210.

Geertz, Clifford
1963 Agricultural Involution: The Process of Ecological Change in Indonesia. Berkeley: University of California Press.

Hagaman, Roberta M., Walter S. Elias, Robert McC. Netting
1978 The Genetic and Demographic Impact of In-Migrants in a Largely Endogamous Community. Annals of Human Biology 5:505-515.

Hassan, Fekri A.
1979 Demography and Archaeology. Annual Review of Anthropology 8:137-160.

Hayden, B.
1975 The Carrying Capacity Dilemma. In Population Studies in Archaeology and Biological Anthropology. A.C. Swedlund, ed. Memoir 30, pp. 11-21. Washington: Society for American Archaeology.

Howell, Nancy
1979 Demography of the Dobe Area !Kung. New York: Academic.

Jochim, Michael A.
1981 Strategies for Survival: Cultural Behavior in an Ecological Context. New York: Academic.

Levine, David
1977 Family Formation in an Age of Nascent Capitalism. New York: Academic Press.

Lewontin, R.C.
1970 Units of Selection. Annual Review of Ecology 1:1-18.

Macfarlane, Alan
1978 The Origins of English Individualism: The Family, Property and Social Transition. New York: Cambridge University Press.

McGuire, Randall and Robert McC. Netting
1982 Levelling Peasants? The Demographic Implications of Wealth Differences in an Alpine Community. American Ethnologist 9:269-290.

Morren, G.E.B.
1977 From Hunting to Herding: Pigs and the Control of Energy in Montane New Guinea. In Subsistence and Survival: Rural Ecology in the Pacific. T.P. Bayliss-Smith and F.G. Feachem, eds. NewYork:Academic Press.

Netting, Robert McC.
1972 Of Men and Meadows: Strategies of Alpine Land Use. Anthropological Quarterly 45:132-44.
1974 The System Nobody Knows: Village Irrigation in the Swiss Alps. In Irrigation's Impact on Society. T.E. Downing and M. Gibson, eds. Tucson: University of Arizona Press, pp. 67-75.
1976 What Alpine Peasants Have in Common: Observations on Communal Tenure in a Swiss Village. Human Ecology 4:135-46.
1981 Balancing on an Alp: Ecological Change and Continuity in a Swiss Mountain Community. Cambridge: Cambridge University Press.

Orlove, Benjamin S.
1980 Ecological Anthropology. In Annual Review of Anthropology. B.J. Siegel, A.R. Beals, S.A. Tyler, eds. Palo Alto, CA: Annual Reviews, pp. 235-338.

Rappaport, Roy A.
1971a Nature, Culture, and Ecological Anthropology. In

Man, Culture, and Society. H.L. Shapiro, ed. London: Oxford University, pp. 237-267.

1971b The Flow of Energy in an Agricultural Society. Scientific American 244:116-23.

Richerson, P.J.
1977 Ecology and Human Ecology: A Comparison of Theories in the Biological and Social Sciences. American Ethnologist 4:1-26.

Schofield, R.S.
1970 Age-Specific Mobility in an Eighteenth Century Rural English Parish. Annales de Demographie Historique, pp. 261-74.

Street, J.
1969 An Evaluation of the Concept of Carrying Capacity. Professional Geographer 21:104-107.

Vayda, A.P. and B. McCay
1975 New Directions in Ecology and Ecological Anthropology. Annual Review of Anthropology 4:293-306.

Vayda, A.P. and R.A. Rappaport
1968 Ecology, Cultural and Non-Cultural. In Introduction to Cultural Anthropology. J.A. Clifton, ed. Boston: Houghton Mifflin, pp. 476-98.

Wiegandt, Ellen
1978 Past and Present in the Swiss Alps. In Hill Lands: Proceedings of an International Symposium. J. Luchok, J.D. Cawthon, M.J. Breslin, eds. Morgantown: West Virginia University Books, pp. 203-208.

Part 3

New Directions in Resolving the Problems of Hierarchical Level, Scale, and Data Collection

10. Remote Sensing, Discovery, and Generalizations in Human Ecology

Introduction[1]

In a recent survey by Ebert and Lyons (1980) of anthropologically-oriented uses of remote sensing, there is a clear emphasis on research into the human ecology of past and present populations. With regard to contemporary populations only, I will make the argument here that studies of human ecology and exploration of the boundaries of ecosystems have rarely had a method as powerful as that offered by remote sensing. For example, remote sensing can help discover unsuspected human and environmental interactions. It can also test how widely local observations apply to larger areas. In addition, the Olympian or "bird's eye" point of view which remote sensing affords makes possible quantitative

---

[1]Fieldwork has been made possible by grants from the National Science Foundation (NSF BNS-77-15622), from the City University of New York (CUNY PSC/BHE 11787E and 13981) and the Wenner-Gren Foundation for Anthropological Research. The invaluable support of Barbara Bury, Tina Cary, and Nora Conant as associates in the field is acknowledged. The advice of Arnold Hopf, agronomist and former administrator in Sigor, Francis Cherogony, District Commissioner of West Pokot, and Parmeet Singh, Central Bureau of Statistics, Nairobi, is also warmly acknowledged. An NSF Scientific Equipment Grant (#79-14954) made possible acquisition of the IMPAC image analysis system. The CUNY Computer Center has been most helpful in facilitating Landsat data transfers and analyses. The opinions expressed herein are those of the author and not necessarily those of the sponsoring agencies or the many persons who have generously contributed their time and commentaries.

measures of biotic associations, their areal extent, and their changes through time.

The synoptic quality of remote sensing data is such that identifying and quantifying "transitional areas" or ecotones is accomplished as readily as mapping major "heartlands" or ecozones. Furthermore, remote sensing is useful in estimating the impact of development projects on local peoples and their surroundings. Perhaps most generally, Arensberg (1981) has noted that partly because of the scales involved (entire populations, communities and settlements can be studied in their wider settings) and partly because of the many and various interactions involved remote sensing represents something of a return to the holistic point of view so important in anthropology and no less essential in ecology.

Of all the advantages which remote sensing offers the human ecologist, the emphasis here is on discovery of interrelationships between a population and its environment and testing wider applications of observations originally made within a strictly local frame of reference. Discovery and testing both involve problems in boundary definition and boundary recognition (see Ellen, this volume). Insofar as boundaries should be operationally defined so as to represent ongoing processes and these processes themselves are inferable from changes in plant cover, then remote sensing data may prove of great theoretical as well as practical value. A project now underway asks the question of the extent to which physiographic features (such as ridgelines), biotic features (such as broad classes of plant cover) and cultural distributions (such as subsistence systems) all do or do not coincide as boundaries . . . and what difference this makes in how one perceives ecosystem functioning as necessarily including human populations. Not all ecologists (especially those whose training has been in the "natural sciences") are willing to admit the human presence as a controlling force, let alone as "benign" a force as I have claimed the Pokot exert over their rangelands in East Africa. Full development of how remote sensing methods can help resolve such boundary recognition problems as: what is a region? what is a zone? what constitutes a transitional area or ecotone? is set aside in favor of a closer look at remote sensing as a tool for testing generalizations and for discovering interrelationships in human ecosystems.

Remote sensing data may be acquired on the ground, from conventional aircraft, and from satellites such as the Landsat series in polar orbits around Earth. All three data sources are integrated in what is called the "multi-stage" approach. This simply means that ground observations, all aerial photography, and analysis of the Landsat spectral data are integrated and brought to bear on a locally defined problem. The use of satellite data is emphasized here because it is still less well known than, for example, aerial photography. Features of the Landsat data are outlined below, and in the following section illustrations are made of the use of Landsat in testing local observations over large areas and as a tool for discovering a possible property of human ecosystems.

Remote sensing in East Africa is receiving major support from donor nations as well as host countries. This is not the place to summarize all the work that is going on but special mention must be made of the research by the Lund University group (Rapp and Hellden 1979), the US/AID Regional Remote Sensing Center in Nairobi, the Kenya Rangeland and Environmental Management Unit, the United Nations Global Environmental Monitoring System, and, among individual efforts, the pastoralist human ecology project in Turkana District (see Little, et al., this volume). Much of this research, like my own, shares a common stress on active, on-ground investigations combined with the use of remote sensing. Priscilla Reining (1972, 1974) was one of the first to insist on the integration of anthropological fieldwork with remote sensing. My own work in the Pokot Test and Monitoring (TAM) area in Kenya is emphasized in what follows simply because illustrative materials are more accessible.

Some Elements of Satellite Remote Sensing

Because excellent texts on remote sensing exist (e.g., Lillesand and Kiefer 1979) and summaries for the non-specialist have been available for some time (Hielkema 1980; Conant 1978; Lyons and Avery 1977; Conant, Reining, and Lowes 1975), the following remarks are offered more as a reminder than as a complete summary of the Landsat system. First of all, all Landsat data are, by law, entirely in the public domain and can be ordered by anyone. The system design is such that each Landsat satellite is over the same area every 18 days, at the same time of day (about 9:30 a.m., local time). The repeatibility of the system offers the rare opportunity of, in a way, returning to the "field" for further data gathering and making measures of change. The temporal dimension of remote sensing is too often neglected in favor of "one shot" analyses.

The primary data in remote sensing are the result of complex energy-matter interactions on the Earth's surface. The Landsat satellites acquire the data by sensing the

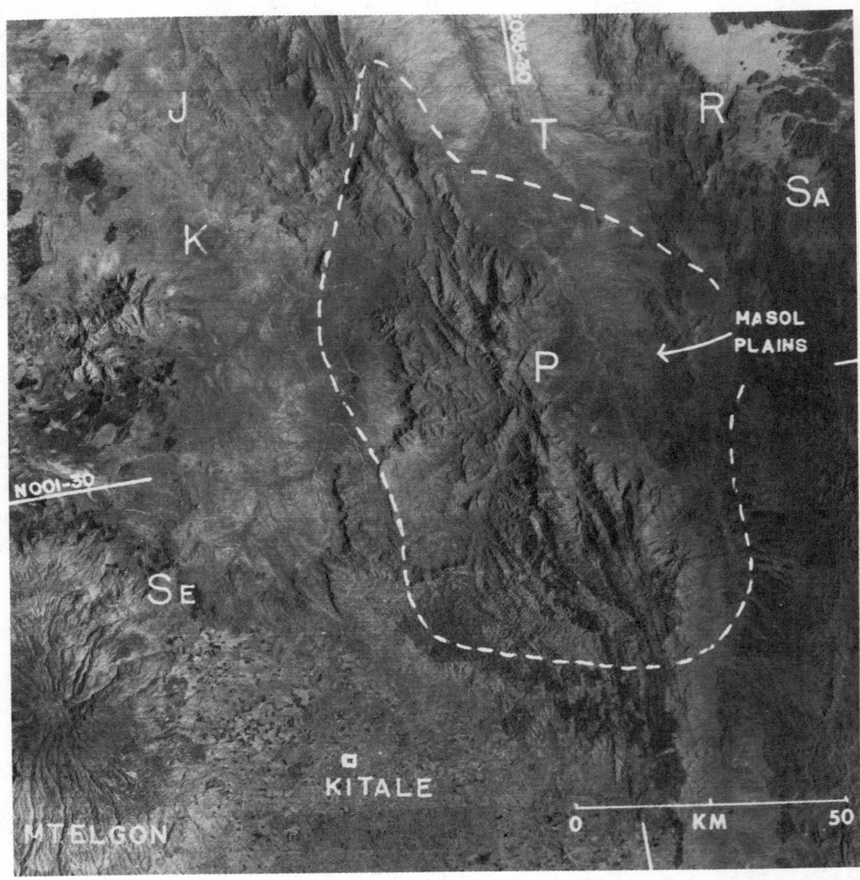

Figure 10.1 The Pokot (P) in northwestern Kenya. Landsat MSS scene 21107-06413, Band 6, 02/02/78. The scale is about 1:1,000,000. The dotted line shows the approximate area of highlands and lowlands exploited by Pokot farmers and herders using the traditional subsistence techniques of shifting cultivation and open range livestock management. These subsistence techniques are still practiced by most Pokot and their neighbors: Karamojong (K), Jie (J), Turkana (T), Rendile (R), Samburu (Sa), and some Sebei (Se). In 1974 the Pokot fled from the Masol Plains because of uncontrolled raiding, and settled in the area marked as P. See text and Figure 10.2. Note that in Figure 10.1 traditional farms are not visible primarily because of their small size and irregular shapes. Industrial and mechanized agriculture in the area of Kitale and the lower slopes of Mt. Elgon shows up as a mosaic of rectilinear field patterns.

reflected energy in 4 bands of the electromagnetic spectrum. When in range of a ground receiving station, the data are radioed to Earth. A present Landsat "scene" consists of more than 30×10^6 data values which, when arranged spatially, represent an area 185 x 185 km on the Earth's surface. Such a scene is composed of more than 7×10^6 picture elements or "pixels." Every pixel can be characterized by its values for the 4 bands sensed by the multi-spectral scanner (MSS) aboard the satellite. The resolving power of the MSS aboard the first 3 Landsat satellites has been about 70m; Landsat 4 will have a resolution of about 30m; the European Space Agency "Spot" satellite, when and if it is launched in a year or so, will have a resolution of perhaps 10m.

The primary Landsat data are reflectance values; they can be used to construct imagery, but this imagery is strictly a secondary product. The imagery looks like a photograph (see Figures 10.1 and 10.2) but it is not; and because the imagery is visually familiar, it is often treated as a primary source from which interpretations can be made directly. In some cases this may work, but in others it will not. For example, the large fields maintained by commercial agriculturalists are visible in the lower part of Plate 1, a Landsat 2 MSS image of Mt. Elgon and northwestern Kenya, and a road project and airstrip are clearly evident in Plate 2, which is a Landsat "return beam vidicon" (RBV) image of part of the same area as in Plate 1. But nowhere in either the MSS or RBV imagery are the swiddens, settlements, or herding areas of traditional subsistence systems to be "seen" as such in the imagery. They can be inferred from the spectral data from which the imagery is made. The full power of the system only becomes available through computer assisted analysis of the original data values.

"Improvement" in the resolving powers of the satellites may obscure important large scale environmental relationships by presenting the user with too much detail or with too small an area for the relationship to be expressed. For some purposes--for example, detecting possible locust breeding sites among vegetation "blooms" over vast desert areas (Hielkema 1980)--spectral values related to a large area pixel (as in the NOAA weather satellites) are preferable to those tied to a pixel of much smaller area (as in Landsat). One NOAA satellite image covers an area about 500 times that of a Landsat scene.

Another reason for not treating the imagery as a primary data source is that often an image will be computer "enhanced" so that edge relationships are narrowed and "border" pixels (those having mixed or ambiguous spectral

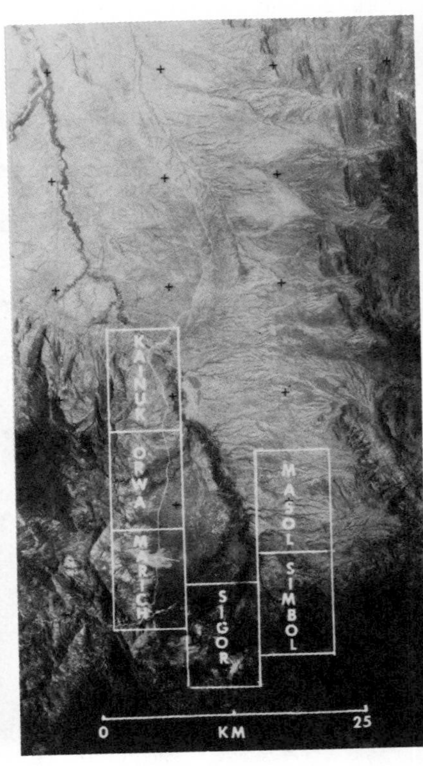

Figure 10.2 Landsat RBV image 30950-06584-B, 10/10/80. The scale is about 1:500,000. The image on the left is unretouched (with the exception of the scale bar) and shows the area in Figure 10.1 under the P and west of the arrow indicating the Masol Plains. The NORAD road project shows up as a north trending line with an airstrip perpendicular to it in the lower portion of the image. The image on the right is identical except for the square brackets showing the approximate locations of the IMPAC spectral data analysis units. Each IMPAC analysis area is about 7 x 10 km. Changes in the spectral data are related to the spread of <u>Acacia spp.</u> in the Masol and Simbol analysis areas. An increase in vegetation patchiness is related to intensification of human activities as one moves south along the NORAD road from Kainuk to Marich. See text.

values) are assigned to one category or another. In such fashion "sharper" images can be built up. Cosmetic enhancements, however, may disguise what is so important in the real world--the fuzzy areas of transition or ecotones between contrasting zones. This directly affects the problem, mentioned earlier, of recognizing and operationally defining boundaries and boundary related phenomena such as ecotones. Perhaps the imagery should be left "unretouched" and used as a guide into the original spectral data on the computer tapes. These data can be analyzed by programs available for use on large "main frame" computers, using a program like ORSER (Turner, Applegate and Merambeck 1978), for example, or more recently on "desk top" microcomputers using an interactive analysis program like IMPAC (Egbert 1979).

The Pokot TAM Area in East Africa

National Science Foundation (NSF) funding and Government of Kenya approval to establish the Pokot Test and Monitoring (TAM) area was awarded in 1977. In effect, this meant a return to the area which was first studied in 1961 as part of Walter Goldschmidt's original project *Culture and Ecology in East Africa*.[2]

Plate 1 is an image of a full Landsat scene with Mt. Elgon in Uganda in the southwest corner. The scale is approximately 1 to 1 x 10^6. The dotted line roughly encloses "Pokotland," the highlands and plains exploited by Pokot farmers and herders of West Pokot District, Rift Valley Province. Unlike the Maasai, who in the colonial era were split off from their farming base and today are almost totally dependent on outsiders for grain, the Pokot farmers and herders have remained in close touch with each other, with the exchange of personnel and surplus produce remaining very much alive (Conant 1965, 1982).

The neighbors of the Pokot are Karamojong, Jie, Turkana, Rendile, Samburu, and Sebei. The large-field systems of intensive agriculturalists and livestock managers of the Kitale/Trans Nzoia area are clearly evident in the lower portion of Plate 1.

Plate 2 is an RBV image collected by Landsat 3 on October 1, 1980. Its spectral range is close to "panchromatic"; the nominal scale is 1:500,000. The area

---

[2]Supported by NSF Award G-11713 and Public Health Service grant MH-04097.

shown is approximately that under the "P" of Pokot in Plate 1. On the left in Plate 2 the RBV image is shown unmodified; on the right IMPAC microcomputer analysis units have been superimposed. Each IMPAC unit is about 7 x 10 km.

Generalizing a Local Observation over a Wider Area

Analysis of these IMPAC units for 1973 and 1978 has helped confirm a complex and unexpected relationship between Pokot herding families and the rangelands they have been exploiting on the Masol Plains for many hundreds of years and possibly a millenium. The relationship has to do with the maintenance of an extensive grassy cover needed by Pokot Zebu cattle and the containment, through the browsing activities of goats and the annual burning over of the rangelands, of thorn bush and thicket involving several varieties of *Acacia* spp. Acacia, if not kept in check, spreads rapidly at the expense of the grassy cover.

This is what happened beginning in 1974 when the Pokot were forced from the Masol Plains by uncontrolled raiding for cattle. Many of the raids were mounted from Uganda and were carried out with motor vehicles and automatic weapons. Unlike traditional raiding patterns in which casualties were deliberately kept low, the new raids involved the attempt at annihilation of Pokot women, children, and men in their camps and homesteads. The herding families abandoned the Masol Plains.

In less than 5 years nearly impassable bush-forests or dense thickets of thorn tree (*Acacia* spp.) grew up. In 1973 about 24% or almost 2000 ha. of the Masol rangeland area analyzed (8000 ha.) were in bush/thicket. About 38% or almost 3100 ha. were grassy. In 1978, for the same analysis area, dense thicket amounted to almost 50% of the area and the grassy cover was down to 13% (Conant 1982). In other words, the plant cover which developed in the human *absence* was far less benign than the mixture of grass and shrub and trees maintained by the human *presence*. And while there has been almost certainly an absolute increase in plant biomass in parts of Masol, this increase can be considered--from the point of view of the Pokot and Turkana (and no one else was using the area)--a case of "green desertification."

It should be noted the original observations about the loss of grasslands and the spread of Acacia were made by the Pokot herders themselves (Komolingolei, Lomortum, and others) during fieldwork in 1977. A casual observation was made about what had been happening since the rangelands had been abandoned in 1974. This remark touched off further queries, leading to confirmation of the spread of Acacia for a large part of the Masol and Turkana plains by analysis of the Landsat spectral data. That is, remote sensing was used to test how widely a local observation could be generalized over a larger area. The conclusion reached seems of some significance: in parts of East Africa traditional subsistence activities are necessary for the maintenance of a benign environment as the local people themselves perceive it.

This finding leads in turn to other considerations which illustrate Arensberg's remark, noted earlier, about the holistic, interactive aspects of remote sensing as applied to human ecology. We could ask what was important in the traditional herding subsistence system in maintaining a check on the spread of the thorn tree and, hence, the maintenance of the grassy cover? The answer seems to be that among Pokot, as well as some of their neighbors, women are the main managers of goats, which can outnumber cattle by as many as 10 to 1. Since goats are the day-to-day "predators" of Acacia, their management by women may be crucial for the survival of the men-managed cattle. Thus we are encouraged to reconsider not only the importance of goats in East African mixed herds but also the role of women as environmental managers in East African herding societies.

Discovering a Complex Interrelationship

Plate 2 shows the existence of a major road running along the western edge of the Masol plains. The road continues on into Turkana District to the north and eventually will go all the way to the Kenya's frontier with the Sudan. The road, which was originally a minor track, has been a project of the Norwegian Agency for Development (NORAD). To facilitate the project an airstrip was constructed alongside the road and is also seen in Plate 2. The road and airstrip first began to show up in the Landsat data in 1973/74, at about the time Pokot herding families were abandoning the Masol plains because of the intense raiding there. Pioneer refugee settlements were set up east of the NORAD road in the foothills of the Cherangani and Sekerr mountains.

In testing for the spread of Acacia as described above, it was noted that the data for the NORAD road area indicated increasingly patchy vegetation as one moved south. This violates a common expectation in Pokotland: patchiness of plant cover tends to increase as one moves north into drier areas. IMPAC analysis units were set up as shown in Plate 2 where they are labeled as K for Kainuk, O for Orwa and M for Marich. The IMPAC areas shown as Mas for Masol, Sim for Simbol, and Sig for Sigor are all away from the road. They contrast with the refugee settlements in terms of elevation, spoil and plant cover as well as settlement history, size, and intensity of ongoing activities.

The pastoral families in the K/O/M areas were engaged in some shifting cultivation as well as management of the small herds remaining to them after the flight from Masol. Subsistence efforts were areally extensive but seemed to involve minimal disturbance of the surrounding areas.

The Marich "M" area, however, showed a sharp contrast in spectral values between its northern portion where there were some refugee families and the southern portion where there was (and still is) a major work camp for road construction purposes. Spectral values for the north of the Marich area were relatively homogeneous and were interpreted as indicating a light but not particularly patchy plant cover. In the south, however, the values were highly mixed, indicating patchy vegetation with bare soil between patches. By "mixed" are meant the percent standard deviations (%SDs) for all four MSS bands, plus a fifth band which is the ratio of Bands 2 and 4. This band has been found useful in compensating for factors affecting all four bands equally (Lillesand and Kiefer 1979:378-379) as well as in estimating rangeland quality (Tucker 1978). The %SDs for 1973 and 1978 were measured for each of the IMPAC areas in Plate 2. From 1973 to 1978 changes in %SDs for the southernmost Marich area were +10.7; in the intermediate Ortum IMPAC area they were +7.5; and for the northern Kainuk area they were +4.8.

A series of comparisons were then made with the second series of IMPAC analysis area which were all located <u>away</u> from the NORAD road and which all have different elevations and soil/plant associations. But parts of the Masol and Simbol areas are similar to the refugee road areas insofar as they have small populations engaged in light cultivation and the management of small herds. In the Masol and Simbol "refugee" areas vegetation is less patchy than in Sigor, which for many years has been operated as a "frontier" administrative outpost. Among other features, Sigor has a work camp, police barracks, and a hospital/aid station. Human activities in the Sigor area are intensive; like much of the area around the newer Marich work camp, spectral values are highly mixed indicating once again patchy vegetation associated with intense human activity.

The 1973 to 1978 changes of %SDs in the second series of IMPAC analysis units were +8.3 for Sigor, +6.1 for the refugee area in Simbol and +4.6 for Masol. The density of population in Marich and Sigor areas, the mechanical manipulation of soil with machinery, the stripping of vegetation by workers in search of fuel, and clearing still other areas for motor yards, garages, administration, and living quarters, all contribute to exceedingly uneven plant cover and hence the most mixed spectral values for Sigor in the off-road series and also for southern Marich in the on-road series.

Thus a preliminary discovery is that increases in %SDs may have as much to do with intensification of human activities as it does with settlement history, size, or local environment factors (such as a north-south cline in diminished rainfall, so that everything else being equal, the expectation is of more patchy vegetation to the north). In the present case, not everything else was equal, and intensified cultural activities in Marich and Sigor are the likely proximal cause of the increase in %SDs and vegetation "patchiness" to the south rather than to the north. Investigation is now underway to see if different areas in different environments but sharing a similar degree of heterogeneity in spectral response also share similar levels and kinds of cultural activities. For example, the Kainuk (K) IMPAC analysis area in Plate 2 also contains, besides a refugee settlement, a Dutch minor irrigation scheme on the border of Pokot and Turkana Districts. The data are being examined to see if the intensified activity in Kainuk shares the same statistical patterns (%SDs in all 4 bands as well as the ratioed bands) through time as the Marich and Sigor areas. Additional Landsat tapes are being analyzed for intermediate dates to see if the discovered relationships between intensification of activity and increasingly mixed spectral responses hold up through time as well as space.

Conclusion

Remote sensing can contribute to human ecology by providing a method for testing local observations for their wider applicability. If this represents a shift from particularistic studies to more testable generalized findings, so much the better. A second contribution of remote sensing is as a tool for discovering unexpected interrelationships between human activities and the surroundings in which they take place: that is, the entire ecosystem, including humans. Projects intensifying agricultural and rangeland use are likely to have effects far beyond those of the project sites themselves. While the use of remote sensing in developing areas is nowhere near as perfected or routinized as Paul and Mascarenhas (1981) suggest, there seems little question that spectral data analysis will become an increasingly common tool in the future. But neither now, nor then, will remote sensing ever replace investigation on the ground. It seems likely that in the best anthropological tradition more fieldwork rather than less will be necessary as remote sensing becomes a tool for discovery and as a method for extending generalizations about ecosystem relationships over wider areas.

References Cited

Arensberg, Conrad
1981 Cultural Holism through Interactional Systems. American Anthropologist 83:562-81.

Conant, Francis P.
1982 Thorns Paired, Sharply Recurved: Cultural Controls and Rangeland Quality in East Africa. In Anthropology and Desertification. Brian Spooner, ed. London: Academic Press. In press.
1978 The Use of Landsat Data in Studies of Human Ecology. Current Anthropology 19(2):382-4.
1965 Korok: A Variable Unit of Physical and Social Space among the Pokot of East Africa. American Anthropologist 67(2):429-434.

Conant, Francis P. and Tina Cary
1977 A First Interpretation of East African Swiddening via Computer-assisted Analysis of 3 Landsat Tapes. Proceedings, 1977 Symposium on Machine Processing of Remotely Sensed Data. Laboratory for Applications of Remote Sensing, Purdue University, West Lafayette, Indiana.

Conant, Francis P., Priscilla Reining and Susan Lowes
1975 Satellite Potentials for Anthropological Studies of Subsistence Activities and Population Change. Report of a National Science Foundation Research Workshop. Washington, D.C.

Ebert, James I. and Thomas R. Lyons
1980 Remote Sensing on Archaeology, Cultural Resources Treatment and Anthropology: the United States of America in 1979. Aerial Archaeology 5:1-19.

Egbert, Dwight
1979 IMPAC: Image Analysis Package for Microcomputers. Greenport, N.Y.: Egbert Scientific Software.

Hielkema, Jelle U.
1980 Remote Sensing Techniques and Methodologies for

Monitoring Ecological Conditions for Desert Locust Population Development. Rome: Food and Agriculture Organization.

Lillesand, Thomas M. and Ralph W. Kiefer
1979 Remote Sensing and Image Interpretation. New York: Wiley and Sons.

Lyons, T.R. and T.E. Avery
1977 Remote Sensing: A Handbook for Archaeologists and Cultural Resource Managers. Washington, D.C.: National Park Service, U.S. Department of Interior.

Paul, Charles K. and Adolfo C. Mascarenhas
1981 Remote Sensing in Development. Science 214:139-145.

Rapp, Anders and Ulf Hellden
1979 Research on Environmental Monitoring Methods for Land-Use Planning in African Drylands. Lund, Sweden: Lunds Universities Naturgeografiska Institution.

Reining, Priscilla
1974 ERTS-1 Data and Anthropology: Carrying Capacity Estimates for Sites in Upper Volta and Niger. Paper presented at the annual meetings, American Anthropological Association, Mexico City.
1972 ERTS Image Analysis: Preliminary Report on ID# 1080-10163, Site North of Segou, Republic of Mali, West Africa. Springfield, Virginia: National Technical Information Service.

Tucker, Compton J.
1978 Red and Photographic Infrared Linear Combinations for Monitoring Vegetation. Greenbelt, Maryland: NASA Technical Memorandum 79620, Goddard Space Flight Center.

Tucker, Compton J., William H. Jones, William A. Kley, and Gunnar J. Sundstrom
1981 A Three-Band Hand-Held Radiometer for Field Use. Science 211:281-283.

Turner, B.J., D.N. Applegate and B.F. Merambeck
1978 Satellite and Aircraft Multispectral Scanner Digital Data User Manual. Office for Remote Sensing of Earth Resources (ORSER). University Park, Pa.: The Pennsylvania State University.

Daniel R. Gross

11. Ecosystems and Methodological Problems in Ecological Anthropology

General ecology is hierarchically subordinate to evolutionary biology. It deals with the structure and function of living systems and provides insight into the mechanisms of microevolutionary change, particularly that of selection. The ecosystem concept is a leading tool of ecology, but it is understood in different ways by different authorities. For some, it refers to any delimitable area of nature; for others it refers to specific models of energy flow or nutrient cycling. Some definitions attach notions concerning change and stability in ecosystems. All the definitions include the notion of a system whose variables interact in definite ways, including elements of the living and non-living environment. Other papers in the volume have critiqued some uses of the ecosystem concept, e.g., to assume homeostasis without specific evidence, to reify the ecosystem as if it were an organism itself, to confuse different levels of analysis and others. These are weighty criticisms and should be taken into account in any use of the ecosystem concept.

One utility of the ecosystem concept in anthropology has been to extend the ecological approach first proposed by Steward to cover aspects of human behavior as belonging to a more general class of biobehavioral phenomena and not to a presumably unique class of cultural phenomena. Within this general paradigm, a number of original and useful studies emerged such as Rappaport's (1968), Vayda's (1961), Netting's (1968), and Thomas' (1973). These investigators asked some serious questions about the problems posed by human ecological studies although none so serious, in my opinion, as to require that the ecological approach be discarded.

One of the most impressive gains of the ecosystems approach was that it led investigators to make more and better measurements in the field than had previously been attempted and then to investigate the interrelations of variables. Not only could environmental and behavioral variables be precisely measured, but also quantification made possible mathematical modeling and testing of hypotheses. Precision itself, as critics pointed out, was not sufficient to establish the validity of some of the claims that were made. The present state of affairs appears to be one in which even more and better data are required in order to validate ecologically-oriented hypotheses. This has both advantages and dangers. The advantage is that our studies will become more reliable and replicable as the scope and precision of measurement increases. There is a danger of becoming obsessed with measurement, hyper-specialized and chronically unable to complete studies. A further danger, on which I shall comment later, is that ecological studies may become so micro-focused that their relevance for broader phenomena of widespread occurrence may be seriously reduced.

The ecosystem concept, while it may have led some investigators astray, provided a guide to the interactions between people and their environments. For any particular problem, reference to the ecosystem may suggest the kinds of measurements to be made in the field, and it provides models of how these variables may be related. Upon first confronting the ecosystem concept, one might gain the impression that the investigator must measure virtually everything in order to understand the interrelationships in nature. In practice, this is seldom the case. Ecological anthropologists are not generally simple-minded inductivists who relate everything to everything else. They usually examine the relationship between a limited number of variables in accordance with a model of ecosystem functioning, e.g., a model of predator-prey relationships, a model of an optimal diet (see Smith, in this volume), or a model of nutrient cycling in a particular biome. In any given case, a large number of potentially influential variables must be ignored in order to examine the specific question at hand. Thus, paradoxically, while the ecosystem concept proposes that everything is systematically related to everything else, investigators in the field restrict the number of variables to a selected few. The use of an ecosystem model, in biology or in anthropology, cannot substitute for theory that is coherent and that can yield testable hypotheses.

Hypothesis-testing--or what many anthropologists call "problem-oriented research"-- has become dominant in contemporary academic anthropology. Very often the hypothesis is only implicit, or it is stated in the form of a critique of a previous theory. For example, an ethnographer goes to the field to try to show the inadequacy of a model of peasant cognition as a way of understanding peasant agricultural decisions. Ecological theory, and the ecosystem concept, may be useful in orienting the formulation of hypotheses and framing of a research design. In my opinion, we cannot frequently draw hypotheses directly from ecological theory. Rather, the concept of the ecosystem serves as a framework within which we can formulate and test hypotheses. Thus ecological theory in anthropology takes a hybrid form, combining with ideas generated in other contexts or even under different paradigms. At a minimal level, the investigator may choose a biobehavioral variable as the indirect measure of something he or she wants to examine, e.g., relative well-being. At another level, an investigator may examine the relative success of two populations in adapting to an environment.

Ecological research is compatible with materialist and political economic paradigms in anthropology. This is because the starting point of their analysis is the way in which people interact with nature in order to produce and reproduce. Some critics attack the ecological position for allegedly treating religion and other aspects of culture as epiphenomena (e.g., Godelier 1972). In spite of the apparent differences, there is still much on which ecologically-oriented anthropologists and political economists ought to agree. There is general agreement that a particular social formation is the outcome of an historical process and that populations and cultures cannot be investigated independently of their context. Both approaches stress the influence of production and exchange. Finally, both approaches are nomothetic, seeking to establish valid generalizations about sociocultural development.

I should like to devote most of the remaining space to a consideration of some basic methodological issues faced by ecological anthropologists, and others with similar objectives. The basic question may be stated as follows: how can anthropologists with their particular research techniques stressing intimate, contextualized knowledge of living human communities, and their recognized expertise in conducting case studies, achieve valid generalizations about social and ecological process? It may be helpful to examine the methodological forms which many of our studies take in order to clarify the benefits and pitfalls of each.

Let us take as a point of departure, a study designed to explain the consequences of a particular kind of change in a particular area or region, e.g., the introduction of a new cash crop in northeastern Brazil, the development of European slaving in West Africa, or perhaps the response of the Plains Indians to the horse. There are many other kinds of questions to be asked; I have merely picked a very common type. There are at least three basic ways of approaching such questions; all are aimed at the same basic objectives, i.e., understanding the basic processes of stability and change in human society. The different modes may be summarized under the following headings: comparative analysis, cross-sectional analysis, and longitudinal analysis. Each is a variety of the experimental method in a context in which the variables cannot be manipulated as in a laboratory. The principal obstacle which these approaches attempt to overcome is that social processes unfold within time frames which often make them inaccessible to direct observation. The three modes are different ways of conducting studies which take time into consideration but which are more controlled than conventional historical research. The three modes are compatible with each other and often are employed simultaneously. The choice of mode depends on the constraints of time and resources on the investigation.

<u>Comparative analysis</u> involves selecting homologous social units widely separated in space which are believed to be similar in certain aspects of structure and function. Often such comparisons are conducted through the literature or comparison of the community studied. Techniques are rarely standardized, and the investigator must proceed on the assumption that significant differences are <u>not</u> due to differences in field technique. Comparative analysis can yield generalizations about causal or developmental processes, but it is most revealing when correlations can be detected between variables in systems which differ in one or more key respects. Because rigorous controls cannot usually be applied, fine-grained statistical analysis is usually impossible. Reliance on the literature for cases inevitably skews the sample in favor of the biases of the available literature.

There are many examples of comparative analysis. One which may be a kind of "classic" is Murphy and Steward's "Tappers and Trappers" (1956) which compared two primarily village-organized societies, the Mundurucú who occupy a tropical environment in Central Brazil and the Montagnais-Naskapi who occupy the sub-arctic boreal forests of Labrador. The comparison deals with the introduction of trader-based commodity exchange involving the gathering of a dispersed resource (natural latex for the Mundurucu, animal pelts for the Montagnais-Naskapi). The study suggests that both societies, while different in many respects, converged on a family-level of organization due primarily to the organizational demands of their productive system. The novelty of the study lies in the fact that the habitats and earlier cultural styles of the two groups are highly contrastive. The proposed mechanism accounting for the convergence is very compelling, and nothing reported in the two studies suggests that any other factor might be responsible. Nevertheless, it is possible that some other variable, unnoticed by the investigators, was in fact the cause of the convergence. Additional case studies would help to clarify this issue, especially if they were chosen in such a way as to avoid excluding cases where the connection does not obtain.

Cross-sectional analysis is usually conducted in a field setting within a single, relatively homogeneous area. The purpose of cross-sectional analysis is to detect differences in otherwise similar segments of cultural or social units that have been exposed to known influences which may have produced changes. Cross-sectional analysis also aims at discovering regularities in processes occurring over time spans longer than the time allotted for the investigation. It accomplishes this by treating different segments of a unit as if they represented different points in a time series. For this reason, cross-sectional analysis may be particularly important in applied studies where recommendations must be forthcoming within a short period.

The basic idea of this mode is to examine different communities or segments of a larger population which have been exposed to known influences at different points in time. The key assumption in cross-sectional analysis is that the various units of analysis differ only in regard to a specific, known influence. Where the influence is a recent disturbance, the assumption is that all units were once very similar to each other. In other words, cross-sectional analysis attempts to find comparable units in order to hold all variables but one constant. Measurement techniques can often be standardized in cross-sectional analysis and samples of adequate size can be drawn.

The assumption that two communities are comparable may be difficult to demonstrate. In fact this is one of the thorniest issues of contemporary ethnography. The absence of conventions and criteria for establishing the comparability of two human groups is a reflection of the underdevelopment of anthropological theory. In fact, one of the most frequent objections raised to ecological research in anthropology is that the investigator has not considered some additional factor which was not a variable in the original research. A highly particularist focus is still dominant in many areas of ethnology. Multiple events may impinge in different ways on otherwise comparable communities. The investigator in the field may have difficulty in ascertaining exactly what perturbations took place and just when they occurred. Increasing the sample size increases the confidence that exotic or unknown influences have not affected the results. But unless resources are unlimited, it may be impossible to build a large sample precisely because of the level of detail at which so much anthropological research is carried out.

An example of this mode is a study done by Gross et al. (1979) of acculturation among four native groups of Central Brazil. The four groups live in similar (but not identical) habitats, speak related languages and have similar histories. Through time-allocation studies, it was determined that two of the groups were far more involved in market exchange than the others. The history of each village population was reconstructed using documents and native informants and approximate dates were reconstructed using an "event calendar." The study revealed the effects of long-term environmental circumscription on shifting cultivators. As the availability of land diminished and fallow periods perforce reduced, the productivity in food per unit of labor went down, and once abundant nutrients became scarce. These factors account for the variation in commitment to market activities. Other ecological studies using cross-sectional analysis include Moran's comparison (1981) of different settlements along the Trans-Amazon Highway in Brazil in which he identified colonist experience with tropical forests as a key factor in explaining variation in cropping and other farm management strategies.

Cross-sectional analysis is more powerful than comparative analysis because greater standardization in measurement can be achieved and because the investigator is more assured of the comparability of the units. The trade-off between ethnographic detail and sample size still obtains, however, and the possibility that some unknown factor has affected the dependent variable cannot be definitely eliminated.

Longitudinal analysis is possible when there is sufficient time to observe directly the changes taking place in a community at various points in time. Because of the rates at which sociocultural change occurs, longitudinal analysis may require tens of years to yield results. But, there is no more reliable means for understanding change over time in human populations. In longitudinal analysis, processes unfolding in time may be directly observed together with the factors thought to be responsible for them. One assumption which longitudinal analysis makes is that the particular time span over which observations are made is "typical" in terms of time-dependent variables such as rainfall and "historical" factors such as warfare, etc. In longitudinal analysis, there usually is no question of comparability of units since specific sites may be revisited repeatedly. Longitudinal analysis is perhaps the "ultimate" in terms of controls and accuracy in naturalistic observation. Its greatest drawback lies in the time-span required to conduct longitudinal studies. Planners can rarely wait long enough to obtain results from longitudinal studies before implementing programs. Some familiar examples of longitudinal studies in anthropology include Mervyn Meggitt's long term study of the Mae Enga (1977) and the long-term field research conducted by Richard Lee (1980), Henry Harpending (1970), Silberbauer (1981), Yellen (1977), and others among the !Kung San of Botswana. Nevertheless, even when sites can be revisited over intervals as long as several decades, it may be difficult to observe processes of change which unfold very slowly. The modern world with vastly accelerated communication and transportation presents yet another problem. The very rapidity of change means that changes often occur in bundles combining several factors which we would prefer to maintain analytically separate. Thus, even the most painstaking longitudinal study of a human community may not be adequate to permit discrimination of the particular factors at work.

Archeologists, and ethnohistorians, of course, have the luxury of analyzing change over very long periods of time. The main drawback for archeologists is that they cannot observe the changes themselves taking place but must rely on the physical residues of human activity as evidence. Ethnohistorians must rely on the sometimes haphazardly recorded evidence which has accumulated. An example of longitudinal analysis in ethnohistory is provided by Adams and Kasakoff's novel study of marriage patterns in New England communities reported on in this volume. Even though they cannot directly verify the accuracy of the data they are using, they can have some confidence that the demographic variables they employ were measured with relatively high accuracy and validity.

As stated above, the three modes of analysis are not mutually exclusive and they may be interwoven in such a way as to provide important support for each other. For many research problems, an optimal field technique might be a hybrid, "micro-macro" approach. First, micro-focused field studies should be carried out in one or more communities, or other social units, in order to gain a first-hand account of the actual social and ecological dynamics. If possible, the selection of units of analysis should be "stratified" in accordance with known variation within the inclusive social unit. Micro-focused field studies lasting for periods of months or years are still the most accurate way of obtaining valid and reliable data on social and ecological structure and function. This is because the ethnographer gains intimate knowledge of local matters, witnesses more aspects of life, and may be permitted to observe much more than any casual visitor. Still, there is no way to verify how representative the local level study was unless the investigator casts a wider net. This is done by systematically investigating selected parameters of the phenomenon under investigation by means of a random sample at the regional level (however this may be defined). In other words, the ethnographer conducts a survey to verify the extent to which processes observed at a local level are replicated globally.

One example of this approach may be found in Gross and Underwood's study of undernutrition induced by work and related caloric deficits among the children of sisal workers in Northeastern Brazil. The process was first identified by detailed dietary intake monitoring at the level of the commensal unit (usually a co-resident household). One class of worker households was judged especially liable to caloric deficits because of extraordinarily high energy requirements of tasks performed by the principal wage earners. The extent of this phenomenon was verified by a survey of 100 households which showed that children in certain workers' households were more likely to show nutritional deficits than others (Gross and Underwood 1971). The next step, unfortunately not feasible, would be to compare survey results for different communities within the region which showed different levels of involvement with the sisal industry. This would constitute a cross-sectional analysis whose results would theoretically show a greater tendency toward undernutrition in communities where the dependence on sisal was greater. Finally, a longitudinal study may be undertaken, in which the same individual children and communities surveyed in 1968 would be surveyed again, say, in 1988, to determine how the influence of sisal agriculture had actually been played out in the long run. One paradox of the longitudinal method is that other conditions might have changed, making the points along the time series non-comparable. Thus, under some conditions, cross-sectional analysis may be more accurate.

There has been an unfortunate tendency, in recent years, to cast doubt on the validity of an ecological model. While critics have pointed to real shortcomings, the result has been that many anthropologists have either prematurely abandoned the ecological approach or engaged in highly particularistic data-collecting sprees. The early proponents of the ecological approach (e.g., Steward, Sahlins, Service) urged that it be comparative and they inaugurated a new era of studies which were very influential, e.g., Sahlins' Social Stratification in Polynesia (1958), and Steward's People of Puerto Rico (1956). As later investigators urged the adoption of the ecosystem as the principal unit of analysis, the objections of critics became more harsh. But the reaction has been out of all proportion with what was proposed. Pejorative phrases like "vulgar materialism" have been heaped on the ecologists because they sought to understand cultural behavior in its environmental context.

One line of response has been to suggest that the only context within which to understand culture is within the meaningful aspects of culture itself (e.g., Sahlins 1976). Another tack has been to proclaim that the social organization of production has causal priority over adapative behavior (e.g., Godelier 1972). The consequence of these approaches is to return anthropology to 1915, to Kroeber's proclamations that anthropology is a purely historical science, that it is folly to speak of causality and that "culture comes from culture." The ecological approach and cultural materialism in general suggests that culture grows out of the concrete problems which people must solve in their everyday life. It does not purport to explain every aspect of culture, but it does suggest a way of understanding the fundamental outlines of social action in any society. The ecosystem concept is one useful item in the ecologist's toolkit because it provides a framework within which to test hypotheses. While the fundamental questions of anthropology will continue to grow out of general social and historical issues, the ecosystem concept may yet serve us well as a guide to the investigation of those questions.

References Cited

Godelier, Maurice
1972 Rationality and Irrationality in Economics. London: NLB.

Gross, Daniel R. and Barbara A. Underwood
1971 Technological Change and Caloric Costs: Sisal Agriculture in Northeastern Brazil. American Anthropologist 73(3): 725-740.

Gross, Daniel R., George Eiten, Nancy M. Flowers, M. Francisca Leoi, Madeline Lattman Ritter, and Dennis W. Werner
1979 Ecology and Acculturation among Native Peoples of Central Brazil. Science 206:1043-1050.

Harpending, Henry
1976 Regional Variation in !Kung Populations. In R.B. Lee and I. DeVore, eds. Kalahai Hunter-Gatherers. Cambridge, Mass.: Harvard University Press.

Kroeber, Alfred Louis
1915 The Eighteen Professions. American Anthropologist 17(2):283-288.

Lee, Richard
1980 The !Kung San. New York: Cambridge University Press.

Meggitt, Mervyn
1977 Blood is their Argument. Palo Alto: Mayfield Publishing Company.

Moran, Emilio
1981 Developing the Amazon. Bloomington: Indiana University Press.

Murphy, Robert F. and Julian Steward
1956 Tappers and Trappers: Parallel Processes in Acculturation. Economic Development and Culture Change 4:335-355.

Netting, Robert McC.
1968 Hill Farmers of Nigeria: Cultural Ecology of the Kofyar of the Jos Plateau. Seattle: University of Washington Press.

Rappaport, Roy A.
1968 Pigs for the Ancestors: Ritual in the Ecology of a New Guinea People. New Haven, Connecticut: Yale University Press.

Sahlins, Marshall
1958 Social Stratification in Polynesia. Seattle: University of Washington Press.
1976 Culture and Practical Reason. Chicago: University of Chicago Press.

Silberbauer, George
1981 Hunter and Habitat in the Central Kalahai Desert. Cambridge, UK: Cambridge University Press.

Steward, Julian H. (ed.)
1956 The People of Puerto Rico. Urbana, Illinois: University of Illinois Press.

Thomas, R. Brooke
1973 Human Adaptation to a High Andean Energy Flow System. University Park, PA: Department of Anthropology, The Pennsylvania State University. Occasional Papers in Anthropology, No. 1.

Vayda, Andrew P.
1976 War in Ecological Perspective. New York: Plenum Press.

Yellen, John
1977 Archaeological Approaches to the Present. New York: Academic Press.

Emilio F. Moran

12. The Problem of Analytical Level Shifting in Amazonian Ecosystem Research

The Problem of Level Definition[1]

The ecosystem approach, because of its focus on the hierarchical level of organization above the population and the community, tends to emphasize macro-level processes such as trophic exchanges, nutrient cycling, and system maintenance. As a consequence past studies using an ecosystem perspective seemed to have a strong functionalist bent that overlooked historical and evolutionary considerations; witness the debate between "functionalists" and proponents of historical/evolutionary models (cf. Rappaport 1977; Diener et al. 1980). What fuels this debate is the underlying basis for their differences--the differing specificity of their levels of analysis disguised under the cover of "the ecosystem" as the unit of analysis.

The shift in the use of the ecosystem as concept to its use as a unit of analysis may be responsible for obscuring the multiple hierarchical levels within ecosystems. It has not been sufficiently recognized that each level's structural and functional relations obscure relationships observable at other levels, particularly as one moves from micro to macro

---

[1]The research on which this paper is based is the result of four fieldtrips over the past decade. Research trips were made possible by funds from the Social Science Research Council, the National Institutes of Mental Health, the Council for the International Exchange of Scholars, and the National Science Foundation. None of these organizations are responsible for the views espoused herein. I wish to thank Dennis Conway, William Denevan, Jim Eder, Roy Ellen, and Ivan Karp for their critical comments on an earlier version of this paper.

levels. The greater the scope of the level, the less visible details of group and individual behavior and ideology appear.

One of the major works in shaping the ecosystem view was Howard T. Odum's Environment, Power and Society (1971). In that book he invited scientists to use the detail eliminator or "macroscope" to overcome the attention to detail that had kept us from seeing the workings of ecological systems (Odum 1971:10). In that book he glossed over the differences between parts and the whole of large, inclusive ecosystems while suggesting that there are enough similarities between the workings of compartments and the whole to permit describing the former at the macro-level rather than as having distinct properties (1971:60). Nowhere in that fundamental work on energetics is there any effort to caution readers as to the problem of level shifting and its analytical consequences. These problems, however, are evident in current Amazonian research and policy-making.

Recent Amazonian studies are characterized by a number of recurrent dilemmas: is the Amazon ecosystem fragile or not? (Farnworth and Golley 1974) Are its soils fertile or sterile? (Alvim 1978; Meggers 1971) Can state-level societies in the region persist without destroying the habitat? (Carneiro 1957, 1961; Meggers 1954, 1971) After examining the available literature, I would contend that some of the heated debates about Amazonian ecosystems reflect a tendency to generalize about processes at one level of analysis from data and research carried out at another level. The problem is traceable to how the processes at one level obscure relationships at other levels. In this paper I explore the implications of level shifting for understanding human ecological interactions generally, and in the Amazon Basin in particular.

The articulation between micro- and macro-levels of analysis is still undergoing conceptual and methodological development. The disciplinary confines of most investigators (see Bennett, this volume) are responsible for this current state and for a tendency to work within a given level, to the exclusion of others. This sort of problem has recently surfaced, for instance, in debates between molecular biologists and evolutionary biologists. While there is little doubt that data on differences in nucleotide sequence found in the DNAs of related species will provide more accurate reconstruction of phylogenies, "the changes in the molecules do not necessarily directly reflect the evolutionary history of the group from which they were taken" (Lewin 1982:1091). Thus, on the one hand, molecular biologists seek to provide us with a neucleotide sequence to understand evolutionary processes whereas evolutionary biologists attempt to provide a time-based model emphasizing species interactions and environmental change. As Lewin has aptly stated, "evolution is a hierarchical process operating at several levels, each important in its own right. Nevertheless, it is prudent to ensure that analytical tools are applied only at appropriate levels. The trick is to agree which levels are accessible to which tools" (1982:1091).

Availability of Data

The relevance of this issue for social and ecological scientists lies in how a given level of analysis may influence one's interpretation of problems such as low agricultural productivity and its social structural implications. Amazonian research, whether anthropological, agronomic or ecological, has been mostly site-specific. Much of the research has taken place in sites about to be affected by "development" and there has been little time for systematic baseline coverage of habitat types, for assessing the impact of various technologies per habitat type, and for collecting representative aggregate data of major social, ecological and economic indicators. Perhaps the most systematic sampling carried out in the Amazon has been by agronomists (Sombroek 1966; Falesi 1972; IPEAN 1974; Nicholaides et al. 1983). But even these surveys have restricted themselves to sites within close proximity of the Amazon river (Sombroek) and the new penetration highways (Falesi; IPEAN), thereby omitting many of the habitat types. However, even with adequate sampling at one's chosen level of study, hierarchically more complex levels of organization must be sampled as well if "systemic" conclusions are to be drawn.

The question before us is, can site-specific studies (micro-level) be the appropriate basis of "region-wide" statements and analyses (macro-level)? A moment's reflection will tell us that such extrapolations seldom work. Phenomena at a given level may have analogs at other levels but they are not identical (Gould 1982:386). Sliding between levels, by making statements about individuals from aggregate data, has been termed the "ecological fallacy" (Robinson 1950). It is generally understood that micro- and macro-levels of analysis have distinct systems of relationships and answer different questions. For example, paraphrasing Gould, populations contain so many individuals that small biases in mutation rate can rarely establish a feature but the analog of mutation pressure at the species level, directed speciation, may be a powerful agent of evolutionary trends.

Directed speciation (i.e., directional bias toward certain phenotypes in derived species) can be effective because its effects are not easily swamped by differential extinction due to the restricted number of species in a clade and because biases in the production of species may be more prevalent than biases in the genesis of mutations (Gould 1982:386). Macro-level studies rely on aggregate data from a broad and representative sample of the universe in question. Micro-level studies rely on careful observation of individuals in a population in order to understand the internal dynamics of that population. A macro-study is not only bigger than the sum of the micro-studies, it is structurally different. Economics long ago distinguished between macro- and micro-economics. Demography while still dominated by the macro-approach has in recent years spawned micro-demographics of small communities--even households (cf. Kosinski and Webb 1976).

Geographers have been particularly aware of the scale problem in reference to trying to comprehend a large region while studying small areas within it. McCarthy et al. (1956:16) noted that "every change in scale will bring about the statement of a new problem and there is no basis for assuming that associations existing at one scale will also exist at another." The caveats of the 1950's have given way to calls for integration of the macro- and micro-levels of analysis but bringing together what are different processes remains a challenge (Beer 1968; Dogan and Rokkam 1969).

Choice of Level and Analytical Implications

The analytical implication of levels chosen in research is part of the larger question faced by scientists when they delimit their scope of study to "feasible" questions. What are the implications of setting those particular bounds to the relevance or completeness of analysis? What is less frequently noted is that the conclusions at each of these levels are distinct and, yet at the same time, each one is relevant to a complete understanding of human behavior. The results of a community study, for example, may not be generalized to a whole society, but the internal structure of a community is relevant to understanding how a community is affected by larger external forces (Epstein 1964:102). If one started with the "state" or national level, however, it might appear that these larger external forces shape the life of local communities in relatively similar ways (Watson 1964:155; Blok 1974; Schneider and Schneider 1976). The focus on the community, on the other hand, shows individuals responding actively to actually subvert or alter these external forces, not passively accepting them (Bennett 1967; Eder 1981; Moran 1981).

It has not been sufficiently recognized that each level's scope obscures relationships observable at other levels, particularly as one moves from local research to regional or national levels (Devons and Gluckman 1964:211). The greater the scope, the less details of group and individual behavior and ideology are analytically recognized. There are, for example, significant differences in the mean demographic behavior of small and large populations because of greater variation in the former. Since population distribution is usually uneven, small areal units have a wider range and variance of population distribution than larger units such as countries or large regions like the Amazon. Likewise, since mobility mainly occurs over short distances, such patterns are critical to micro-demographics but they appear as insignificant factors when aggregated as compared to natural changes in population (J. Clarke 1976). Thus the relative significance of migration versus natural change depends more on the size of the area studied (i.e., the level of analysis) than on real demographic differences. This "scale-linkage" problem remains incompletely resolved (cf. Haggett 1965).

Anyone familiar with the ecosystem concept will readily recognize that the ecosystem is a flexible unit defined by the needs of the researcher. Its use seldom, if ever, facilitates replicability nor is it obvious on reading the conclusions of a study what the scope of the study had been given the tendency to shift levels between field data and theoretical discussion. The positive uses of the ecosystem concept are many and in no way do I wish to denigrate the many ways this concept emphasizes the interconnectedness of the living and non-living components of the biosphere. What I wish to point out, however, is that while reference to the ecosystem as one's unit of analysis has produced results that address important human ecological relations within a single level--they need not apply to the whole of the human adjustments. A given ecosystem study is a model of horizontal structural and functional relations and is confined to a given level. Its "holism" is level-specific.

Geertz (1963) was the first anthropologist to argue for the usefulness of the ecosystem as a unit of analysis in social/cultural anthropology. In *Agricultural Involution* (1963) he tested Steward's emphasis on subsistence and found it wanting. He showed by a broad use of historical records that Indonesia's agricultural patterns, for example, could be understood in terms of the economic restrictions of the Dutch colonial authorities. In fact, Geertz used the region of Indonesia as his ecosystem level. He identified two contrasting agricultural systems within the broader ecosystem and discovered the explanation for their differing development in the varying historical pressures of Indonesia's colonial economy.

In another use of the concept, Rappaport's study of ritual and ecology in the New Guinea Highlands (1968) defined the ecosystem unit in terms of the material exchanges of a local population. How could one compare the Geertz and Rappaport studies which deal with ecosystemic interactions at different levels? In the last chapter of Pigs for the Ancestors (1968) Rappaport acknowledged that a local population engages in material and nonmaterial exchanges with other local populations which, in the aggregate can be called "regional populations." These, he suggests, are likely to be more appropriate units of analysis for long-range evolutionary studies given the ephemeral quality of local populations (1968:226). Unfortunately, other anthropologists did not follow this insight regarding the differences between relatively synchronic micro-level studies and diachronic, macro-level approaches like Geertz's.

From this contrast of the varied uses of the ecosystem unit by Rappaport and Geertz, and from the examination of debates surrounding the human occupation of the Amazon Basin (Lathrap 1970; Meggers 1971; Carneiro 1957; and more recently Hames and Vickers 1983), I began to examine the possible association between differing levels of analysis and major points of disagreement in human ecological and Amazonian studies. Anthropologists have long used local communities as their fundamental units of study wherein a cultural or ethnographic method could be applied (Steward 1950:21). Most scholars have been quite aware that individual communities are part of larger wholes but such functional interdependencies have seldom been a part of the analysis. It has been common in anthropology to study local communities to quantify certain variables or to study populations before the full impact of the modern world reaches them (Rappaport 1968; Nietschmann 1973; Waddell 1972; Baker and Little 1976; to name but a few recent ones). While all these researchers recognize the value of addressing larger populational and ecological units, they chose to limit the scope of the investigation for the sake of precise and efficient data gathering. In such studies, the community is seen as a "closed" system for the purposes of analysis.

Localized studies provide insight into family structure, subsistence strategies, labor inputs, health and nutritional status, flow of energy, socialization, and cultural institutions. Studies at this level, however, cannot address issues of social evolution, explain changes in the economic structure of society, patterns of economic development, or political economy. These issues can be addressed only by a different type of research method emphasizing historical, geographical, economic and political change over time.

Regional analyses add a very different and much needed insight into the processes of human adaptation. A regional study emphasizes historical and economic factors and considers many local-level phenomena as secondary to the historical forces at play (cf. Braudel 1973; Smith 1959; Bloch 1966). One may note both Geertz (1963) and Bennett (1969) predominantly use historical factors in explanation in their regional analyses. Bennett defined the region of the North American Northern Plains in terms of its historical unity (1969:26). He was able to explain the adaptive strategies of four distinct ethnic groups in terms of differential access to resources, differential access to power loci, and social/cultural differences. Thus, while he was able to flesh out the social/cultural details of the population by local interviews and study of ethnic interactions, a full understanding of the operative forces required aggregate data from social and economic history of the data.

The choice of proper level can come only from a recognition of the appropriate level at which one's questions can be addressed. Julian Steward's difficulties in achieving his goals in his ambitious Puerto Rico research project (Steward 1956) can be traced to a failure to shift from his micro-level analysis of a group's "culture core" to the necessary macro-level analysis of the Puerto Rican political economy. Steward's earlier micro-level studies had successfully generated sophisticated analyses of the internal structure of patrilineal bands and their articulation with selected habitat features (Steward 1955). The multilineal evolution goals of the Puerto Rico study needed to move beyond the study of specific human/habitat interactions towards a dynamic model of structural transformations. The articulation of Puerto Rican communities needed to be related to external social systems through which many community features could be understood through time.

Questions about levels of analysis and the scale of sampling appropriate to given research interests helps shed light on some of the major debates about human occupation of the Amazon. An examination of the levels at which generalizations have been made will serve both to suggest the articulation between levels and to identify some of the major gaps in our current knowledge about the area.

Levels of Analysis and Amazonian Soils

The problem of level shifting emerges at the outset as one of the fundamental problems in the ability to differentiate between Amazonian soils. Most maps available are at a scale of 1:100,000 to 1:500,000. These macro-scale maps show the soils of the Amazon to be primarily oxisols (latosols) with a small area of inceptisols (alluvial soils) along the floodplain (National Academy of Science 1972). If the connection is attempted between these soils and human use of them, as is often the case, discussions will emphasize that these soils are poor and their utilization is restricted to long fallow swidden agriculture with shifting of fields every two to three years due to rapid declines in fertility caused by the loss of the limited nutrients made available after the burn (McNeil 1964; Gourou 1966; Meggers 1971; Goodland and Irwin 1975). A great deal of the pessimism about the potential of the Amazon is based on this level of analysis.

But how representative is the available data? Does it provide an adequate enough representative sample of the whole Basin to permit macro-level generalizations such as those above? Reliance, until recently, on the simple dichotomy between the floodplain and the uplands, comprising 2% and 98% of the area respectively, is at a level of generality not likely to generate systematic scaling of the Amazonian regional system and implies that each of the two areas are more homogenous than is the case. Studies done elsewhere have noted that variability increases with movement towards the more micro-scale units in the sampling process. For the Amazon there is no available soil mapping at a scale that permits observation of specific soils except for a few isolated localities (Furley 1980; Ranzani 1978). Is the absence of such detailed micro-scaled maps critical?

When one changes level from the Amazon as a whole to specific sub-regions, the homogeneity suggested at the regional level rapidly yields to extreme local variability. Instead of two soil types, three to five are noted. Not only is there increased detail in visible soil types but even the areal extent of soil types may be misjudged (Ranzani 1978). A technologically sophisticated aerial survey of the Amazon using sideways-looking radar (RADAM 1974) at a scale of 1:100,000 observed that the dominant soil type in the sub-region of Maraba were the ultisols. However, localized study by Ranzani in Maraba (1978), at a scale of 1:10,000, concluded that oxisols constituted 65%, entisols 22%, and ultisols <u>only</u> 13% of the soils in the area in question. Scale is important when such variability is present.

Whereas maps at a scale of 1:100,000 to 1:500,000 may be useful in addressing questions about geologic history, geomorphology, and general questions about the relationship between soils and biotic productivity, speciation, and climate, they are of little use in addressing questions about human use of resources, the social organization and structure of human communities, and their adaptive strategies. Maps in the order of 1:20,000 and up are not useful for land management. A planner or a researcher using such a map will assume that all the soils labeled with a particular name will have the same characteristics as does a "typical profile." Such a macro-scale map might suggest that farmers can move from place to place with a uniform land management approach and expect similar results everywhere. This has been, in fact, a dominant viewpoint in anthropological writings about the Amazon tropical rain forest peoples (cf. Wissler 1926; Meggers 1971). Given the lack of micro-scale studies in a sufficient number of areas by systematic sampling, it has been easy for investigators to dismiss variations as "non-representative" and to accept the macro-scale as more accurate. Such a decision is incorrect from the point of view of geographical sampling and its analytical implications (Duncan, Cuzzort and Duncan 1961).

From the point of view of regional policy, reliance on macro-scale maps has had serious consequences. The decision to focus government directed colonization along Brazil's Transamazon Highway in the Altamira region of the Xingu River was based on political and economic priorities based on the identification of medium to high fertility Alfisols which appeared to dominate the region (IPEAN 1967). This decision was based on the extrapolation of a few soil samples to the region as a whole. As a result, colonists were placed on all available lots as they arrived since soil quality was thought to be homogeneous. Also, a uniform set of crops was required in order for colonists to obtain bank credit. Most farmers who followed the directives of the bank obtained low yields and defaulted on their loans. It was not until the colonists were all settled on their land that micro-level soil sampling was carried out by Moran (1975), Smith (1976) and Fearnside (1978) in the Altamira area and by Ranzani (1978) and Smith (1976) in the Maraba region. These investigators discovered that the soils of the area are a patchwork, with radical differences in nearly every kilometer and even from one neighbor's plot to another. Thus, the soils of Altamira were highly variable with the medium to

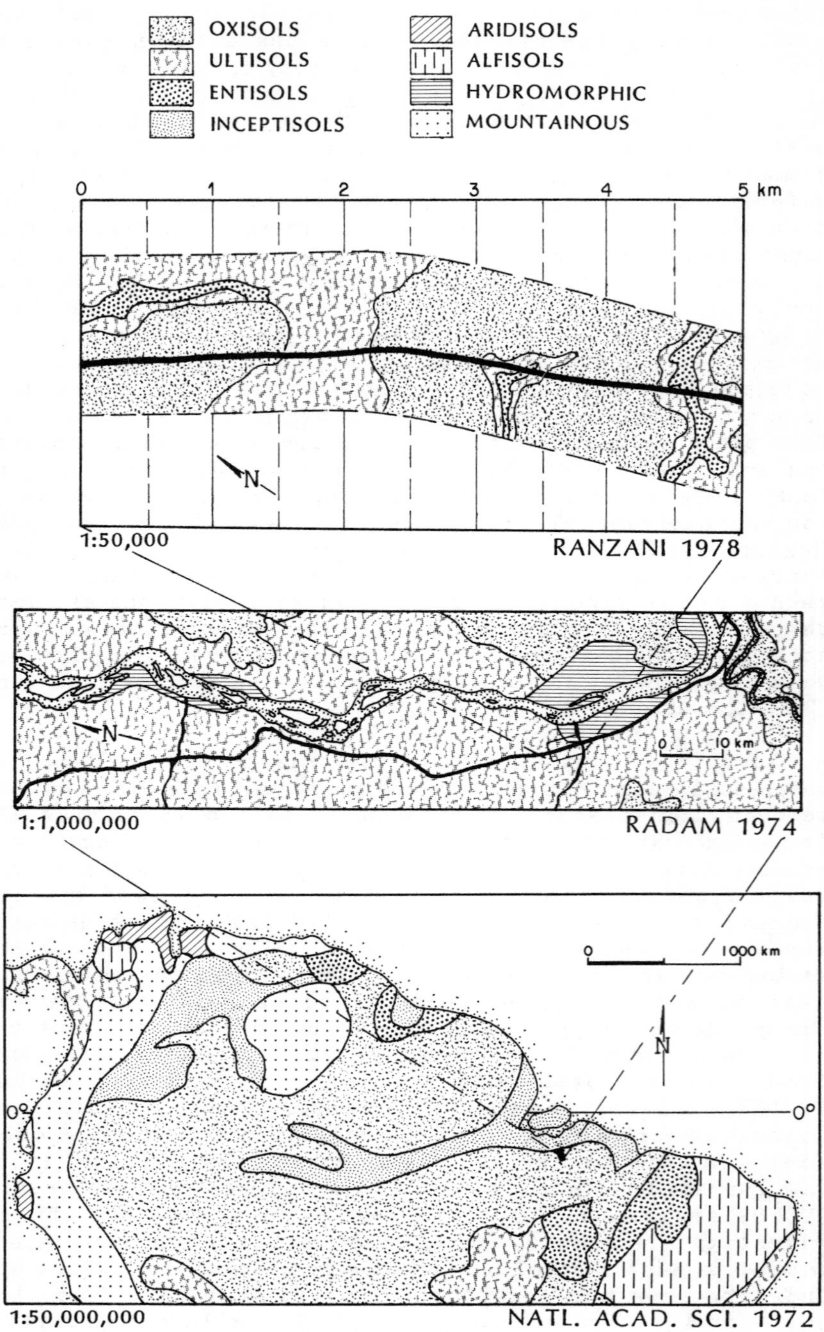

Figure 12.1 Changing evidence for major soils found in a region as a function of scale.

high fertility alfisols making up only 8% of the total soils and scattered in small patches (see Figure 12.1).

Recognition that land use planning and agronomic decisions can only be accurate at the micro-level could have led to a different pattern of land occupation, a less homogeneous effort at agricultural extension, reduced likelihood of loan defaults, and many other problems that affected the performance of farmers in the Transamazon (Moran 1981).

Levels of Analysis and the Provision cf Agricultural Inputs

Macro-level analyses often have noted that in the Amazon the lack of sufficient credit was a major obstacle to increases in food production. In the Amazon Basin, analysts have added that the archaic system of *aviamento*, wherein riverine traders controlled the supply of goods to the Amazon interior, and long term credit extended at exorbitant rates, was a fundamental cause of the region's perpetual state of underdevelopment (Wagley 1953; Santos 1968). The macro-level solution to this situation was to provide credit at favorable rates through the normal channels of the Bank of Brazil. In making such a policy decision, planners failed to take into consideration micro-level constraints to the use of capital resources such as (a) the structure of local social relations, (b) the costs of monitoring the credit worthiness of a rural population in a rain forest region, (c) the differential experience of farmers with bank credit, and (d) the traditional forms of allocating cash inputs. Nor did the planning process allow for the imperfections in the local-level administration of resources by government agencies. Credit institutions were unable to release funds in accordance with the agricultural schedule of the specific areas in question. Extension agents were unable to gain access to fields in order to monitor the progress of farm work yet continued to require elaborate procedures designed to monitor credit worthiness.

The aggregated data showed a high rate of credit default; however, the reasons for such defaults could only come from farm management surveys--micro-level studies at the level of the individual farm, which were not part of the monitoring process. Micro-level analysis of credit has shown its cost to be unreasonably high. Loans cost not the 7 percent per annum "face" cost but 50 percent, due to lost labor time in obtaining release of funds (Moran 1975). Moreover, lack of previous experience in using agricultural credit led to misallocation.[2] Farmers with little managerial background tended to consume their loans rather than apply them to the intensive use of limited areas (Moran 1981).

Credit institutions were also not attuned to the micro-level agronomic constraints to cereal production in some parts of the Amazon Basin. While cereals can be grown in the Amazon Basin, they are more susceptible to pests and diseases and require soils of higher initial fertility than do root crops (Moran 1975, 1981; Smith 1977, 1982). Though cereals could be grown well on Alfisols, they do not fare so well on Oxisols and Ultisols. They also usually require substantial fertilizer inputs after the first or second year of cultivation, but levels of fertilizer input for tropical soils have as yet to be worked out per crop and per soil type (Tropical Soils Research Program 1976:137). The banks, however, gave credit for cereal crops only, despite the patchy availability of Alfisols and the higher cost of inputs that they required.

Not only was planning affected by the inappropriate macro-perspective to land planning but so was the evaluation of farmer performance. Whereas some farmers familiar with the Amazon refused to go along with the practices promoted by the government and obtained good yields from their diversified agricultural operations, the use of aggregate production data, rather than individual farm management surveys hid the differential performance of farmers and led to a reduction of government support to the whole small farming population. Elsewhere I have shown (Moran 1979b, 1981) that the Amazonian caboclo population[3] had precise knowledge of forest resources, soil types, and had better results than farmers following practices promoted by the planners. The caboclos' use of the region's resources (Moran 1974) was more complete, more rational and more efficient than that of outsiders. Instead of identifying farm strategies that worked, the aggregate analysis provided no details on what management practices worked but only that the output did not meet national expectations set before the

---

[2]Fewer than 21% of farmers had had previous experience in dealing with banks for financing agricultural work (Moran 1979c).

[3]Caboclo refers to the racially mixed rural population of the Amazon. As a sub-culture it adopted aboriginal subsistence techniques and Portuguese social forms (cf. Wagley 1952, Moran 1974).

project began.[4] At the evaluation stage the agencies involved used inappropriate quantitative tools to measure farmers' productivity, to identify limiting factors and to correct actions. All that the aggregate analysis could do was balance the output of the sector against the total inputs provided. The analysis did not show, and could not show, that the inputs were not timed to the needs of farmers, that institutional performance was a constraint in itself, and that the technological inputs were in part responsible for the low yields in two out of the three years measured.[5]

The aggregated data from the banks and the government agencies showed that low amounts of rice, corn and beans had been marketed by Transamazon farmers. These low production levels were attributed to "low level" of technology in use and the "lack" of entrepreneurial spirit among the farmers. It was a case, as Wood and Schmink (1979) have reminded us, of "blaming the victim." The negative evaluation of farmer performance comes as no surprise, though, when one considers the inappropriateness of the data. Input/output data for a sector created a mere three years before could have hardly yielded results capable of explaining poor performance. Only micro-level farm management investigations could have revealed those factors.[6]

Discussion

Human adaptation and social differentiation do not occur in a vacuum. This process of social reproduction reflects the adaptation of the population to local habitat, to the economic and structural relations within nation-states, and

---

[4]The projected yields were unrealistic in the extreme given the uncertainties of farming and the lack of baseline surveys of soils, climate and input prices. In fact, farmers did reach those yields--but only on the fifth year after settlement.

[5]The 1972 rice harvest was reduced in no small part due to the promotion of a seed type inappropriate for the humid tropics (i.e., developed for the semi-arid Northeast with a short growing season). The 1973 season was hampered by unusually high rainfall, flooding and fungus infestations resulting from the high moisture. Unfinished roads made it impossible for farmers to market the produce they obtained (Moran 1981).

[6]While it can be argued that the evaluation process was political rather than economic, it can be argued that even if political aspects could be left out the level of analysis could not have yielded any other results.

to the ability to function within the social field provided by an incipient socio-economic setting in a rain forest environment.

One proposed solution to the limitations found in past ecological analyses has been to move the field towards the adoption of microeconomic models (see Smith, this volume). However, this is one of the most problematic of all solutions for ecological anthropological research given the crucial difference between ecological and economic theory. Both economic and ecological theory recognize that individual decisions, in the context of hierarchies of group organization, structure the system. Economics describes the process as one of individual firms seeking to survive and maximize their utility within the constraints present--making them analogous to ecological systems. However, ecologists tend to argue that the behavior of individuals at <u>all</u> levels of group organization is subject to natural selection on the basis of relative fitness. Economists, by contrast, make a distinction between the decision-making process at the individual level and the level of the firm. Whereas firms are assumed to act to ensure survival, individuals are assumed to aim at maximizing consumption. By making it an assumption that individuals are more concerned with immediate consumption than they are with survival and reproduction, economists have created a profound theoretical problem for the study of human ecosystems. Human ecosystems are inextricably bound to system of <u>values</u>, however culturally-defined (see Bennett, this volume). Thus, it is of fundamental importance to understand how our value, or economic, systems relate to ecological systems. Bernstein (1981:326) believes that the absence of feedback about the effects of macro-decisions on the local environment in larger economic and political systems is responsible for the failure of such systems to respond adequately to perturbations. Whereas it is relatively easy to see the connection between crop rotation and yield in a village plot, it is difficult to establish the causes and effects of acid rain on several states downwind from the power plants. Ecological and economic scientists need to develop a coherent theory of decision-making that avoids the inconsistent assumptions between levels of organization currently present. While it may not be completely erroneous to assume that individuals seek to maximize their utility, neither is it far-fetched to note that they also seek their survival and reproduction and that the latter is more fundamental to individuals than is maximization of consumption.

The social and ecological future of the Amazon and its people are constrained by a centralized macro-level approach to planning and implementation which did not begin in 1964 but has deep historical roots (Roett 1972). The priorities set by the State for the development of the Amazon were national in scope: to improve Brazil's foreign exchange balance, to promote national integration, and to reduce social tensions in the Northeast. In none of the planning documents is there mention of how the macro-economic objectives of the project would articulate with the complex micro-economic and micro-ecological processes at the level of individual farms and farm production dynamics.

The choice to use macro-economic planning took place because of the structure of the Brazilian bureaucracy and the preference of centralized states to aggregate inputs in formulating policies. Hirschman has pointed out that planners tend to be biased against programs that involve technological uncertainties and prefer to provide support to large corporations rather than many local small holders (1967:39-44). Thus, the problem is general to all complex bureaucratic structures. In Brazil's case that structure is also remarkably centralized (i.e., authoritarian), which makes the structure of decision-making even less amenable to inputs from micro-level studies. The more centralized the structure of decision-making, the less able it is to process complex information incorporating the variability present in any areally extensive system. As a result, decision-making is insensitive to micro-level variability and tends toward homogeneization of both environmental and social variables. Economists have noted that economic policies in Brazil since 1964 have increased the gap between income groups to a more evident distinction between haves and have-nots. While economists agree that such a long-term process is destabilizing, it has not led to a reconsideration of the basic assumptions responsible for this process. Ecologists have also noted a tendency to treat the Amazon as a forest, of which any part can be cleared with equivalent results. The results have been destructive of forest and of the capital they represented. The question which is central to the future of Amazonian ecosystems is whether or not the structure of the Brazilian bureaucracy is capable of adjusting its policies to include inputs from specific sites to optimize productivity and conservation per site. The implications of such a structural change on the human populations is explored in another volume (Moran 1983).

There is increased recognition that the Amazon is very heterogenous and probably varies a great deal in fragility and/or resiliency from place to place. We already know that white sand/black-water river watersheds are particularly susceptible to "desertification" (Herrera et al. 1978; Uhl

1983). The soils are extremely variable throughout the Basin and demand site-specific strategies of utilization. Clearly, areas with low initial soil fertility should be protected from predatory forms of exploitation and reserves created to prevent a breakdown in the closed nutrient cycle of the forest. Macro-level approaches are too insensitive to variation and to feedback on local environmental and social impacts to permit the development of the necessary site-specific strategies of resource use in heterogeneous ecosystems. What is needed is a "nested" approach to resource use that builds up systematic sampling of sub-regions, districts and localities so that information feedback flows from specific sites through each level of the hierarchy in order to permit adjustment to variation.

Conclusion

For the purposes of field research, it is seldom practical to try to investigate more than one level. But as the two debates reviewed above suggest, to shift levels between data and analysis is analytically inappropriate and obscures the complex processes being studied. Levels are hierarchically structured and exhibit both vertical and horizontal interactions. Ecosystem research normally focuses upon horizontal interactions within a given level. Vertical hierarchical organization has received much less attention in ecological anthropological research and remains problematic both theoretically and methodologically (cf. Pattee 1973; Gould 1982; Lewin 1982).

Minimally, the first requirement in overcoming the current dilemma is the recognition of the distinctiveness of levels of analysis. Once they are recognized, the differences between levels pose little difficulty for specific empirical studies with limited and clear objectives (cf. Gross, this volume). A study of a sample of groups in a rural community makes it possible to generalize about group structure, although not about the structure of, say, "peasantries." To arrive at the latter type of generalization requires systematic comparisons of a, representative sample of rural groups and of their interactions with the larger society. In short, the research design must be adapted to the level of organization to be explained and explanations confined to that level. Each explanation "nests" within the other level and operates within the general constraints set by the other level (see Golley, this volume). Thus, while each hypothesis is restricted to a particular level of analysis, structural and functional aspects of ecosystems are affected by processes at other levels. Each hierarchical level adds a layer to our understanding of the total human adaptational situation.

While we should all aspire to the integration between macro- and micro-level explanations, this integration cannot be achieved by mixing levels between the data-gathering and the interpretational stages. Synthesis can only result from preliminary separation of micro- and macro-analyses. Only after the level-specific processes have been interpreted can we hope for a reintegration of the levels.

References Cited

Alvim, P. de T.
1978 Perspectivas de Produção Agrícola na Região Amazonica. Interciencia 3(4):243-249.

Baker, Paul T. and M. Little (eds.)
1976 Man in the Andes. Stroudsburg, PA: Dowden, Hutchinson and Ross. US/IBP Synthesis Series, No. 1.

BASA (Banco da Amazônia, S.A.)
1971 Programa Especial de Crédito Rural. Belem, Pará: BASA.

Beer, Stafford
1968 Management Science. Garden City: Doubleday.

Bennett, John
1967 Microcosm-Macrocosm Relationships in North American Agrarian Society. American Anthropologist 69:441-54.
1969 Northern Plainsmen. Chicago: Aldine.

Bernstein, B.B.
1981 Ecology and Economics: Complex Systems in Changing Environments. Annual Review of Ecology and Systematics 12:309-30.

Bloch, M.
1966 French Rural History. Berkeley: University of California Press. Originally published in 1931.

Blok, Anton
1974 The Mafia of a Sicilian Village, 1860-1960: A Study of Violent Peasant Entrepreneurs. New York: Harper and Row.

Braudel, Fernand

1973 The Mediterranean and the Mediterranean World in the Age of Philip II, Two Volumes. New York: Harper and Row.

Carneiro, Robert L.

1957 Subsistence and Social Structure: An Ecological Study of the Kuikuru. Ph.D. Dissertation, University of Michigan.

1961 Slash-Burn Agriculture: A Closer Look at Its Implications for Settlement Patterns. In Man and Culture. Anthony F. Wallace, ed. Fifth International Congress of Anthropological and Ethnological Sciences.

Clarke, J.

1976 Population and Scale. In Population at Microscale. L. Kosinski and J. Webb, eds. New Zealand: Commission on Population Geography.

Devons, E. and M. Gluckman

1964 Conclusion: Modes and Consequences of Limiting a Field of Study. In Closed Systems and Open Minds. M. Gluckman, ed. Chicago: Aldine.

Dogan, M. and S. Rokkan (eds.)

1969 Social Ecology. Cambridge, MA: MIT Press.

Duncan, O., R.P. Cuzzort, and B. Duncan

1961 Statistical Geography: Problems in Analyzing Areal Data. Glencoe, IL: Free Press.

Eder, Jim

1981 Who Shall Succeed? New York: Cambridge University Press.

Ellen, Roy

1978 Problems and Progress in the Ethnographic Analysis of Small-scale Human Ecosystems. Man 13(2):290-303.

1979 Introduction: Anthropology, the Environment and Ecological Systems. In Social and Ecological Systems. P. Burnham and R. Ellen, eds. London: Academic Press.

Epstein, A.L.

1964 Urban Communities in Africa. In Closed Systems and Open Minds. M. Gluckman, ed. Chicago: Aldine.

Falesi, Ítalo Cláudio
1972 Solos da Rodovia Transamazônica. Belem, Pará: IPEAN. Boletim tecnico No. 55.

Farnworth, Edward and Frank Golley (eds.)
1974 Fragile Ecosystems: Evaluation of Research and Applications in the Neotropics. New York: Springer-Verlag.

Fearnside, Philip
1978 Estimation of Carrying Capacity for Human Populations in a Part of the Transamazon Highway Colonization Area of Brazil. Ph.D. Dissertation: University of Michigan, Department of Biological Sciences.

Furley, Peter
1980 Development Planning in Rondonia based on Naturally Renewable Resource Surveys. In Land, People and Planning in Contemporary Amazonia. F. Scazzocchio, ed. Cambridge: Cambridge University, Centre for Latin American Studies.

Geertz, Clifford
1963 Agricultural Involution. Berkeley: University of California Press.

Gluckman, Max (ed.)
1964 Closed Systems and Open Minds: The Limits of Naivety in Social Anthropology. Chicago: Aldine.

Goldscheider, C.
1971 Population, Modernization and Social Structure. Boston: Little Brown.

Goodland, R.J. and H.S. Irwin
1975 Amazon Jungle: Green Hell to Red Desert? Amsterdam: Elsevier.

Gould, S.J.
1982 Darwinism and the Expansion of Evolutionary Theory. Science 216:380-7.

Gourou, Pierre
1966 The Tropical World. 4th edition. New York: Wiley.

Haggett, P.
1965 Scale Components in Geographical Problems. In

Frontiers in Geographical Teaching. R.J. Chorley and P. Haggett, eds. London: Methuen.

1983 Adaptive Strategies of Native Amazonians. New York: Academic Press.

Herrera, R., C. Jordan, H. Klinge, and E. Medina
1978 Amazon Ecosystems: Their Structure and Functioning with Particular Emphasis on Nutrients. Interciencia 3(4):223-231.

Hirschman, A.O.
1967 Development Projects Observed. Washington, D.C.: Brookings Institution.

IPEAN (Instituto de Pesquisa e Experimentação Agropecuária do Norte).
1967 Contribuicâo ao Estudo dos Solos de Altamira. Belem, Pará: IPEAN. Circular No. 10.
1974 Solos da Rodovia Transamazonica: Trecho Itaituba-Rio Branco. Belem, Pará: IPEAN.

Katzman, M.T.
1976 Paradoxes of Amazonian Development in a "Resource-starved" World. Journal of Developing Areas 10(4):445-460.

Kosinski, L. and J. Webb (eds.)
1976 Population at Microscale. New Zealand: Commission on Population Geography.

Lathrap,D.
1970 The Upper Amazon. London: Thames and Hudson.

Lewin, R.
1982 Molecules come to Darwin's Aid. Science 216:1091-2.

McCarthy, H.H., J.C. Cook, and D.S. Knos
1956 The Measurement of Association in Industrial Geography. Dept. of Geography, University of Iowa.

McMaugh, T.H.
1982 Adaptation can be a Problem for Evolutionists. Science 216:1212-14.

Meggers, Betty
1954 Environmental Limitations on the Development of Culture. American Anthropologist 56:801-824.

1971 Amazonia: Man and Culture in a Counterfeit Paradise. Chicago: Aldine.

Ministerio da Agricultura
1972a Altamira 1. Brasilia D.F.: INCRA.
1972b Amazonia: Uma Alternativa para os Problemas Agràrios Brasileiros. Mimeographed Manuscript.

Moran, Emilio F.
1974 The Adaptive System of the Amazonian Caboclo. In Man in the Amazon. C. Wagley, ed. Gainesville: University of Florida Press.
1975 Pioneer Farmers of the Transamazon Highway: Adaptation and Agriculture Production in the Lowland Tropics. Ph.D. Dissertation, University of Florida.
1977 Estrategias de Sobrevivencia: O Uso de Recursos ao Longo da Rodovia Transamazonica. Acta Amazonica 7(3):363-379.
1979a Human Adaptability: An Introduction to Ecological Anthropology. N. Scituate: Duxbury Press. Published in 1982 by Westview Press.
1979b Strategies for Survival: Resource Use Along the Transamazon Highway. Studies in Third World Societies 7:49-75.
1979c Criteria for Choosing Homesteaders in Brazil. Research in Economic Anthropology 2:339-359.
1981 Developing the Amazon. Bloomington: Indiana University Press.

Moran, Emilio F. (ed.)
1983 The Dilemma of Amazonian Development. Boulder, Colorado: Westview Press.

National Academy of Science (NAS)
1972 Soils of the Humid Tropics. Washington, D.C.: National Academy of Sciences.

Nelson, Michael
1973 The Development of Tropical Lands: Policy Issues in Latin America. Baltimore, MD: The Johns Hopkins University Press.

Nicholaides, J., et al.
1983 Crop Production Systems in the Amazon Basin. In The Dilemma of Amazonian Development. E.F. Moran, ed. Boulder, Colorado: Westview Press.

Nietschmann, Bernard
1972 Between Land and Water. New York: Seminar Press.

Nugent, Stephen
1981 Amazonia: Ecosystem and Social System. Man 16(1):62-74.

Pattee, H.H. (ed.)
1973 Hierarchy Theory. New York: Brazilier.

RADAM (Radar da Amazonia)
1974 Levantamento de Recursos Naturais. Vol. V, Rio de Janeiro: Ministerio de Minas e Energia.

Ranzani, G.
1978 Alguns Solos da Transamazonica na Região de Marabá. Acta Amazonica 8(3):333-355.

Rappaport, Roy
1968 Pigs for the Ancestors. New Haven, CT: Yale University Press.

Robinson, W.S.
1950 Ecological Correlations and the Behavior of Individuals. American Sociological Review 15:351-57.

Sanchez, Pedro and S.W. Buol
1975 Soils of the Tropics and the World Food Crisis. Science 188:598-603.

Sanchez, Pedro, et al.
1972 A Review of Soils Research in Tropical Latin America. Raleigh: North Carolina Agricultural Experiment Station Technical Bulletin 219.

Santos, Roberto
1968 O Equilibrio da Firma Aviadora e a Significação Economica. Pará Desenvolvimento 3:7-30.

Schneider, J. and R. Schneider
1976 Culture and Political Economy in Western Sicily. New York: Academic Press.

Schuh, G. Edward
1970 The Agricultural Development of Brazil. New York: Praeger.

Smith, Nigel
1976a Transamazon Highway: A Cultural Ecological Analysis of Settlement in the Lowland Tropics. Ph.D. Dissertation, University of California, Berkeley, Department of Geography.
1977 Influencias Culturais e Ecologicas na Produtividade Agricola ao longo da Transamazonica. Acta Amazonica 7:23-28.
1982 Rainforest Corridors. Berkeley: University of California Press.

Smith, Thomas
1959 The Agrarian Origins of Modern Japan. Stanford: Stanford University Press.

Sombroek, W.g.
1966 Amazon Soils. Wageningen: Centre for Agricultural Publ. and Documentation.

Steward, Julian
1950 Area Research: Theory and Practice. New York: Social Science Research Council.
1955 Theory of Culture Change. Urbana, Illinois: University of Illinois Press.
1956 The Peoples of Puerto Rico. Urbana, Illinois: University of Illinois Press.

Tropical Soils Research Program
1976 Annual Report 1975. Raleigh, North Carolina: Soil Science Department, North Carolina State University.

Vickers, William
1979 Native Amazonian Subsistence in Diverse Habitats: The Siona-Secoya of Ecuador. Studies in Third World Societies 7:6-36.

Waddell, Eric
1972 The Mound-Builders. Seattle, Washington: University of Washington Press.

Wagley, Charles
1952 The Folk Culture of the Brazilian Amazon. Proceedings of the XXIX Congress of Americanists. Chicago: University of Chicago Press.
1953 Amazon Town. New York: Macmillan.

Wagley, Charles (ed.)
1974 Man in the Amazon. Gainesville, Florida: University of Florida Press.

Watson, W.
1964 Social Mobility and Social Class in Industrial Communities. In Closed Systems and Open Minds. M. Gluckman, ed. Chicago: Aldine.

Wissler, Clark
1926 The Relation of Nature to Man in Aboriginal America. New York: Oxford University Press.

Wood, C. and M. Schmink
1979 Blaming the Victim: Small Farmer Production in an Amazon Colonization Project. Studies in Third World Societies 7:77-93.

John W. Bennett

13. Ecosystems, Environmentalism, Resource Conservation, and Anthropological Research

Informal Foreword

This paper--really an essay, or a philosophical rumination--has three main objectives: it is, first, a kind of polemic against the tendency to dichotomize human culture and behavior from the physical environment which sustains them. Secondly, it attempts to describe, by means of three case studies, the complex ways modern humans use and degrade the environment, and to suggest the kind of research activities which anthropologists--and other social scientists--must engage in to make a contribution to the unravelling of these complex processes. Third, it speaks for the need for a normative perspective--a viewpoint which takes reasoned, biased positions on the problem of resource use and abuse and proceeds toward scholarly attempts to examine them empirically.

There is a hypnotic appeal, especially to academics, in the scientizing mode of thought and rhetoric, of splitting hairs and avoiding political entanglements. Concepts like that of the <u>ecosystem</u> give us a comfortable sense of precise and rigorous knowledge of the way the environment works. Less often acknowledged is that if we neglect the major influence on the environment--humans and their institutions--this knowledge is of little meaning. While anthropologists perform archaistic studies of odds and ends of humanity, municipal authorities struggle with the chemical, geological, economic, and political problems of toxic wastes--with little help from social scientists. Agricultural research provides clever answers to the problem of increasing yields without ruining the soil and water, but rarely concerns itself with the problems of decision-making among farmers who must make a living and function as members of communities.

We talk about "sustained yield" of resources: a fine conservationist principle that has attracted little work by the social sciences on how to put it into practice in a competitive and individualistic economy, with the partial exception of economics. Entrepreneurial production--rapidly becoming the dominant form of production in the world--is rarely compatible with ecosystemic principles, and hence one wonders, again, if ecosystem and other concepts like it have any relevance to the real world. This world includes humans who struggle to survive and to realize their goals in a human society and culture. If these factors are not somehow built into our ecological science, we are all monuments to futility and elitist pomposity. This view has an acknowledged bias: it is scholarship and science from a jaundiced perspective, and let the chips fall where they may.

Formal Introduction

The paper contains two general and familiar ideas about the relationship of the concept of ecosystem to human affairs: first, if the human use of the physical environment is to be brought into some kind of balance, both human and physical factors must be conceived as a single system, i.e., a system in which human needs are satisfied *and* the yield of the resource is maintained. As things stand now, human needs come first, and only then adjustments are made in resource practices which may reduce exploitative use. Most of these adjustments, I suspect, simply displace exploitation or destructive use into some other system. The second, and perhaps not so familiar, idea is that the most important human factor in ecosystems is not some exotic force or process embodied in biological theory, but represents the purposes and actions of humans in real social contexts, i.e., human ecology *is* human behavior (Bennett 1980).

Politics, social change, greed, profit, self-actualization, ethics, and philosophy are all aspects of the human engagement with the physical environment, and these factors must be incorporated into our understanding of human ecology if we are to achieve a more sustainable use of the world. Human ends must be related to environmental ends; the quality of life must be synthesized with--and perhaps politically subordinated to--the quality of the environment. If ecosystem means dynamic balance between resource and sustenance, this requires a restructuring of human purpose and cultural, political, and moral problems.

While these ideas were articulated in the idealistic ecology movement of the 1960's and '70's, its successor, the organizational environmental movement of the later '70's and

'80's, has largely surrendered them in favor of an acceptance of the institutionalization of regulation of resource practices. Such regulations have failed, in large part, to attack the fundamental issue, which is the persistent priority of human demands on the environment.

The role of anthropology--or any other social discipline--in this situation must be dual: (1) to conduct research on the way physical phenomena become absorbed into human systems of needs, wants, and profit-seeking: a process I have called the "ecological transition" (Bennett 1976:2-5). This effort should not be simply an analysis of how humans use physical or natural phenomena to survive and realize their aims (the transformation of Nature into "natural resources"), but a normative inquiry obsessed with the question of whether the transformation process is generating environmental costs which future generations must somehow pay. That is, the human-centredness of our social disciplines must give way to a concept of "socionatural systems"--systems of effort and impact of humans on Nature, in which humans are part of the larger whole. The politics of need and want satisfaction must be included in the data protocols.

(2) The second role of these disciplines is even more difficult: the need to raise serious questions about fundamental social and ethical values of the 20th century--in particular, the dominant theme of self-gratification. These values need to be viewed with reference to the costs generated by efforts to realize such goals. Social scientists should take the leadership in documenting these costs, but even more important is the necessity of finding alternatives. Reduced expectations is the pathway of the rest of the 20th century: how can this pathway be reconciled with the dominant ethos? How can a culture of mass indulgence be realigned toward a culture of austerity and more modest expectations? Above all, how can we create a mass culture more concerned with posterity than with self-gratification in the here and now?

Ecosystems and Human Systems

The concept of system, originating in mechanical and biological investigations in the 1940's, was originally an arcane notion attracting workers in interstitial scientific and humanistic fields. By the 1980's, the concept has become commonplace in many fields, including the social sciences, and is extensively used as an analytic concept in applied fields like management and communications. The original philosophical tradition survives in General Systems Theory, a highly theoretical inquiry not to be confused with studies of empirical systems (for a typical treatment, see Laszlo 1972).

Ecosystem is really one of the specialized concepts pertaining to empirical systems and consists of a set of generalizations about the interdependent nutritional and populational processes of plant and animal species living in defined physical environments (Tansley 1935 is the pioneer statement). However, during the 1960's, under the stimulus of the idealistic ecology movement, the concept began to be used by non-biological scientists and commentators in new ways. It was proposed that humans, who disturb natural ecosystems, should model their own uses of the physical environment on that of non-human components of ecosystems and should adjust their resource practices so as to insert human activities into ecosystems without strain to the biotic and abiotic components. Likewise, studies have been made in which human institutional processes, like economic behavior, have been proposed as models for ecosystem processes. These various attempts on both sides of the fence have not borne much policy or theoretical fruit, and most efforts seem to be mainly intellectual exercises in analogy (for extensive discussion of this point, see Bennett 1976, Chapter 6).

The basic ideas associated with the ecosystem concept are expressed by the tendency for natural species to exchange energy in such a manner as to create cyclical movement. For example, consumption of natural substances and energy conversions among species can result in a dominance of one species or the overconsumption of given substances, but this imbalance gives way, sooner or later, to compensatory phenomena, such as a rise in a predatory population which reduces the numbers of the dominant form; or the bloom of a new sessile plant form which shifts the dominance to a new consuming species. Such cyclical movements, with maintenance of approximately stable or average energy budgets, are sometimes approximated among human populations, especially low-energy-using and isolated tribal groups, but they do not begin to describe the major course of human ecological history (for further discussion, see Bennett 1976, Chapter 5).

This history was concisely synthesized by Eugene Odum in 1969, in one of the classic papers associated with the idealistic ecology movement of the 1960's and early '70's. In essence, Odum noted that natural systems tend to approach unity or stability in their relations of production to output, subsequent to youthful states where the ratio of production to output was greater than unity. Human systems, on the other hand, increasingly seek maximum output at the lowest possible energy expenditure. Therefore, since human purposes, like profit and gratification, intervene in and influence the process, unity or stability is never reached; the tendency is for demand for yield to increase exponentially and to require ever increasing amounts of energy. These rising costs of production are concealed or charged to other institutional systems. The classic example is, of course, the cost of fossil fuels consumed in crop production, which are charged off to national energy budgets or shunted off to the consumer. Thus, the full cost of food production is disguised. While improvements in fertilization, tillage, and other agronomic techniques may appear to lower the environmental costs of agricultural production by conserving soil or water quality, these procedures may result in increased environmental costs felt in some other sphere. Segmental approximation of ecosystemic balances in human activities thus might be illusory when all of the larger systemic processes are considered.

The crucial issue remains how to maintain high levels of production in order to meet social demands. While the idealistic ecology movement led to a series of environmental strategies which represent "improvements" in accordance with ecosystemic principles, there has been no fundamental change in social goals--demand remains at high levels although some erosion has taken place due to scarcities or rising costs (Hirsch 1976). The question therefore is whether these high levels of demand exerted by human systems on the physical environment can be attained or maintained without irreversible environmental damage or degradation. That is, can we continue to produce at a high want-satisfaction level and safeguard the environment while doing so?

The theoretical issue, then, of the relationship of ecosystem to the human sphere is simply whether or not human or social factors can be incorporated in balanced, sustained-yield ecosystems. That is, are humans part of ecosystems in the sense that their needs can be satisfied without running down the system? Is there a direct or linear relationship between the magnitude of human demands on the environment and the degradation of this environment? Or is the relationship curvilinear; i.e., can degradational processes be modified by superior strategies or technologies and still maintain high yields?

Several considerations arise at this point. First, there is the question of <u>time</u>. Obviously, degradation is a temporal process, taking place at different rates and depending on many factors. If you replace one-fourth of the forests you cut with seedlings, you delay the time it takes to achieve a state of denuded and eroded land; but if the replacement rate is only one-fourth, ultimately the denuded state becomes visible. Yet it is possible to claim, on the basis of replanting activity, that you are meeting some of the conditions of sustained yield. And you can always promise Society (or Nature) that when capital permits you can step up the rate of replanting from one-fourth to 100%. This is a noble promise, but one rarely kept.

A second factor, the circumstances of regeneration or recovery of an altered natural substance or resource, is, of course, also a temporal as well as a material process. No unmodified landscape, once transformed by humans (or any other species), ever returns to its original state because in a sense there is no such "original state." However, one can obtain similar states: equivalent biomass although with new and different species; similar energy potentials and changes, though not identical to the original; and so on. This constant change and recovery of physical phenomena is itself an aspect of evolutionary change; the human contribution is intrinsically no different from that of other species. It is simply quantitatively much greater. Moreover, the recovery rates of natural systems altered by humans tend to be slower and the return to earlier states tends to be less promising or certain. In addition, the chance of further intervention during the process of regeneration is always high. Thus the tendency is toward progressive degradation--or exponential curves of increasing output and exploitation. Eastern Mediterranean forests were slowly destroyed over a period of 2000 years by shipbuilding, goat grazing, firewood, and other uses; they have never recovered. This type of process can be duplicated for countless habitats or ecosystems throughout the world.[1]

But cyclical processes similar to those in natural ecosystems appear segmentally in the human domain. Grazing lands offer examples. Here regenerative capacities are often substantial, and what appears to be abusive or degradational usage may turn out, even in a few years' time, to be a cycle of use and recovery. The concept of "overgrazing," formulated originally by conservationists with little understanding of the practices of either nomadic herders or sedentary ranchers, ignored the tendency of these people to engage in cyclical resource use strategies. However, secular

---

[1]Incidentally, it is in historical contexts of resource utilization like this where anthropologists and archeologists can make salient contributions to our understanding of how humans use Nature (e.g., Cernea 1981).

degradational and erosional patterns exist nonetheless. The conversion of large portions of the North American range to heavy brush cover, often too difficult or costly to remove and to replace with grasses, is a case in point. This example is especially interesting since the brush cover, caused by human abuse of grass, actually represents an increase in biomass over the grass stage. Humans consider it to be a deleterious change for economic not ecological reasons. The case also illustrates the tendency for judgments about ecological matters to become intertwined with human purpose and value.

All modern uses of the physical environment are mediated by institutions. The concept of institution is absolutely crucial to the problem of environment in the contemporary world. However, it is one concept that remains largely unfamiliar to anthropologists; indeed, most anthropologists this writer has talked to recently consider the term to be "sociological." This is due to the fact that anthropological theory was formulated on the basis of studies of societies "without institutions"--in a manner of speaking. That is, the formal-legal constituents of rules and purposes segregated by function, which characterize the institutions of civilization, is a process which was only weakly developed in (formerly) isolated tribal societies. Instead of institutions, anthropologists of the 1920's and '30's believed they had only "culture."

If anthropologists wish to adequately deal with contemporary environmental problems, they will be required to use the concept of institution--or to develop their own version of this fundamental concept. Such a task includes an objective look at the process of change and reform--very much a topic immersed in the "historical present." For example, the history of use of the Great Plains by Americans in the past century offers impressive opportunities for the analysis of how institutions shaped environmental successes and failures: the land survey and its irrelevance for natural topography and resource placement; the institution of freehold land tenure in a region demanding collective use and sharing; high-yield cash-crop agriculture on marginal soils; and so on. Even the rehabilitation measures promulgated by the Roosevelt Administration as a result of the Dust Bowl have been recently reanalyzed as an example of how the best of intentions in environmental management, if not balanced with an appropriate understanding of human behavior, can make the situation worse. Donald Worster (1979) has recently proposed that soil conservation and other subsidized programs cushioned the fears of farmers so that they assumed that soil abuse would be compensated by federal benefits; consequently, they were free to continue abuse management procedures in pursuit of high yields and profits although the market institutions of the nation forced the smaller farmers to opt for such intensive cultivation.

Transient Herding and Rangeland Conservation

Now for some case studies. Tribal herding societies in Africa constitute an unusually complete case of changing resource practices, illustrating shifts from ecologically benign to abusive systems. Sometimes lumped together in the category of "nomadism," these groups in reality offer a wide variety of range utilization patterns involving varying types of settlement, movement, and sequential use of pasturage and water. Their transiency represents an adaptation to marginal resources in dryland environments where rainfall is not sufficient to provide year-round forage at any single location. Hence, movement between pasture areas affording adequate grazing and water at different times of the year evolved over the centuries. Recurrent droughts encouraged the development of a series of organizational devices like the "herd-friend": each herd owner has one or more associates in other regions who are prepared to take part of his herd during periods of local drought, returning them, with suitable compensation, when the drought period is at an end. By moving the animals--and sometimes the residences or camps of the families--reasonable assurance of forage for a herd of reasonably stable size was obtained. The human populations of these groups remained static, grew very slowly, or fluctuated with conditions--as has been the case for most tribal subsistence adaptations where growth or profit was not the main objective (for discussions of the pastoral ecological and development problem, see Oxby 1975; Agency for International Development 1980; Galaty et al. 1981).

Beginning in the colonial period in the 19th century, these ecologically-adapted strategies of livestock and human production began to change under the stimulus of new conceptions of economic effort, and also as a result of altered access to pasturage, due to new political boundaries or new uses for the rangeland. These changes were greatly accelerated in the post-World War II period of independence when the colonies became nation-states, and the tribal people were gradually transformed into citizens who were expected to adhere to new concepts of tenure rights and to fulfill national development objectives. In the past 20 years, the effort to "develop" transient pastoral societies into sedentary livestock ranchers has constituted one of the principal targets of agrarian development in the dryland regions of sub-Saharan, East, and Southern Africa. The U.S. Agency for International Development committed $618 million to such projects over an approximately 12-year period in the 1960's and '70's. The projects were encouraged or initiated by country governments not only in order to increase the offtake of animals and diversify the product (much of the traditional industry was concerned more with blood and milk rather than beef) but also to find substitute occupations for people pushed out of rangelands targeted for crops, plantations, game parks and other uses.

Many of these projects happened to reach a peak of involvement during a period of recurrent drought, (i.e., the Sahelian drought is the best known segment) (see Dalby and Church 1973). The forced modification of transient pasture usage plus drought, plus the frequent failure of the country governments to follow through with promised pasture development and well-drilling, resulted in a deterioration of the dynamic resource-population system. Constrained to limited pasturage, herders followed a variety of strategies: overgrazing, concentration around water sources, ignoring prescribed range areas, migrating across national boundaries, or selling herds and moving to the cities.

These processes, of course, actually began much earlier, under colonial governments, though the period of independence witnessed an acceleration. Rangelands in nearly all of these countries were in a state of deterioration and measures to reclaim pasture and hasten sedentarization were in operation. One approach to the problem of maintaining pastoralist production, while at the same time avoiding pasture abuse and herd fluctuation, involved the allocation by governments of large tracts of rangeland for which no immediate alternative use was foreseen, to herding groups in the form of cooperative or "group ranches." The herders were expected, and sometimes aided, in adapting to these large but much more restricted grazing areas, but on the whole the schemes worked poorly. Large as they were, they were not sufficient in time of drought, and the herd owners felt free to move their animals off them. More fundamentally, the combination of restricted collective pasture tenure and household herd ownership resulted in a "tragedy of the commons" of the classic type. During droughts, or in response to other factors modifying herd size, sales, or production, the owners simply attempted to maximize their production and thus competed for pasture; the end result being badly overgrazed group ranches (for a summary of the group ranch situation, see Oxby 1982). In any case, nowhere in Africa has a balance between resources, people, and animals been established--at least as it existed in the pre-colonial period (for a broad survey of all the issues, see Galaty et al. 1981).

It is perhaps too easy to attribute this collapse of a human-managed ecosystem to the nation-state and its development initiatives. There is, of course, evidence that the traditional system also went out of balance in the past, due to tribal wars, invasions, population increases and other factors. The rinderpest epidemics appear to have been the result of changes introduced by colonial governments (Kjekshus 1977), yet the diseases were present for centuries and native cattle breeds had developed degrees of immunity to the organisms. New, introduced breeds and new strains of the organism resulted in the devastation of herds in the 19th century. There probably were earlier episodes, now lost to history. A sober scientific perspective on the entire problem of African pastoralism would probably acknowledge a fluctuating interaction over centuries between people, animals, plants, disease organisms and other factors; the current troubles may represent the shift to a new ecosystem--or socionatural system--in African drylands. It is too early to say if the present situation represents a progressive and non-regenerative deterioration. The issue here is the fact that human populations have always displayed these cyclical patterns of use and abuse of resources; in some cases the degradation is irreversible; in others, regeneration is possible.

The book by Helge Kjekshus (1977) cited above in connection with <u>rinderpest</u> has a significant general theme: it proposes to demonstrate that contemporary management of herds and rangelands is not the first control system imposed on East Africa. Kjekshus shows that "control" of an ecosystem is a relative matter: beginning in the colonial era, attempts to dominate Nature in East Africa meant increasing production of many commodities but also a series of calamities, from the rinderpest epidemic and the continued difficulties created by the tsetse fly, to the groundnut fiasco, to increasing range degradation and soil erosion. In contrast, the relationship between humans and the physical environment in precolonial times was much more benign, although this can be exaggerated, as previously suggested, since there are indications of cylical epidemics and environmental abuse. However, a recent increase in abusive trends seems undeniable; and for the first time, perhaps one is entitled to fear that range recovery may become progressively more difficult and pastoralism increasingly less viable. This is a matter of some moment since it threatens the contribution of animals to the diet and the productivity of otherwise marginal lands.

So far as anthropological research is concerned, the burst of effort in the past decade has been of inestimable value not only to the theory of cultural ecology--an intra-disciplinary concern--but also to the policy and practice of livestock management and economic development. In fact, the anthropological effort was largely paid for by the development agencies in their desperate attempt to determine why their carefully-conceived schemes went astray. In other words, the impetus came not from the discipline itself but from the participation of anthropologists in real-life issues. For the first time in anthropological research in African pastoralism, basic questions of policy, and of practical effort, were made the primary focus of research. The values involved were openly expressed: the welfare of the herders, as well as of the range and animals, must be a concern of the developers. The writer does not feel he is exaggerating when he says that we now know more about pastoralist societies and ecology than we know about the cultural ecology and livelihood of any other tribal-peasant part subsistence-part commercial production system in the Third World and that this knowledge was gained by making research topics sensitive to real human needs (see Lees and Bates, this volume).

Sustained Yield in Coastal Fisheries

The concept of *sustained yield* is usually offered as the major general objective of resource management systems designed to achieve something like ecosystemic continuity. This concept is ambiguous since it is often not clear whether it refers to the economic product derived from the physical resources or the resources themselves. In addition, every modern resource practice implicates many, not just one species. Sustained-yield management of forests may assure a continuing supply of trees, but with a diminished or vanished supply of other plants and animals living in the natural stand previous to intensive cutting and replanting. But a certain degree of regeneration is even possible here, providing that intact older stands are preserved as a source of other organisms to replenish the cutover tracts. But all this is very expensive in terms of contemporary economic arrangements. Labor, time, and other costs must be added to the product price, something the producers are not usually inclined to do. Tax laws and other instrumentalities may also penalize such management schemes. Sustained-yield versions of ecosystems become a complex matter of costs, prices, profits, laws, and management personnel. The history of forest regeneration on a world-wide basis gives no room for optimism.

In recent years strenuous attempts were made by the U.S. Government to establish sustained-yield management regimes for East Coast fisheries. Overfishing by the multitude of small private fishing boats and companies, particularly in New England, were beginning, in the 1960's, to develop into a classic case of abuse of a "commons": the Atlantic fish school. The evidence took the form of drastic changes in the numbers of fish of various species or in the virtual disappearance of some. Of course, pollution and fluctuating ocean temperatures also play a role, and the evidence is not as decisive as one would wish. But in any case, over-predation by humans was considered to exist. In 1976 the U.S. Government promulgated its Fisheries Conservation and Management Act, considered at the time a model of sustained yield management regulation. Coastal fisheries were extended out to 200 miles, and the general coastlines divided into 8 regions. Each region is supervised by a Regional Council, whose membership includes Federal, State, and industry representatives. The law requires that fisheries be managed for attainment of what is called Optimum Sustainable Yield (OSY); that is, the most you can take and still maintain the fish stocks. This combines both biological and natural factors, plus socioeconomic ones; that is, human activities and needs are supposed to be inserted into the "ecosystem." In essence, this requires some extremely complex trade-offs between fish populations, fish catches, economic costs, and needs of coastal human populations.

The new law and regulatory devices were greeted with optimism by environmentalists, but with skepticism by fisheries peoples. However benign the goals, the law itself made no attempt to define Optimum Sustainable Yield for the simple reason that no one knew how to define it or what types of data to include in the definition. Nor was there any systematic attempt to define the human institutions and activity patterns which modify the physical circumstances. No precedents for sustained yield existed save in the form of seat-of-the-pants management by the fishermen themselves. However, these strategies were site-specific: adjusted to microenvironments and changing physical factors, like wind or water temperature, as well as to social phenomena, markets, and consumption standards. No set of criteria applicable everywhere were visible. In short, the basic information necessary to sustain or manage an ecosystem including human activities in accordance with the law was simply not available in any precise form (see Wilson and Acheson 1981 and other volumes in the study for a detailed history and analysis).

Most of the Regional Councils did make an effort to set quotas on total catches, these quotas adjusted to what little is known about the impact of fishing on stocks and the economic demands of the fishing industry. None of the parties have shown satisfaction with the results: the scientists feel the fish are being depleted; the fishermen resent regulation of any kind; and the Council members acknowledge they are doing their best but basically "pinning tails on donkeys." The issue is simply that the optimal fish catches in terms of conservationist standards do not necessarily correlate with acceptable economic returns to the fishermen. That is, a large catch can mean only modest income if the catch is made up of species which bring low prices on the market. Taste and preference standards influence the marketability of fish as they do other foodstuffs. Moreover, regulation assumes that the major objective of fishermen is to control and even reduce his own catch.

The study done by Acheson and Wilson shows that the current procedures followed by the Councils are uninformed; they reflect the lack of hard data on the components of the system mentioned earlier. There has been no inquiry by the Councils as to what is gained or lost by fishermen when certain regulations or strategies are used. The concept of a trade-off between the demands of the fishermen for income and the species survival of given fish stocks have not formed the basis of the legislation or the makeshift procedures followed thus far. In other words, if human activities are to be inserted into ecosystems, full consideration of the role of various behavioral and socioeconomic factors on the human side need to be integrated with the environmental data. As it stands at present, conservation was conceived largely as a matter of curtailing overfishing, not weaving human interests and needs within the socionatural system. (For comparable discussions of fisheries problems in Asian contexts, see Emmerson 1981).

While conservationists were impressed with the law, the fishermen's attitude might be summarized as a mixture of anger and contempt. Many, if not most, simply ignored the law since it was virtually impossible to enforce due to the lack of precise definitions. Moreover, the concept of OSY, while important, somehow has not attracted the kind of research effort from biologists and resources management specialists it deserves, and the available information by 1981 was no more abundant than in previous years and decades. To establish a sustained yield regime in a complex socionatural system like coastal fisheries would require an extremely expensive multidisciplinary research program--not to mention innovative thinking and experimentation.

However, the Wilson and Acheson research program was at least a first step--an economic-anthropologic partnership between several East Coast universities designed to construct a series of models of local fishing strategies. These models were of two main types: an econometric model of fishing as small entrepreneurial firms with an emphasis on risk and decision-making, and an anthropological model based on concepts of adaptive strategy and cultural factors of influence. Some crossover between the models was worked out, but on the whole, this integration remains to be accomplished. The chief contribution of the research to our understanding of fisheries as a cultural-ecological problem is the ethnographic information on how small fishermen combine information from social sources, their own competitive interactions, practical knowledge of fish behavior, and so on, to forge their own "seat of the pants" strategies. This is certainly an important first step in understanding the larger system of fishing and the conservation problem, but much work remains to be done.

Once again: we are dealing here with the concept of "socionatural system" (Bennett 1980). If human activities are to be inserted into ecosystems, the system itself has to be re-conceptualized: it is not a matter of a "natural" system being invaded by humans, but a complex whole system involving an interaction between the physical resources, animal species, and the human activities. This requires a shift in values as well: human components must be viewed as analytically equal to environmental components. The tendency to take human needs and interests as separate and with an always-higher priority from the environmental is what vitiates attempts to develop true conservationist and ecosystemic-management schemes. There is, of course, considerable room for pessimism as to whether these can be implemented given the deeply-institutionalized human-first consciousness of contemporary institutions.

Surface Mining and Land Reclamation

Another example of an attempt to utilize ecosystemic ideas in resource management is that of surface mining of minerals, particularly coal (see National Research Council 1981). The decision to exploit shallow deposits of coal in several Western states received predictable opposition from conservationists, preservationists, sportsmen, and ranchers, whose economic interests, values, and communities would be disrupted by the mining operations. That is, issues of concern were almost equally divided between physical and social concerns. The central theme of protest over surface mining for a generation has been the visual appearance of the spoils banks following extraction. This concern has taken the form of persistent attempts to obtain legislation designed to require companies to restore the landscape to its original condition.

The Surface Mining and Reclamation Act of 1977 was the culmination of this campaign; and while the Act did not completely satisfy its conservationist proponents, it represented a major step in establishing a degree of environmental responsibility in the industry (the Reagan administration issued a revised and weakened set of implementing regulations in 1983). The original law required that a minimum performance standard be adhered to in mining operations which transform the land surface and soils. The term "reclamation" is used in the Act throughout, although the word in the past has been associated more familiarly with natural "wastelands" to be developed for agricultural or recreation uses. "Restoration" is a more accurate term since the law provided for measures which would "restore the land affected to a condition capable of supporting the uses which it was capable of supporting prior to any mining, or higher or better uses of which there is reasonable likelihood. . ." (SMRA, Sect. 515(b)).[2]

The case also illustrates another important issue: the importance of aesthetic interests in the management of resources and their restoration or reclamation. This factor became one of the most difficult issues in the attempts to adhere to the provisions of the Act. Restoration of a mined surface for agricultural uses, industrial or residential development, or recreational purposes are found to be in conflict with aesthetic interests in a great many instances. The preservationist goal is to make the lands look like they did before mining; the value is placed on the scenic appearance or on the "native" contours and vegetation. Since in a majority of cases the vegetation, and in many cases the very contours of the land were previously modified

---

[2]My brief excursion here into the semantics of the problem is deliberate in order to illustrate another important facet of the attempt to bring humans into relationship with ecosystems. Since government becomes the court of last resort, one must be attentive to the nuances of legal and legislative language because regulation requires enforcement, which becomes a legal process.

by human activities, these goals are somewhat ambiguous. More important is the fact that reclamation of spoils and land levelling for agricultural purposes in many or most regions is more successful if the underburden soil material is left exposed, after a degree of levelling and re-contouring, since this material has been found to be more fertile than the original topsoil. If recreational uses focus on water facilities, like sloughs or ponds, the rugged spoils contours may be preferable to levelling. In desert regions where the original vegetation was extremely sparse and heavily modified by grazing, restoration to this condition is easily done but this simply returns the land to an extremely low-productivity state. And so on.

Analogous to the fisheries legislation, the surface mining Act did not define the varying definitions of restoration or reclamation, nor did it base its provisions on research in different environments and biomes. Above all, the trade-offs and benefits of different uses of mined land before or after reclamation were not described. Nor are there provisions for involving local people in decisions on the pattern of reclamation. As in the fisheries case, the human activity factor was not included systematically in the specifications. This was to some extent deliberate since the issue was known to be extremely complex, and it was expected that application of the Act would develop and vary as experience accumulated. However, insufficient provision for such experimental modification was included. The Reagan Administration's modified regulations permit these flexibilities but also leave a series of loopholes which strongly suggest that the real intention is to return to the pre-1977 situation which absolved companies from responsibility. This may be contrasted to the situation in European countries, for example, Germany, where restoration of mined lands, in accordance with wishes and needs of local populations, have been a standard provision of law and a budgetary item in mining economics for many years.

The Act generated widespread controversy as soon as it went into effect. Questions about its provisions and basic philosophy were asked not only by mining companies, with their obvious vested interests in non-enforcement, but also by environmental groups concerned with the problem of alternative strategies of treatment of the land for different purposes following the mining activity. Community-oriented groups were concerned with the failure of the Act to clearly specify that local people should be consulted about the nature of the reclamation or restoration instead of making this a mandatory matter defined by Federal regulation. This concern generated enough political steam to encourage various groups in the Carter Administration to request the National Academy of Sciences-National Research Council to undertake a research project aimed at clarifying the whole issue.

Ultimately two NRC committees were appointed, one of them concerned with technical matters and the other with a fully multi-disciplinary inquiry into the role of land, soil, economics, and cultural interests involved in surface mining activity in American society. This committee worked for three years to collect information from published and field sources on the various conditions of surface mining and land restoration in various parts of the country where the activity was taking place--in particular, Appalachia and the northern Great Plains. The result was a report (NRC 1981) which while suffering from the usual ills of research-by-committee nevertheless managed--for the first time--to officially define the problems of surface mining both in terms of sociocultural factors and purely economic and technological factors. That is, the report is a kind of "cultural ecology" of surface mining. It will not be reviewed as such by the American Anthropologist because anthropologists rarely identify cultural ecology as anything that exists outside of their own specialized arena of research subjects (tribals, peasants), but it is a document in this field, nevertheless. As such, it indicates the magnitude of the tasks before us: the sheer cost of assembling a thoroughly multi-disciplinary team of expensive experts to work for three years to produce something like a general-systemic model of a complex instrumental activity and that such cost can only be borne by the Federal government.

As one who participated in the work of this committee, I can testify to the fact that anthropologists were listened to carefully and that the anthropologists listened carefully to the economists and technical people. The work of such groups as the Anthropology Resource Center, which has shown a commendable interest in the impacts of energy development on Amerind reservation groups (Jorgensen et al. 1978), was taken seriously, and representatives of that research effort were asked to make presentations to the committee. All of this is to the good; if it does not generate immediate relief or implement social change, one must be patient. It is too easy to be cynical; anthropologists must work hard to be heard; but their message, when delivered intelligently and not truculently, begins to register.

This case illustrates the way ecosystem becomes absorbed into a matrix of human intentions, values, and economic activities. The goal of simply returning a landscape to a natural state is largely meaningless since it is difficult to define the nature of the previous state and its value to humans. Once a physical environment has been altered, questions of relative costs and benefits immediately arise. If, in a pluralistic society, there is no general consensus on the array of costs and benefits, then these must be determined through a complex social process involving dialogue between various interests. Each of these interests, or uses of the land, may have a different definition of what constitutes a balance between human interests and those of the environment. Biological standards of ecosystemic functioning are thus not sufficient to decide the case. Once again, the system must be re-conceptualized as a socionatural entity in which humans are defined as responsible components with other components of the system. This means subjecting human interests to a dispassionate scrutiny and making hard choices between these interests. Thus, systemic thinking in the resources field becomes a political process as well as a sociopsychological one.

Concluding Remarks

These considerations raise some important issues concerning how ecological science is to be used in practical environmental affairs. Ecosystem is one of those concepts that seems to acquire a life of its own: once the concept proved its usefulness as a way of analyzing interdependencies and processes among living species and physical phenomena, ecosystem became a reality: ecosystems existed. Hence we are persuaded to search for and to *find* ecosystems; and their properties are likely to be idealized. In the early idealistic ecology movement, the fact that some subsistence-tribal societies were represented as approximating ecosystemic homeostatic properties was the occasion to recommend similar behavior for modern society, ignoring the fact that modern society operates on entirely different principles of resource use and with differing social and economic power magnitudes. While the exegesis based on the ecosystem concept formed a significant critique of these destructive practices, it could not supply remedies.

The remedies, as the later organizational environmental movement and its experiments in regulation and legislation has found, lie in everyday institutional forms and behavior. Ultimately the meaning of a total ecosystem is to be found in ourselves, not in Nature. If we are to insert ourselves into Nature in some sophisticated and constructive way, we must study ourselves as much as we study Nature, perhaps more.

Several research tasks have high priorities. In my opinion, one of the highest concerns the way different organizational forms and institutions establish high probabilities for specific resource practices. Are cooperative forms more conducive than competitive ones to resource conservation? Are collective property institutions like those of the Hutterites more congenial to a sense of guarding resources for posterity than individualistic frames? Are market pressures and profit motivations more exploitative than centrally-planned systems? A carefully-conceived and planned comparative study of these institutional forms, with systematic variation in other variables like population, climate, crops, and extractive modes of utilization, might begin to give us the information we need. The need for this type of information is critical in Third World countries where development programs in agriculture and industry have wrought havoc on the physical environment.

A second major task concerns the way societies allocate and control their use of resources. This task must begin with research on the institutions and organizations that any society have available to make resource decisions and organize the transformation of these resources into products or energy. How resources are used and distributed is governed, as noted earlier, by sets of rules which are as yet only generally understood. Intense research needs to be done on particular systems of resource utilization and transformation: mining, petro-chemicals, cropping, fisheries, timberlands, and so on. Such studies must include the politics and economics of the institutional system, as well as cultural values and habits which influence the power structure. Anthropologists have a vital role here since their ethnographic case-study method can be easily adapted to such research. Prototypes already exist: the recently-accumulating new material on African pastoralists in the development process is an example.

However, the problem is not one a single discipline can solve. A concept like socionatural system is the key, and this concept would require intimate collaboration among several disciplines in order to be effective as a research frame. So the main problem of defining cultural ecosystems becomes one of overcoming the social and cognitive barriers to collaborative work by people from different branches of scholarship. A culturally-oriented ecosystem or socionatural system concept is largely a structure of cognitive interdependence among people who at the present time are required to find their rewards in life largely in the form of personal intellectual satisfaction and by the prestige gained by impressing their disciplinary colleagues. The reinforcement of this segregative social process by the structure of the modern university is one of the more depressing aspects of the problem.

As things stand now, intimate relationships among disciplines are largely interdicted by the structure of the professions and the universities (for a discussion, see Bennett 1981, and other papers in the same volume). This sort of work can occur only in organizational settings outside universities or in sheltered zones inside the institutions, like research institutes enjoying outside funding. Government agencies are responsible for much constructive work of this kind, but this era may be drawing to a close due to financial constraints. Integrative research and scholarship, related to the pressing environmental problems of the age, will have to depend largely on enterprising and enthusiastic individuals who band together and attempt to overcome the early-20th century institutions that imprison them. Interdisciplinary research on socionatural systems is the main survival task of science; yet it is the one thing our vaunted establishments of learning and knowledge find it most difficult to sponsor. To realize the goals of scientific integration and system management of resources, we must change the arrangement of cognitive categories in the human mind and the social forms these create. This is a formidable task indeed.

References Cited

Agency for International Development
1980 AID Program Evaluation Report No. 4. The Workshop on Pastoralism and American Livestock Development. Washington, D.C.: U.S.A.I.D.

Bennett, John W.
1976 The Ecological Transition. New York and London: Pergamon Press.
1980 Human Ecology as Human Behavior. *In* I. Altman, A. Rappaport and J. Wohlwill, Human Behavior and Environment, Vol. 4. New York: Plenum Press.
1981 Social and Interdisciplinary Sciences in U.S. MAB: Conceptual and Theoretical Aspects. *In* E.H. Zube, editor, Social Sciences, Interdisciplinary Research and the U.S. Man and the Biosphere Program. Workshop Proceedings. U.S. MAB, Dept. of State, and the University of Arizona, Tucson.

Cernea, Michael
1981 Land Tenure Systems and Social Implications of

Forestry Development Programs. Washington, D.C.: World Bank. World Bank Staff Working Paper No. 452.

Dalby, David and R.J.H. Church
1973 Drought in Africa: Report of the 1973 Symposium. London: University of London Center for African Studies.

Emmerson, Donald K.
Rethinking Artisanal Fisheries Development. Washington, D.C.: World Bank. World Bank Staff Working Paper No. 423.

Galaty, John, D. Aronson, and P. Salzman
1981 The Future of Pastoral Peoples. Ottawa: International Develoopment Research Center.

Hirsch, Fred
1976 Social Limits to Growth. Cambridge: Harvard University Press.

Jorgensen, Joseph G. et al.
1978 Native Americans and Energy Development. Cambridge, Mass.: Anthropology Resource Center.

Kjekshus, Helge
1977 Ecology Control and Economic Development in East African History. London and Nairobi: Heinemann.

Lazlo, Ervin
1972 Introduction to Systems Philosophy. N.Y: Gordon and Breach Science Publishers.

National Research Council.
1981 Surface Mining: Soil, Coal, and Society. A Report Prepared by the Committee on Soil as a Resource in Relation to Surface Mining for Coal. Washington, D.C.: National Academy Press.

Odum, Eugene
1969 The Strategy of Ecosystem Development. Science 164:262-269.

Oxby, Clare
1975 Pastoral Nomads and Development. London: International African Institute.
1982 Group Ranches in Africa. Pastoral Network Paper 13D. London: Overseas Development Institute.

Tansley, A.G.
1935 The Use and Abuse of Vegetational Concepts and Terms. Ecology 16:284-307.

Wilson, James A. and James M. Acheson
1981 A Model of Adaptive Behavior in the New England Fishing Industry. University of Rhode Island and University of Maine Study of Social and Cultural Aspects of Fisheries Management in New England. Report to the National Science Foundation, Vol. III.

Worster, Donald
1979 Dust Bowl: The Southern Plains in the 1930's. New York: Oxford University Press.

Index